The Identities and Practices of High-Achieving Pupils

Also available from Continuum

Justice and Equality in Education, Lorella Terzi
Sociology, Gender and Educational Aspirations, Carol Fuller

The Identities and Practices of High-Achieving Pupils

Negotiating Achievement and Peer Cultures

Becky Francis, Christine Skelton and Barbara Read

continuum

Continuum International Publishing Group

The Tower Building   80 Maiden Lane
11 York Road   Suite 704
London SE1 7NX   New York NY 10038

www.continuumbooks.com

British Library Cataloguing-in-Publication Data
A catalogue record for this book is available from the British Library.

ISBN: 978-1-4411-2156-1 (paperback)
       978-1-4411-5719-5 (hardcover)

Library of Congress Cataloging-in-Publication Data
Francis, Becky.
The identities and practices of high-achieving pupils : negotiating achievement and peer cultures / Becky Francis, Christine Skelton and Barbara Read.
   p. cm.
Includes index.
ISBN 978-1-4411-5719-5 (hardcover) — ISBN 978-1-4411-2156-1 (pbk.) — ISBN 978-1-4411-9923-2 (ePub) — ISBN 978-0-8264-2177-7 (PDF) 1. Gifted children—Education. 2. Gifted children—Social conditions. 3. Academic achievement. 4. Academic achievement—Sex differences. I. Skelton, Christine. II. Read, Barbara, 1969- III. Title.

LC3993.2.F73 2012
371.95—dc23
                                       2011024514

Typeset by Newgen Imaging Systems Pvt Ltd, Chennai, India
Printed and bound in India

Contents

Acknowledgements

The authors would like to thank Taylor and Francis and Wiley Blackwell, and the editors of *Educational Studies*, *British Educational Research Journal*, *The Sociological Review*, and *British Journal of Sociology of Education* for their permission to use data and arguments first appearing in articles in these journals. Chapter 3 uses ideas and quotations that appeared in Skelton, C., Francis, B. and Read, B. (2010) 'Brains before "Beauty"?' High Achieving Girls, School and Gender Identities, *Educational Studies*, 36:2, 185–194. Some arguments and data in Chapter 4 first appeared in Francis, B. (2009) 'The role of The Boffin as abject Other in gendered performances of school achievement', *The Sociological Review*, 57:4, 645–669. Some of the material in Chapter 5 first appeared in Read, B., Francis, B., and Skelton, C. (2011) Gender, popularity and notions of in/authenticity amongst 12-year-old to 13-year-old school girls, *British Journal of Sociology of Education*, 32:2, 169–183. Details for the Taylor and Francis publications can be found at: http://www.informaworld.com. And some of the discussion in Chapter 7 first appeared in the Equal Opportunities Commission Working Paper Series *Breaking Down the Stereotypes: Gender and Achievement in Schools*.

Becky wishes to thank Dan, Ben and Louis for putting up with her typing away 'out of hours' to finish the book. Barbara would like to thank her friends and family, especially Helen, Gemma, Ed and Louise, for all their love and support during the writing of the book and the life of the project itself.

We want to thank the ESRC for supporting our work on high-achieving young people and their gender constructions, and Continuum for supporting the book. Finally, we thank the schools and young people that participated in the study.

Introduction

What were your school days like? Were they good times or bad? Most of us tend to romanticize our school experiences at least to some extent, with narratives such as their being 'the best days of our lives' being common.[1] Yet similarly most of us can remember incidents of bullying/being bullied, physically or psychologically; most can remember kids who were perpetually picked on; and some of us would have been such a child. Most of us would know someone, and some of us would have been someone, who found school 'hell'. School institutions are peculiar worlds within worlds, each with their own particular culture, and each class developing its own relationship dynamics. Time moves more slowly in childhood – schooling can seem like an eternity, and hierarchized relationship networks in schools can be intense. It is for such reasons that, as Holland et al. (1998) observe, for many young people the apparent import of academic achievement and attainment pales into relative insignificance compared to that of relationships with peers. And as we shall discuss in this book, many studies have gone further and suggested a direct relationship between maintenance of peer relations (popularity) and underachievement.

It is this relationship between popularity and achievement at school that this book sets out to discuss. But what is novel about this book is that, while a range of studies look at *under*achievement and its relationship to peer popularity, this book focuses predominantly on the experiences of *high*-achieving pupils.

The research preoccupation with underachievement, rather than achievement, reflects two factors. The first is contemporary policy obsessions with 'standards' as indicated by education credentials, and the related market for education: perceptions of policy success and the success of individual schools within the market both rely on the driving up of educational achievement, with a resulting focus on underachieving pupils. We discuss the manifestation of these policies and resulting discourses a little more below, and in far greater detail in Chapter 1. The second reason, which may account for a sociological focus on underachieving kids prior to the contemporary policy trends elevating education credentials, is what Delamont (2000) identifies as a fascination with anti-school boys ('hooligans') and their practices, among sociologists of education. As Walkerdine (1990) has also argued, male sociologists in particular seem to have been fascinated by working-class 'lads' disengaged from education, perhaps because 'hanging out' with these rebellious boys gave ethnographers a sense of anti-establishment, hyper-masculinity. Certainly as Walkerdine observes, these researchers often showed little interest in girls' behaviours in relation to their studies, or criticality into the misogynist behaviours of the boys. But whatever the reasons, this comparative lack of attention to *achieving* pupils comprises an important omission, especially given that analysis of the constructions of high-achieving young people may provide insights and implications for the understanding of underachievement.

Policy Preoccupations with Attainment

The last thirty years has seen a trend towards an increased blurring of public and private funding in education in certain Western nations, including the UK (Ball, 2007). In the UK there has been a gradual marketization of schooling: although curriculum is centralized with a National Curriculum, there have been a range of policies devolving funding and governance arrangements: from the Conservatives' 'grant maintained schools' in the 1990s, to the New Labour academies in the 2000s, and the coalition government's application of grant maintenance principles to their expanded academies policy in 2010. School 'league tables' are used to publicly document schools' exam results, informing families about a school's 'success' and hence supposedly facilitating choice for families regarding which school children attend. The reality has proven very different, with parents with sufficient cultural and financial capital closely engaging with the information available and often moving into the local catchment areas of successful schools in order to guarantee their children a place. Such trends have created a highly diverse and increasingly socially distinct market, as in some areas house prices become inflated around particular schools, and working-class families who might previously have been in catchment areas are squeezed out by a sudden catchment contraction due to the influx of wealthier families into the area. Such families then do not have the purchasing power to pursue similar strategies. The painful consequences of such patterns are evidenced both statistically (by research showing that working-class pupils tend to be concentrated in poor schools), and qualitatively (by research demonstrating the internalization of failure that children who perceive themselves as attending a 'rubbish' school experience).

Within this environment it is unsurprising that, as the mechanism for market information, education credentials have become elevated in import. This foregrounding of credentials over content of education has promulgated an intense educational instrumentalism, for policy, schools and middle-class parents. There is a great deal of concerned talk in government and opposition circles about the over-focus on '5 A*–C grades, including Maths and English' at GCSE (until recently the key indicator for pupil achievement in England: the indicator of 'good/expected achievement' in England for pupils at age 16 has become progressively more demanding through the last decade, beginning with 5 A*–Cs, then in recent years 5 A*–Cs including maths and English, and most recently with the coalition government's introduction of the English Baccalaureate (EBac), denoting a narrow portfolio of 'traditional' subjects at the General Certificate of Secondary Education (GCSE) which young people must succeed at to qualify for the 'EBac'). This focus on credentials is seen by many, including some politicians, as distracting from the meaningful content of pupils' learning. And there is policy anxiety about the scale of influence of league tables compared with what they can actually tell parents about the quality of the school concerned. But nevertheless, in spite of this concern, league tables have been maintained in England (unlike some other parts of the UK), presumably as they comprise such a fundamental component in realizing the market in education – which successive governments have remained committed to as an imagined driver of quality. Schools are assessed by the Office for Standards in Education, Children's Services and Skills (Ofsted) inspectors (Ofsted also provides information to parents) according to their achievement rates. Schools are aware that this is what motivates families to seek school places – to which funding is attached – hence schools are in turn compelled to focus on education credentials. And for parents, the assumption of these credentials as a prime, even exclusive, indicator of school quality becomes normalized and unquestioned.

Necessarily underpinning the league table mechanism is a draconian testing regime, discursively positioned to support 'standards and effectiveness', and producing the credentials articulated in the league tables. Although Standard Assessment Tasks ('SATs') tests have been dropped at Key Stage 3 (11–13 years), and have been dropped in primary schooling in Wales, they are so far maintained across other educational key stages in England, rendering

English children some of the most nationally tested in the world. This being said, given drives towards global standardization and comparison/competition, informed by data collection by organizations, such as the Organisation for Economic Co-operation and Development (OECD), European Union (EU), publishers of international higher education league tables and so on, and the increasing positioning of education institutions as part of a global education market, such credentialization and routine testing is an increasing feature of other education systems. This trend is integrally linked to the influence of neoliberal policies in many Western nations, wherein education has been repositioned as a fundamental economic driver.

Although this idea has become normalized in the past thirty years to the extent that it is now often unquestioned (at least by government), it is important to remember that economic competitiveness has not always been the rationale for the funding of education. Previous rationales have included instilling religion and national identity (Wolf, 2010). However, neoliberalism takes human capital theory as its premise – whereby state education systems are seen as supplying young people with the necessary skills and knowledge to enable them to efficiently fulfil national workforce needs, and hence to bolster the national economy in a global marketplace. Education credentials, secured through national examinations (or even international examinations), are seen as indicators of such education, in spite of increasing anxiety from employers, policymakers and others that the content of the National Curriculum does not necessarily closely match workforce requirements.

In this credentialized context, patterns of achievement, and especially *under*achievement, have become foregrounded, and seen as reflective of the success or failure of government policy drives to raise standards. This situation has resulted in an acute awareness (and often increased anxiety) concerning pupils' relative educational 'achievement', among policymakers, practitioners, parents and pupils themselves. As we go on to relay more fully, in talking to the high-achieving young people in our study, we were shocked to find the extent of their knowledge about their own precise position in attainment hierarchies within their schools, and how far this forensic and overt concern and hierarchization of achievement had come within the school environment.

This international foregrounding of achievement has resulted in a raft of materials geared at raising the achievement of different groups (notably boys, and in the USA, African American pupils). However, within this work there has been very little attention to high-achieving pupils. The distinctions and hierarchizations produced by the focus on achievement and credentials has served to officialize what was once limited to the preoccupation of a few parents and fans of IQ testing – the construction of 'gifted and talented pupils'. Ofsted inspections include assessment as to how far children delineated 'gifted and talented' are acknowledged and 'extended' by schools, and there are now a plethora of books and materials produced to facilitate this aim. However, there has been little sociological work done even on this group of pupils, let alone the wider group of pupils who are generally high achieving.

Gender and Achievement

One unanticipated outcome of the publication of school league tables in Britain was the moral panic about boys' underachievement, which has continued unabated to the present day. The media publication of achievement statistics, which included a gender breakdown, highlighted the point that since the replacement of the old 'O' level examinations at age 16 (the then school leaving age) with GCSE exams, girls were catching up with boys in the traditionally masculine subjects of maths and science, whereas boys had made no similar gains in the traditionally feminine fields of English and languages. Hence it appeared that girls were outperforming boys overall; and since that time girls have gone on to close the gap with boys at maths and science (although boys still outperform girls at higher level maths), while boys as a group continue to lag behind at language and literacy. This realization on the part of media commentators that boys were not outperforming girls to the extent they had presumably assumed has precipitated a now long-standing stream of articles (revisited periodically on the publication of exam results) bewailing boys' position, and often constructing them as victims of a feminized schooling system, feminist educators or the crisis in masculinity. Several points are notable from a feminist perspective, and have been repeatedly articulated by feminist researchers – for example, that there was no national outcry and panic in the preceding period when boys were seen to be outperforming girls; that achievement is informed by other factors such as ethnicity and social class (the latter being the strongest predictor of achievement in the UK), so that some groups of boys continue to outperform other groups of girls; and that an obsession with overall pan-subject statistics masks wide variations in achievement in different subject areas.

Nevertheless, the panic has been sustained, and vast amounts of government attention, materials, diktats to schools, research funding and funding of initiatives to 'raise boys' achievement' have been dedicated on this basis. This experience has been shared in a number of other countries, most notably Australia, and more recently in a host of others including the USA. Much research, including some of our own, has demonstrated how the focus on boys and direction of materials and resources towards them has been detrimental to girls' education, and sometimes to that of boys too (see e.g. Skelton and Read, 2006; Charlton et al., 2007). There tends to be an assumption in commentary on 'boys' underachievement' that all girls are now achieving, and hence they are not a concern as their needs are being met. However, not only does research show that certain groups of girls – including white and minority ethnic working-class girls – continue to underperform in comparison to other particular groups of girls and boys, but also evidence shows that girls continue to face a host of issues in their schooling. Girls' achievement is shown to remain a pertinent issue by studies highlighting the costs (and often repudiation) of high achievement for some girls (Walkerdine et al., 2001; Archer, 2005; Renold, 2006; Jackson, 2006a). Subject preference and uptake remains strongly patterned by gender (Paechter, 2001; Francis and Skelton, 2005), and school continues to be a prime location for the production and perpetuation of gender subjectivities and inequality.

Constructions of gender difference have themselves been shown to impact on achievement in a variety of ways. It is dominant constructions of femininity that render high achievement potentially problematic for girls; but also a raft of research has suggested that high status constructions of 'laddish' masculinity in schools interpolate boys in behaviours detrimental to their achievement. These research findings are elaborated in the proceeding chapters. However, suffice to say here that it was this body of research on gender and achievement, to which we have contributed, that motivated the study on which this book is based – an exploration of the gender identities of high-achieving pupils.

As well as research showing how educational high achievement does not sit comfortably with dominant constructions of gender, there is also a substantial body of evidence recording the policing and punishment to which children not 'fitting' traditional constructions of gender may be subject to by their peers. Reading these bodies of research on the problematics of high achievement given the threat to pupils' gender identities, one might conclude that very few young people must be able to maintain social acceptance with peers as well as achieve highly. But as any teacher will report, high-achieving, popular kids do exist, and are actually relatively plentiful. Yet though such pupils might be seen as especially interesting sociologically, if there has been scant research on high-achieving pupils, research on popular high-achieving pupils has been virtually non-existent. Therefore our study deliberately set out not only to include pupils who are simply high achieving, but also pupils who sustain the balance of achieving academically while remaining popular with peers.

This book, then, sets out to examine the identities of high-achieving pupils, with a focus on gender, and the ways in which the social constructions of gender and the pupils' gender subjectivities relate to their high achievement. Within this we also attend to three different groups: high-achieving pupils who simultaneously maintain strong popularity in the classroom; high-achieving pupils who are less popular but not directly stigmatized for their achievement; and those high-achieving pupils singled out as 'boffins' or 'geeks'. We aim to provide an understanding of their performances of selfhood in the classroom, and their experiences, and the ways in which gender informs these aspects. We also document how achievement impacts on popularity, and the relation between popularity, achievement and binary constructions of gender. In investigating and articulating the findings from our research and the wider literature, we hope to inform practice for those working with pupils: in highlighting the sensitivities and variety of pressures that constrain pupils' identities and behaviours, we hope to inform policy and practice for both high-achieving and underachieving pupils. And crucially, we hope that the book will provide a better understanding of the implications and consequences of the educational policy terrain which places so much emphasis on attainment and credentials, for pupils in schools.

What the Different Chapters Do

Chapter 1 considers the ways in which 'high achievement' is conceptualized – generally (e.g. in education policy), and here in our book. Hence examples from recent educational policy will be provided to illustrate our arguments concerning conceptions of achievement evident in contemporary education policy, and the discourses underpinning these conceptions. In particular, the chapter looks at how 'achievement' is predominantly and narrowly focused on pupil 'attainment' in examinations and schools' 'effectiveness' in enabling pupils to achieve the prescribed standards. For example, the development of policies around educational 'excellence', gifted and talented support, and so on, have reshaped the organization and management practices of schools. Such policy interventions and their impacts for social equality will be considered.

Building on Chapter 1's account of the policy terrain and preoccupation with narrow conceptions of achievement, Chapter 2 will elucidate the theoretical perspective adopted in the book. This is a feminist approach informed by poststructuralism, and includes applications of Judith Butler's theories, as well as elaboration of our own recent developments of Bakhtin's work in application to gender identity. The chapter therefore sets out developments and debates in gender theory, from socialization and sex role theories in the 1970s, to social constructionist and poststructuralist contributions in the 1980s and 1990s, and most recently critiques and challenges arising in new ways of approaching the conception and analysis of gender. The chapter then concludes with an outline of the methods adopted in our study from which some of the data discussed in the book is drawn, and issues arising.

The different aspects facilitating pupils' high achievement are drawn out in Chapter 3. We begin by exploring what made high-achieving pupils similar, and/or facilitated their achievement, discussing the different approaches, views and experiences shared by these pupils. We found that being recognized publicly by the school as 'high achieving' facilitated shared approaches to academic work amongst boys and girls that were irrespective of their gender, social class and ethnic background. These were: (1) being well regarded by the school which afforded them high status and which also encouraged their motivation and commitment to school work; (2) feeling part of a supportive group with many pupils talking of the importance of the class 'getting on' or 'bonding' as a whole; (3) having effective relationships with teachers. (However, individual performances of 'selfhood' differed considerably according to social class, ethnicity and gender, as we elaborate in this chapter and in other chapters.)

The second part of the chapter sets out our arguments concerning tensions between popularity and academic application/high achievement, looking at what pupils say about this. Particularly, we engage the point that while much research has shown this tension to be an issue for groups of boys (and an impediment to their learning), in our study it was girls who articulated the greatest anxiety in this regard. Here we will draw out the pupils' conceptions of 'balance' between popularity and achievement. A means by which both girls and boys could manage their cleverness yet not be seen as a 'boffin' was to be regarded as popular by classmates. Those pupils nominated as 'popular' were (irrespective of social class and ethnicity) highly connected both socially and in terms of school work. This was made easier for them by their physical 'good looks', fashionable dress style and particular constructions of subjecthood, as will be elaborated in Chapters 5 and 6. However, not all the high-achieving pupils had the abilities, skills or indeed 'good looks' that enabled them to maintain this balance, and many pupils – especially less popular girls – expressed anxiety in this regard. The chapter concludes by discussing some of the strategies adopted by these pupils in negotiating the difficult balance between high achievement and social acceptability.

Chapter 4, 'Boffins and Geeks', builds on the notion of 'balance' elucidated in Chapter 3, exploring divergences, organized around the commonly perceived tension between popularity and achievement. Hence this chapter focuses on the behaviours and classroom positioning and experiences of those identified as 'boffins' (swots). The *consequences* of 'imbalance' between academic application and sociability are a key focus for the chapter.

An account of different conceptualizations of 'geekdom' is provided at the outset, with discussion of the various terms applied ('swot', 'boffin', 'boff', 'geek', 'keeno', 'nerd', etc.), and of the subtle distinctions between these various terms. Data from our study is then drawn on to illustrate the experiences of pupils labelled as 'boffins', and how these relate to social class, 'race' and (especially) gender. We elaborate our findings on the positioning of The Boffin in classroom relations and hierarchies with reference to Hannah Arendt's work on pariahs and parvenus, conceiving The Boffin as a pariah. Within this marginalization of 'boffins' it is argued that the construction of academic diligence as feminine leads boy 'boffins' to be positioned as effete, and consequently at risk of homophobic bullying. We argue that, in the hyper-heterosexual world of the school, 'boffins' are constructed as sexually deviant: boy boffins constructed as 'gay', and girl boffins constructed as asexual (again, we shall illustrate these arguments with examples from our data). Hence we show how the positioning of 'boffin' works as a deterrent to other pupils in being identified as too academically applied. However, the chapter also addresses the various capitals and counter-discourses available to 'boffins', both in education and in 'geek counter-culture'.

Chapters 5 and 6 focus on a group of pupils whose practices have not yet been thoroughly documented – high-achieving popular pupils. The chapters discuss their perceptions and behaviours in the classroom in relation to social identity ('race', social class and especially gender), analysing how they maintain their popularity with peers (a particular focus of Chapter 5), and the various means by which they simultaneously manage their academic achievement (the particular focus of Chapter 6).

Hence Chapter 5 focuses on the ways in which children's 'peer cultures' and friendship group dynamics influence and constrain the complex and fluid 'identity work' of secondary school pupils. In particular the notion of 'popularity', and the ongoing, constantly shifting (re-)construction of differential boundaries of status and prestige amongst different individuals and groupings are explored. The chapter investigates pupils' own (often ambivalent and/or contradictory) conceptions of 'popularity'; the degree to which popularity relates to 'good looks' and being 'fashionable'; their constructions of and (dis)identifications with the nebulous, differentially statused 'subcultural' groupings identified within schools (such as the 'emos' and the 'chavs'); the contradictory desires of many pupils to both 'belong' to a group and to be seen as a unique 'individual'; and the policing of boundaries and the complex internal dynamics of pupil friendship groups. The chapter examines the ways in which such performances of identity (and their interpretation by others) are infused with culturally dominant discourses relating to gender, class and 'race', whilst sometimes also working to disrupt such discourses.

The various ways in which high-achieving popular pupils achieved their simultaneous popularity and academic success are explored in Chapter 6. Their gender subjectivities, and the ways in which they used gender performance to maintain their popularity, comprise a key focus.

Hence we elucidate the different ways in which high-achieving popular pupils maintained their popularity through their particular classroom behaviours. As well as the good looks and fashionability discussed in the previous chapter, we found other key factors facilitating popularity including sociability in and beyond the classroom. This sociability was underpinned by a strong investment in heterosexuality for high-achieving popular boys and girls, and popularity was also ensured via particular constructions of gender. These productions of gender and (hetero)sexuality of course differed for boys and girls, and examples from the study data will be provided to illustrate this point. However, the high-achieving popular pupils' productions of gender also included strong elements of contradiction and plasticity – this will be discussed with reference to our conception of 'gender heteroglossia' (elaborated in Chapter 2).

We establish that high-achieving popular pupils maintain their 'balance' between sociability and achievement by their sociability in the classroom. How, then, do they avoid this mitigating against their academic success?

The chapter addresses the specific strategies via which high-achieving popular pupils manage to maintain their school work, and avoid alienating the teacher, in spite of their sociability with peers. These include careful identity work in maintaining particular constructions of 'self' with teacher and peers, and gaining kudos from friendships with more disruptive, less high-achieving pupils. But the chapter also highlights how our research findings belie the notion that all boys are embarrassed by academic success, or that pupils necessarily jeopardize such success in order to maintain popularity.

The final chapter draws together the key findings and arguments made in the book and articulates their implication for educational policy and practice. Chapter 7 begins by summarizing the key points made in previous chapters, situating them within the neoliberal policy terrain. Specific attention is given to the ways in which processes of distinction are formally encouraged via neoliberal educational policy, and the implications for educational (in)equalities. Before attending to implications for practice, we elaborate the theoretical developments and their implications as suggested by our findings and theoretical analyses, drawing out the specific promise of Bakhtin's conceptions of heteroglossia and monoglossia for analysis of social identity. Next, we draw out implications of the contents of the book for policymaking, raising questions around tensions between effective facilitation of narrowly conceived productions of 'achievement', and social justice/inclusive understandings of education. Finally, we elaborate the implications of these debates for practice; again reflecting on some of the tensions at stake (does one attempt to improve the system from within, or to challenge the system itself?), and concluding by setting out recommendations for better facilitation of achievement, within a more inclusive conception of education.

Note

1 Emma Perry (2010) found this discourse common even among offenders, virtually all of whom had had profoundly difficult experiences of the education system.

The Policy Context: Educational 'Standards' and Human Capital

1

Chapter Outline

'How did you get on at school today?' These are often the first words school pupils hear when they get home at the end of the day. Parents say their children greet this question with anything from a grunt, to 'boring' or 'same as usual'. We can all probably remember why we weren't more forthcoming when asked this question: after all, there's nothing interesting in going over what lessons we'd had and we certainly weren't going to tell our parents about our conversations or what we'd done with our friends during the break periods. But has anyone ever asked parents what it is they actually want to know when they ask their children how they got on at school that day? In the absence of any findings from a bona fide research study, enquiries of parents waiting at the gates of a local primary school threw up similar responses. They wanted to check if their child was okay, and hadn't been unhappy or upset; they also wanted to find out what they had been up to all day; and several mums (as it was only mothers at these particular school gates) said they wanted to find out how well their child had done in their maths/spelling tests or in reading to the teacher. In other words, when it came to this last point, 'How did you get on at school today?' was code used by the mums to ask their offspring whether they had 'achieved' in their school work. 'Achievement' is a word that has permeated educational policy in the UK, Australia, Europe and North America for at least the last 15 years (Apple, 2004; Francis and Skelton, 2005). In the UK, Europe, Australia and Canada worries about the gender gap between boys and girls has occupied educational policymakers' concerns (Martino et al., 2009) whilst in the USA it has been the achievement gap between white students and African American and Hispanic students which has been the focus of debate (Chubb and Loveless, 2002). However, 'achievement' is a far more loaded term than it appears to be at first sight. When policymakers talk about pupil 'achievement' they are inevitably drawing attention to children's performance in examinations – for example, in the UK this would mean the number of pupils gaining five A*–C grades at GCSE or what level they had reached in their SATs. The clue as to what policymakers mean when they talk about 'achievement' is revealed in the name of the SATs (standard achievement tests); that is, the focus is on a narrow interpretation of 'achievement' whereby what children score or 'attain' in examinations is the sole critical factor.

Of course, this concern with pupils performing competently in school examinations has been of central importance for well over a hundred years – that is, ever since the need for entry qualifications for universities and for certain jobs have been around. But, as has frequently been pointed out over this time, whatever is considered to be of concern in schools at any one historical point is a reflection of the existent relationship between the economy, culture and politics (Brown et al., 1997). Today, as in earlier periods, the focus is on the child to do the best they can, and for the school to provide a learning environment that will help the child to do well. However, the political background context has shifted radically with a move away from the assumption that schools are doing all they can to enable children to reach their highest potential to one that implicitly views schools as not always trying hard enough and needing to be made accountable when pupils fail to 'attain' the prescribed grades in examinations (see later discussions on human capital and neoliberal theory). What we intend to do in this chapter is to set out how narrow notions of 'achievement' are and how these have come to be equated with pupil 'attainment' and 'school effectiveness' by educational policymakers. We will explore constructions of 'achievement' in contemporary policy, and how such achievement is patterned by gender, as well as other aspects of identity such as social class and 'race'. Before beginning to do this we will first offer some insights into what concerns sociologists of education when talking about 'achievement' as distinct from 'attainment'.

Who is an 'Achiever'?

In this book, we see 'achievement' as largely socially produced. As such, we use the term 'achievement' rather than 'ability' (as the latter term refers to something more innate). This is not to preclude acknowledgement that, for example, severe physical impairment can constrain 'achievement'. However, we do see achievement as relative, and hence retain a strong scepticism towards approaches that suggest fixed 'levels' of ability (for example, MENSA's (www.mensa.org.uk) faith in IQ tests as an indicator of intelligence, or the notion of gifted and talented underpinning 'gifted and talented' policies in England).

As we go on to show, the evidence for social impact on achievement is overwhelming. A raft of historic and contemporary sociological and economic research demonstrates the impact of capital – both social and financial – on educational achievement. Understandings of 'high' and 'low' achievement depend on context, and change according to family, school, local authority and country (as international measures such as OECD Programme for International Student Assessment (PISA) research demonstrates in the latter case). Our own research supports this contextual relationality of 'achievement', as we shall explain. Research shows that the more diversified and marketized educational systems are, the more socially segregated achievement becomes (in other words, the wider the social class gap for achievement, with working class/poorer children underperforming in relation to their wealthier peers), as those with greater financial and social capital have stronger purchasing power within the education market. For example, middle-class parents have the educational and 'systems' knowledge to research the 'best' schools in their area, to liaise effectively with educational personnel on behalf of their children, and to provide networks, advocacy and information to support their children's educational trajectories. Financially, even if not choosing private education for their children (in England uptake of private education stands at 7 per cent), middle-class parents are more likely to be able to afford to move home to access the best schools (which often dramatically inflate house prices in the surrounding catchment area), and to purchase additional tuition, resources and 'educational/cultural experiences' for their children.

We want to illustrate some of these points by considering what factors are brought into discussions about pupils' achievement. One of the regular conversations one of us have with third year undergraduates taking an *Education and Culture* degree is 'what do you think of when you describe an "achieving student"'? Unsurprisingly, the undergraduates start by describing someone first and foremost in terms of attainment whereby anyone achieving is seen as scoring the higher grades for assignments and presentations. In order to obtain these grades such a person is assumed to possess the kinds of personal characteristics on which that attainment is based such as industriousness, intelligence and being a high flier. The question always comes up as to whether someone can be an achieving student if they don't get good grades and aren't particularly intelligent, industrious or highflying. The immediate reaction is 'no' but on further reflection someone can always bring to mind an example of a student who might well be considered to be an achiever even though they did not appear to do particularly well academically.

An illustration of the kinds of conversations had could be summarized by 'Chloe': a fictitious student used here to exemplify how 'achievement' is more than simply the acquisition of good academic grades. Although 'Chloe' is a fictitious character, her practices are familiar to us as lecturers, and will likely resonate with other lecturers reading this account. In her final undergraduate year Chloe found herself struggling with her dissertation on gender roles in children's reading scheme books. She had chosen this as her topic as she wanted to go into primary teaching: her tutor had suggested she select a topic that would enable her to demonstrate an interest in children's literacy at interview for a place on a teacher training course. By her own admittance, Chloe didn't really enjoy studying and had come to university because her family expected her to, as well as to be with her friends and have a good time. When she came to discuss the writing up of her dissertation with her tutor it rapidly became apparent that she hadn't actually carried out any interviews with the children, looked at the children's reading schemes or spoken to the teacher. Rather perplexed, Chloe's tutor asked her why she had not collected any data during her two weeks in school. Chloe told her tutor that she had not really paid too much attention in the module on gender or the one on researching in schools and so had used her visits to primary classrooms to 'help out' as she wasn't sure what she should be doing with the children. This meant she had ended up with virtually nothing to write about for her dissertation. As the grade for the dissertation was a substantial part of the marks for the final year and because she was clearly going to get a low score for it, Chloe was worried that she would not get the 2.1 degree she required to get onto a teacher training course. Chloe went on to scrape a 2.1 degree in no small part due to the efforts of her parents (in helping her to challenge the grades she was given for her work) and obtained a place on a teacher training programme. As with her undergraduate degree study, Chloe did not secure good grades for her written assignments or for her school placements on the teacher training course but she did manage a bare pass. She then obtained a teaching position at her old private school.

So although Chloe did not match the profile of a 'high achiever' as initially described, she was undoubtedly a winner of the educational stakes. How was she able to succeed in securing the degree and job she wanted given her unwillingness to study and lack of motivation and application?

Where this example of 'Chloe' is useful is because, in discussing what we think of when talking about an 'achieving student', a whole range of apparently disconnected factors come into play. When students are considering what kinds of things give some people an advantage over others, they talk about such features as appearance, social class, college from which a degree is obtained. For example, 'Chloe' might be advantaged by being white, middle-class, blonde-haired, blue eyed, slightly built, attractive and popular; she may have been educated at a private school; she might be doing her degree at one of the UK's prestigious research-based universities. 'Chloe's' middle-class position, her privileged (ethnic) 'whiteness', her cultural capital (knowledge of how to use the educational system to advantage; Bourdieu, 1986a) and her gender working together to produce an acceptable, appropriate (stereotypical) female primary teacher. Of particular debate in these discussions is whether students who do not manifest these opportunities, characteristics, attributes and so forth are as successful. For example, if 'Chloe' was black or Asian, working-class, or had undertaken her degree and teacher training at less prestigious institutions would she have secured her 'ideal' career as a teacher? The answer to that is it is most unlikely. As statistics on attainment show, the interplay of gender, social class and ethnicity have significant ramifications for attainment in examinations.

'Achievement' and 'Attainment': Gender, Social Class and Ethnicity

If we look at the attainment of pupils in England in GCSE – the examinations students sit aged 15 – the statistics show how certain groups appear to do exceptionally well whilst others continue to underperform. What is of particular interest is that, although the UK, Australia, Canada, and more recently

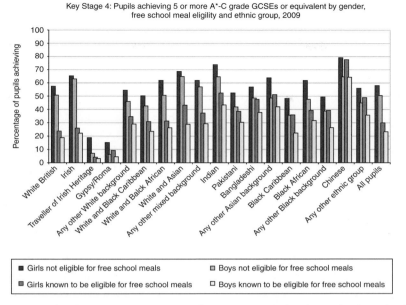

Figure 1.1 Pupils achieving 5 or more A–C grades GCSE or equivalent by gender, free school meal eligibility and ethnic group.

Source: Department for Education (2010) Statistical First Release: GCSE and Equivalent Attainment by Pupil Characteristics in England, 2009/10.

the USA, have targeted boys' underachievement as the issue teachers need to pay attention to in schools, the statistical evidence shows that the *gender* gap is one of the smallest gaps in performance. It is socio-economic, that is social class, differences which reveal where the substantial gaps in attainment lie (Figure 1.1).

When looking at these statistics it should be noted that the effect of socio-economic factors on student achievement is measured by relating examination success to children who take Free School Meals (FSM). Eligibility for FSM is widely used in UK educational research as a measure for identifying social class (e.g. Cassen and Kingdon, 2007). It is a far from satisfactory indicator for a range of reasons (see Hobbs and Vignoles, 2007), however, eligibility for FSM does indicate that the young people concerned are from disadvantaged families, and as other records which would provide more accurate identification of parental social class are not kept, educational researchers often use FSM as the best available indicator. There have been ongoing debates about the accuracy and validity of the indices used to measure inequality since the 1930s (Gorard

Table 1.1 Percentage of those achieving 5 A*–C Grades at GCSE including English and Mathematics.

	Non-FSM Boys	Non-FSM Girls	FSM Boys	FSM Girls
Asian Indian	65	74	43	53
White British	51	58	19	24
Black Caribbean	36	48	22	36

Figures rounded up to nearest percentage

Source: Department for Education (2010) Statistical First Release: GCSE and Equivalent Attainment by Pupil Characteristics in England, 2009/10

and Taylor, 2002) and it is likely these will continue until a more satisfactory means of collecting data on social class has emerged. Some researchers have started to move towards using students' postcodes as a means of ascertaining their social class (Hobbs and Vignoles, 2007) but, as yet, official government statistics continue to use FSM status to denote 'socio-economic background'. With this caveat in mind, we can see the effects of social class on attainment. Extracting some of the data from the main table above and putting it into Table 1.1 helps to highlight three points. First, that the gap in achievement between students on free school meals and those not on free school meals is substantial. For example, the gender gap between Asian Indian middle-class boys and girls (those recorded here as Non-FSM) is 9 percentage points and between working-class boys and girls (denoted as FSM) is 10 percentage points. But the attainment gap between Asian Indian middle-class and working-class boys is 22 percentage points, and similarly there is a 21 percentage point gap between middle-class and working-class girls.

A second issue is that despite the concerns that boys are the underachievers, not all groups of girls are outperforming boys in examinations. As can be seen here, 51 per cent of white British, middle-class boys secured 5 A*–C grades GCSE including English and Mathematics in comparison to 24 per cent of white British, working-class girls. Similarly, white British, middle-class boys were more successful than the majority of working-class girls from every ethnic group apart from Asian Indian and Chinese girls.

A third point is that for ethnic groups other than white British, the gender gap is similar to the social class group gap. Social class is clearly of far more significance for the achievement of white British pupils than gender. Whilst in 2009 the gender gap between white middle-class boys and white middle-class girls is only 7 per cent (and 5 per cent for white working-class boys and white working-class girls), the social class differences are much wider. The intra-gender ap between middle- and working-class boys is 32 per cent (and 34 per cent intra gender gap for middle- and working-class white British girls). Compare this to the gender/social class gaps of black Caribbean pupils. For example, the gender gap between black Caribbean middle-class boys and middle-class girls is 12 per cent (in girls' favour); the gender gap between working-class boys and working-class girls is 14 per cent (in girls' favour). Similarly, the social class gap in attainment for black Caribbean middle-class and working-class boys is 14 per cent. The intra-gender gap between middle-class and working-class girls is 12 per cent.

In discussing these differences in performance at GCSE between the various ethnic groups, it is important to bear in mind that the sizes of these groups are variable and so to attempt to draw conclusions is extremely problematic. It is common to hear about the successes of Chinese boys and girls and the underachievement of Gypsy/Roma and Traveller pupils but these are relatively small groups. Furthermore, particularly in the case of Gypsy/Roma and Travellers, there is the matter of how and whether children are identified as belonging to these specific groups. Also, the attainments of students in these various ethnic groups do vary across the years with many making year-on-year gains. For instance, with regard to GCSE results Bhavnani (2006, p.39) found that:

> The results of ethnic minority girls have improved at a much higher rate than white girls over the last two years. For example, the results of white girls have improved by 3 percentage points, whilst the results for Caribbean girls have improved by 9 points.

It is clear then that doing well in examinations is not simply a matter of cognitive abilities, motivation and working hard. Other aspects of our social identities play a part in what we can achieve when it comes to educational success. It was shown in the previous section how Chloe's effective negotiation of the route through to her desired job was partly attributed by the undergraduates to the combination of her cultural capital, social skills, gender, ethnicity and so forth. The following section provides some illustrations of how these various social constructs produce educational opportunities and outcomes.

Illustrations of How Gender, Social Class and Ethnicity Shape Achievement

There is a wealth of research studies that show how students' chances of achievement at school are influenced by their gender, ethnicity and social class (see for example, Francis and Skelton, 2005; Gillborn, 2008; Weis, 2008).

As we have said earlier, governments across the Western world have been concentrating their policy efforts on boys' underachievement despite the statistics demonstrating that successful examination performance is far more complex than a simple matter of gender. Girls are regarded as the winners of the educational stakes because they outperform boys; that is, working-class girls do better than working-class boys, and middle-class girls exceed the achievement of middle-class boys. But, as we have just seen middle-class pupils are much more successful than working-class students. Why is this? Helen Lucey and Diane Reay have written extensively of the ways in which middle-class children benefit from institutional practices of selection, and strategies that promote 'excellence' within state schooling, such as the 'gifted and talented' scheme (Lucey and Reay, 2000; Lucey, 2001; Reay and Lucey, 2003; Reay, 2004). They discuss how these schemes and strategies which are ostensibly aimed at providing 'gifted' working-class children with equal opportunities actually exacerbate notions of working-class academic failure. This happens by way of middle-class children being more likely to be singled out for such schemes. An important point to note is that middle-class children are not singled out for gifted and talented schemes because they are 'brighter' than working-class students but rather they are more likely to have parents who are better equipped to highlight and facilitate their abilities, and even to negotiate the entrance requirements. McNamara Horvat et al. (2006) explain what happened to the daughter of a black, middle-class family in their study who failed to reach a score in her entrance test that would enable her to join a gifted programme. The parents' first reaction after finding their daughter's grade was insufficient to secure her a place on was to enrol her on a school activity that was run by the teacher who organized the programme. The mother spoke to the teacher who informed her that her daughter was indeed bright and perhaps she should be tested privately by a psychologist. She was not the first mother who had gone down this route so the family were able to use their contacts with other middle-class parents to find the name of a psychologist who was familiar with administering the kinds of tests that gifted programmes used to identify 'talented' students. An appointment was made with the psychologist who tested the daughter and the score was, this time, high enough for the parents to go back to the authorities and successfully argue for a place on the programme for this black, middle-class girl.

The middle-class monopoly of gifted and talented programmes means that, even when working-class children are included, they are more likely to drop out, largely because they feel out of place. Diane Reay's research with pupils on these gifted and talented programmes found that:

> In interviews with the working-class 'withdrawers' they all talked about feeling awkward and out of place in the G&T groups claiming that: 'it's not my sort of thing' 'It's for really clever children' none of my friends go so I felt all on my own' 'it's really for posh kids' (2004, p. 82).

These gifted and talented schemes may have been started up with the intention of offering bright working-class children opportunities to get on at school but the context in which they operate exacerbates social class differences. Later in the chapter we look more closely at neoliberal policies on education and discuss how the marketization of schooling and notions of 'free choice' and 'opportunity' mask how achievement and failure is brought about. The focus in neoliberalism on 'individual choice' sets up 'failure' as the fault of the individual who has not taken advantage of the openings on offer rather than looking to it being a consequence of structural inequalities such as social class, ethnicity and gender.

A further illustration of how gender and social class functions to (dis) advantage certain groups has been found in studies of 'school choice' (Reay and Ball, 1998; Walkerdine et al., 2001; O'Brien, 2003; Burgess et al., 2006). It is middle-class parents who are more able to exercise their 'choice' over which school their children will attend, and, according to Stephen Ball (2003), act as 'risk managers' in using their significant social, economic and cultural advantages to access the best schools they can. In contrast, in working-class families children tend to be given a greater say in which secondary school they will attend, and working-class families are more financially constrained in their choice (e.g. they are less likely to be able to afford to move into catchments where there are excellent schools, or to send children to schools far from home; see Cassen and Kingdon, 2007; Perry and Francis, 2010). Research conducted by Burgess et al. (2006) shows that working-class parents are concerned with school quality in identifying a location for their children, but are less likely than their middle-class counterparts to be offered a place, and often have to opt for the local school. Moreover, the working-class girls in Walkerdine et al.'s (2001) study of middle- and working-class girls growing up relied on their social networks rather than their parents to help choose which school they should go to. Their lack of social capital meant that, unlike their middle-class counterparts, their 'choices' were inevitably constrained. Similarly, when it comes to higher education, middle-class girls are more successful in getting a place at the more prestigious, research-based institutions due to familial cultural capital and enjoy a relatively smooth and predictable path to graduation (Reay et al., 2005). Whilst the working-class girls in Walkerdine et al.'s (2001) study did succeed in obtaining a degree, their experiences of getting into higher education and being at university were far more fragmentary and diverse. This shows how even apparently 'free choices' are far from equal and powerfully shaped by social class.

A consequence of not getting into the 'right' school or university has a knock-on effect for students' self-esteem and sense of identity. Lucey and Reay (2000) found that working-class girls consigned to schools not of their choice believed that, as they had ended up at 'rubbish schools', they too must be 'rubbish'. Such perceptions result in working-class students having difficult relationships with education, often culminating in total disengagement with schooling (Sewell, 1997; Osler and Vincent, 2003). Feelings of disappointment, anger and shame at their lack of education were also evident in a study of young people who had not pursued their studies beyond age 16 (Archer et al., 2003). The devastating psychic costs of difficult educational experiences have been identified in much of the literature already referred to in this chapter. For example, Maeve O'Brien (2003) discusses how the working-class Irish girls in her study found the demands on them and the efforts required to achieve high academic performance 'too gruelling, too lonely, unsociable and stressful' (p. 251). She called this process 'moving out' rather than 'moving on' (p. 251), and this notion helps to explain working-class girls' relative underachievement. The studies by Osler (Osler, 2006; Osler and Vincent, 2003) show that negative experiences at school for some girls, via interpersonal, institutional and structural barriers, frequently result in girls' 'disappearance' from education. Of course, it is not just working-class girls who pay a psychic price through their experiences with educational structures.

Although middle-class girls tend to do well at school the expectation of achievement brings with it tremendous pressures. Walkerdine et al. (2001) report that, in some of the middle-class families taking part in their research, success was so expected that anything other than 'excellent' grades was perceived as failure. As a consequence, these middle-class girls, including those who were extremely high-achieving, spoke frequently of their worries about 'not being good enough' (Walkerdine et al., 2001). As Walkerdine et al. (2001) observe, it was as though these girls could *'never* be good enough' to meet the expectations of their parents (see also Lucey and Reay, 2000). Furthermore, these psychic costs can be seen in the self-harming behaviours which are evidenced particularly amongst middle-class girls such as anorexia, bulimia, self-harming and so forth[1] (Reay, 2001, 2006; Evans et al., 2004; Walkerdine, 2003). Such expectations of pupils' achievement based on gender and social class are further intersected by ethnicity.

Whilst from the 1970s onwards studies of 'race' and schooling have drawn attention to a range of pathologizing assumptions about different ethnic groups (e.g. black pupils seen as holding 'disruptive attitudes'; Wright, 1987; Sewell, 1997; Asian girls regarded as quiet, timid and deferent in the classroom; Brah and Minhas, 1985), more recent work has considered the intersectionality of 'race', social class and gender constructions on achievement (e.g. Mirza, 2009). It is important that researchers continue to scrutinize the ways in which 'race' influences teachers' perceptions of pupils and impacts on their classroom and behaviour management. Such explorations highlight underlying racist assumptions that account for the greater number of exclusions from schools of African-Caribbean males (Parsons et al., 2005; Gillborn, 2008). However, research studies specifically focusing on the gender identities and performances of particular minority ethnic groups in relation to education, and the inter-relation of ethnicity and gender in their performances of selfhood are relatively fewer but potentially offer greater insights into 'achievement'. For example, Archer and Francis' (2007) study of British Chinese school students unpicks the relational discourses of 'race', gender and educational achievement evident in teachers' talk. Here they show how the 'ideal' pupil is discursively produced as white, middle-class and male, and how 'Other learners' are constructed in relation to this perception. Specifically, teachers constructed British Chinese boys as achievers, but also, because British-Chinese boys were perceived as non-laddish, 'quiet' and non-interactive, their learning styles and gender constructions were problematized (i.e. as being 'feminine' rather than adequately 'masculine'). The only other construction of British Chinese masculinity evoked by teachers was that of the triad: teachers constructed this (hyper-masculine) position as adopted by 'a few bad apples'. However, there was only *one* form of British Chinese femininity constructed by teachers in their interviews, and this was characterized by passivity, hard work, high achievement, dedication and focus and was both eulogized and pathologized. This construction of British Chinese femininity, which inevitably the girls themselves neither aspired or lived up to, positioned them as 'pure' students who were never contaminated by anti-school attitudes. But, British Chinese femininity was also pathologized and infantilized, and girls were likened to educational automatons – being too quiet, too passive and too repressed. Hence although the majority of British Chinese young people were achieving in the British educational system, this attainment tended to be perceived by teachers as achieved 'in the wrong way' – mainly because their approaches to learning were characterized as diligent and conformist (traits ascribed to 'the feminine' and 'the East') rather than assertive and challenging (traits ascribed to 'the masculine' and 'the West').

These are just a few illustrations of how the intersectionality of gender, social class and ethnicity shape students' achievement at school. In the next section we set out the educational policy context which has mobilized current constructions and understandings of 'achievement.'

Educational Policy and 'Achievement'

The quotation marks around 'achievement' in the title act as a reminder that whilst government policy in countries from North America, to Australia to Europe[2] give it a central place in education discourses these are actually more narrowly focused on 'attainment'. Furthermore, the education system has been referred to as a 'political football' (ATL, 2010; Bujak, 2010) meaning that it is subject to political whims that come and go with different government ministers and administrations, and is constantly being restructured accordingly. As Mansell (2010) observes, incoming governments must be seen to be 'progressive' and transformist, rather than maintaining the status quo. As such, the education system is vulnerable to being constantly modified or totally transformed depending on the caprice of the ruling government. Education as a 'political football' does not only represent power struggles between the political parties of a country but is then also susceptible to deeper, more fundamental, changes. A clear example of this is the impact of the Educational Reform Act (1988) on the UK education system in the late 1980s, which completely altered the way in which the system operated.

The Education Reform Act (1988) made schools subject to the 'marketplace' in the same way that business and industry are. The justification for introducing this sweeping change to how education operated was that the existing system was regarded by right-wing politicians to have been steadily and increasingly influenced by progressive, left-wing ideologies and, as a consequence, was failing children and their parents. As Apple (2006) argues, right-wing politicians in several Western countries adopted similar means of attacking existing educational set-ups: 'this involved the construction of an imagined national past that is at least partly mythologized, and then employed it to castigate the present' (p. 470).

Of course, the educational systems put into place in Western societies following the end of the Second World War in 1945 were not representative of either 'a golden age' in education nor was it an era of damaging organizational and curriculum decisions. In actuality, the period between 1945 and 1973 witnessed significant and 'rapid economic growth and educational expansion against what appeared to be a background of social harmony' (Brown et al., 1997, p. 1). This was a period which was characterized by 'economic nationalism' whereby people were seen as being able to socially progress if there was national economic growth. The three concepts associated with economic nationalism were 'prosperity', 'security' and 'opportunity'. The role of the state was to ensure the delivery of these attributes; that is, to secure continuing economic growth people needed to feel economically secure and this meant the government had to ensure full employment. And the opportunity to ensure there was full employment came through the provision of good, relevant education and social welfare systems.

The demand on the education system made by states adopting economic nationalist policies was to help the most 'gifted and able people', regardless of socio-economic background, so that they were able to take up those jobs which were of central importance and demanded the most skill. Accordingly, what was understood by a good, relevant education system at this point was based on the idea of meritocracy, i.e. educational and social success being the result of ability (specifically IQ) and individual effort. An example from the UK illustrates how such a system worked. Initially, the focus on individual intelligence and IQ led to the organization of schools into three categories and was known as the 'tripartite' system: grammar schools for the most academically able pupils; technical schools for those children who showed particular aptitudes in mechanical or practical sciences; secondary modern schools for everyone who did not have either practical or academic abilities and which provided a basic education in preparation for lower skilled work or, in the case of girls, domesticity (Deem, 1981). However, the UK's deep-seated social class stratification swiftly emerged with the academic grammar schools (regarded as the most prestigious as they were the gateway to universities and the professions) becoming populated by children of the middle classes. Furthermore, the education system was expected to provide a platform for the furthering of democracy whereby children would be mixed together and develop mutual respect, understanding and tolerance. In this period of economic nationalism it is fair to say that, irrespective of political party, there was overall support for the expansion of the educational sector as a way to accomplish both social justice and economic efficiency, yet the tripartite system was entrenching social difference. Hence, there was a shift towards comprehensive education so that children were all put through the same schools. As Brown et al., (1997) have observed, 'the education systems of the Western world expanded to perform their new role of providing the human capital, as it came to be called in the mid-1950s, for the expanding middle-class occupations in industry' (p. 5).

We will return later in the chapter to human capital theory, and what needs to be noted here is that, by the time the education systems of globalized Western countries shifted to reflect neoliberal demands, there was (in the UK and see also in the USA; Apple, 2006) a mixture of schools based on different political orthodoxies. For example, in the UK there were comprehensive schools but also grammar schools, independent schools, public schools and so on.

The rise of global competition accelerated the breakdown of economic nationalism and heralded the current political climate located within neoliberal contexts. Attempting to summarize globalization and education's role within it in a few sentences risks reducing complex and sophisticated concepts and ideologies to banality (for detailed readings on globalization and education, see Apple, 2004; Zajda, 2005; Lauder et al., 2006). Yet it is useful to note that:

> The dominant view of the global knowledge economy, at least from the vantage point of the developed nations, is of a competition between nations in which education plays a key role in outsmarting others in the competition for scientific knowledge and technologies that enable innovation. National prosperity, justice, and social cohesion are therefore seen to rest on the creation of a highly skilled workforce with the knowledge, enterprise, and insights required to attract the global supply of high-skilled, high-waged employment. (Lauder et al., 2006, p. 3)

One of the key differences between the demands on education in globalized societies and their earlier policy contexts based on national boundaries is the shift away from the idea that what the economy needs are citizens with specialized knowledge and skills; rather, a high-quality general education is required. To ensure that schools are providing this high-quality education, mechanisms were introduced that placed them alongside business and industry in forcing them to compete (for pupils, the best teachers, resources and so on). This positioning of schools is located within neoliberal education policies.

Neoliberalism, Education and Schools

Neoliberalism demands that the drivers of business and industry, namely competition, effectiveness and efficiency, are applied to the public sector. However, as has been pointed out by several writers, educational policy in neoliberal societies was under a New Labour government based on 'a curious combination of neoliberalism and neoconservatism' (Whitty et al., 1998, p. 89; see also Apple, 2004). Whilst neoliberalism placed the emphasis on market forces and expected individuals to take responsibility for themselves and to make the kinds of suitable 'choices' that will enable them to become flexible, entrepreneurial, economic subjects, neoconservatism, with its emphasis on testing, auditing and surveillance, acted as a check that the 'right choices' were being made (Hill, 2001; Ball, 2003). Under the coalition (Conservative-Liberal) government the state's role in general has been rolled back and the discourse in education policy has shifted to one of self-reliance and punishment for failure (Mortimore, 2010). Schools are then preoccupied with educational 'standards and effectiveness'.

As two of us have argued elsewhere (Francis and Skelton, 2005), standards and effectiveness have largely been measured by UK's successive governments in terms of 'achievement' in public examinations, particularly GCSE results (tests taken at the end of compulsory schooling). A tool seen by policymakers as making school performance transparent (and aiding parent 'consumers' in their choices in the new education quasi-market) was the publication of 'League Tables'. 'League Tables' first made their appearance in the mid-1990s and depicted the relative achievements of a school's pupils at GCSE exams. These put pressure on schools to show how successful they are in ensuring they 'deliver' pupils with unassailable credentials, as failure to do so means they are unlikely to survive in the 'marketplace'. Thus schools are reliant on their pupil and teacher populations to reach these standards and, inevitably, are seeking out those most likely to help them to do so (Gewirtz et al., 1995). As such, there has been a move from 'student need' (as required in the period of economic nationalism) to 'student performance' and from what the school does for the student to what the student does for the school (Apple, 2004).

Furthermore, there are links between neoliberalism and human capital theory in that neoliberalism draws on the latter to position the individual as requiring skills to equip them for the competitive global marketplace, and to show them as able and responsible for doing so and for their progress (or lack of it). Human capital theory maintains that a country can only remain competitive in a global market by providing the workforce with adequate skills, and with the knowledge to enable them to flexibly adapt to technological innovations. High levels of education across the workforce will, then, result in economic competitiveness and resulting prosperity and low unemployment. So, in terms of achievement, we can see that both neoliberalism and human capital perspectives prioritize educational attainment as ensuring a competitive economy. And, as has already been indicated, the focus on the individual to take responsibility for achievement at school occupies an equal place in what Fairclough (2000) calls a combined moral-contractual discourse; that is, the responsibility of schools is to offer high quality levels of education and the responsibility of pupils is to take up these opportunities.

The pupil or student in neoliberalism is positioned as the market-led individual who produces themselves as 'economic maximisers, governed by self-interest' (Lynch, 2006, p. 3). As Kathleen Lynch goes on to say in discussing the revisioning of liberal-humanism to neoliberalism: 'neo-liberalism has inherited the core values of liberalism in both its humanistic and economic forms. It shares with the classical liberalism, a humanist tradition that defines the person as an autonomous and rational being' (p. 3).

In neoliberalism, the 'individual' sees themselves as 'the centre of action, [–] the planning office . . . [of] his/her own biography' (Beck, 1992, p. 135). As one of the key theorists on 'individualisation' in neoliberal or 'Third Way' theory, Beck implies here that people are the authors of their own lives and are no longer constrained by the 'totalities' of twentieth-century modernity – such as social class, 'race' and gender differences. In what he refers to as 'Second' or 'Reflexive' Modernity inequalities will not disappear, but the individual will produce 'biographical solutions to systemic contradictions' and these will be 're-understood' as personal risks and opportunities (Beck, 2002, p. xxii).

'Individualization' and Education Policy

'Individualization' is of central significance in that it underpins current educational policy in the UK and other global north countries (e.g. Australia, Canada and the USA) (Giddens, 1998; Apple, 2004). What it means in terms of education has been mentioned above in referring to Fairclough's use of the term 'combined moral contractual discourse' evident in the Labour government's (1997–2010) educational policies which offered 'something for something'. Fairclough (2000, p. 39) illustrates this 'something for something' pact by quoting then Prime Minister Tony Blair as saying, 'Our welfare system must provide help for those who need it but the deal that we are trying to create in Britain today is something for something. If we provide jobs we expect people to take them.' But, in addition to this, a further responsibility of the neoliberal state is to promote citizenship. Thus whilst education is seen as a means of producing the 'human capital' (see above) which is critical for economic success (Fairclough, 2000), schools and colleges are expected to achieve this whilst simultaneously encouraging tolerance, respect, active community engagement, social awareness, personal fulfilment and so on (Arnot, 2009). Hence, governments have introduced strategies that, on the one hand, are aimed at promoting achievement through acquiring more and better qualifications, whilst, on the other, ostensibly providing opportunities for all pupils to secure these credentials. An example of this has been the 'gifted' programmes referred to earlier.

'Gifted and Talented' Education Programmes

'Gifted and talented' programmes feature particularly significantly in both the USA and UK, although the USA has a longer history of offering such courses. What is understood by 'gifted' is similarly defined, for example, in the UK as:

> 'Gifted and talented' describes children and young people with an ability to develop to a level significantly ahead of their year group (or with the potential to develop those abilities):
>
> - 'gifted' learners are those who have abilities in one or more academic subjects, like maths and English
> - 'talented' learners are those who have practical skills in areas like sport, music, design or creative and performing arts
>
> Skills like leadership, decision-making and organisation are also taken into account when identifying and providing for gifted and talented children. (Directgov, 2010).

In the USA, definitions do vary slightly from state to state but the majority of programmes are based on the US federal definition of gifted and talented students which asserts:

> Students, children, or youth who give evidence of high achievement capability in areas such as intellectual, creative, artistic, or leadership capacity, or in specific academic fields, and who need services and activities not ordinarily provided by the school in order to fully develop those capabilities. (Public Law, pp. 103–382, Title XIV, p. 388)

In keeping with the aim of gifted and talented programmes offering opportunities for 'bright', working-class children, it is psychological explanations on thinking processes or developmental aspects which have come to dominate studies on gifted girls and boys (Stoeger, 2008). Although Stoeger does not state explicitly why there is this particular focus on gender 'brain structures' we would suggest that it is in keeping with the concerns over 'boys' underachievement', the explanations for which have been largely (albeit misguidingly) attributed to cognitive differences (e.g. Gurian, 2002; Norfleet James, 2007). And, in the same way that psychological explanations of boys' underachievement have been widely critiqued (see next section), any suggestion that cognitive superiority either (a) can be attributed solely to brain functioning or (b) is the means by which 'bright working-class students' are successfully caught up in the net and dropped into gifted and talented programmes, is misleading. As we have shown earlier, the construction of, and access to, gifted and talented programmes is far more complex than simply assuming 'bright working-class' pupils will automatically find themselves on one of these courses.

In neoliberal societies, where schools are in a marketplace and competing to attract the most able students who will enable them to do well in the League Tables, gifted and talented programmes act as a selling point. In the UK and USA, Gewirtz et al. (1995) and Wells and Oakes (1997), respectively, found that middle-class parents were particularly keen on selective schooling processes whereby some (of their) children were seen to be flourishing. As such, the main impetus for schools' 'fast-track' or 'enriched' or 'gifted' programmes 'appears to be *commercial* rather than *educational*' (Gewirtz et al., 1995, p. 169). For parents and pupils, there is a certain amount of social and educational cachet about being 'chosen' for inclusion in one of these programmes. Not least is the organizational management of these programmes that clearly single out these pupils for special attention. For example, the California Department of Education (2010) says that these gifted programmes should consist of 'special day classes, part-time groupings, and cluster groupings'. As has been shown in comparative studies of gifted and non-gifted children it is the process of defining children as gifted that 'causes them to feel that they excel in the academic field and therefore they strive to meet the expectations set for them in the programs built specially for them' (Science Daily, 2009). And, as we have shown earlier, whilst middle-class parental cultural capital operates to secure access to such courses for their offspring (McNamara Horvat et al., 2006), working-class pupils' lack of the same deters them from continuing with such programmes, even when obtaining a place on them (Reay, 2004). Hence although the link between constructions of 'giftedness' and social class/race/gender is rarely acknowledged (given the discursive unacceptability of any analysis which could be considered eugenicist), clearly the concept *is* socially constructed, and is mobilized and/or accessed more easily by particular social groups. This has strong implications in the context for our study of young people who had been designated 'high achieving' (and indeed, many of these young people were assigned to particular 'gifted and talented' programmes).

The discussion in this section has concentrated on how the concepts of neoliberalism, especially those of competition, effectiveness and the responsibility of 'individuals' have shaped educational policies. 'Gifted and talented' programmes have been singled out for discussion as these are of particular significance for our study of high achieving pupils. However, we cannot leave this chapter on educational policy without giving some consideration to the main themes of this book, that is, how gender and achievement has featured in recent years.

Gender and Achievement in Neoliberalist Educational Policy

It is fair to say that 'gender and achievement' only came to occupy a central position in educational policy around the mid-1990s when the League Tables drew attention to girls' outperformance of boys (Francis and Skelton, 2005). Part of the reason why this apparent 'underachievement' of half the school population was important was because of the potential waste of future human capital. Another explanation offered by pro/feminists[3] for the policy focus on boys from 1995 onwards was because it was *boys* that were underachieving. As Pat Mahony (1998, p. 39) argued:

> When the focus was on the alleged underachievement of girls, it took a good deal of persuasion by (mainly) feminists before policy makers would look beyond the innate capacities of girls themselves for explanations of 'failure' in maths and science . . . By and large what was once evidence of the problem *of* girls has now become, not even the problem *of* boys, but the problem *for* boys.

From the outset, feminists have challenged the extent to which *all* boys were actually underachieving and pointed out how social class and ethnicity made a difference to educational outcomes of both boys *and* girls (Epstein et al., 1998; Kenway et al., 1998). However, any arguments highlighting the complexity around gender and attainment in examinations fell on deaf ears for many years. Rather, the response to boys' underachievement on the part of educational policymakers was both swift and interventionist. The main concern lay with boys' failure in literacy and a number of policy documents have appeared suggesting various classroom practices aimed at motivating boys and improving their reading and writing skills (Ofsted, 1993, 2003a,b; QCA, 1998; DCSF, 2007b). These documents offered strategies to teachers that promoted stereotypical notions of boys and perpetuated the myth that all boys approached learning in the same way, that is:

- Boys require tasks based on kinaesthetic learning styles (DCSF, 2007b).
- Boys require more active forms of learning (QCA, 1998).
- Boys prefer non-fiction and non-literary texts (Ofsted, 2003a).
- Boys require 'boy friendly' materials (Ofsted, 2003b).

In addition, these documents suggest that teachers are not always aware of, or sensitive to, boys' emotional, social and educational needs (see especially QCA, 1998; DfES, 2003). As a majority of teachers, especially primary teachers, are women then the implication is that women teachers are not as likely as men teachers to be able to help boys achieve their potential. As such, one of the motivations underpinning the government recruitment drive of attracting more men into primary teaching has been the ongoing underachievement of boys (Francis and Skelton 2005; Martino, 2009).

So in relation to gender and achievement, the policy efforts to raise achievement may be seen as facilitating *boys'* achievement (and their inclusion). Despite all the policies and interventionist strategies, however, there has been

no corresponding improvement in reducing the gender gap. Whilst the performance of boys has improved, so has the performance of girls, thus boys
are still frequently reported in the media and by popularist writers as being
let down by the educational system (McClure, 2008; Palmer, 2010). However,
in educational policy, as the individualized society thesis sees the individual as responsible and mutually obliged, it is no surprise to see policy statements appearing that increasingly express frustration at the apparent lack of
progress among some boys. From a neoliberal perspective, underachieving
boys appear to be unable or unwilling to take up the 'opportunities' that will
facilitate achievement – achievement that is vital for both individual and state
economic success in a globalized economy. Neoliberalism depends on pupils
producing themselves as flexible, responsible, competitive 'individuals' all of
which evoke the 'good' hard-working pupil rather than the 'laddish' school
boy. Within the 'something for something' social ethos discussed earlier,
underachieving boys do not appear to be upholding their side of the bar-
gain. In fact, on top of their own lack of application, they increasingly became
identified as distracting their classmates and teachers, hence impeding those
better-intentioned pupils doing their best to progress. For example, in a
policy document written, interestingly, by the Department of Education but
produced by the Health Development Agency: 'Secondary schools often contain groups of boys who create a culture that is anti-work, anti-establishment
and disruptive to both boys' and girls' education – the antithesis of the positive achievement culture and ethos that a school is hoping to create' (DfES,
2003, p.14). What we can see here is the shift away from discourses around
boys that position them as 'victims' (e.g. 'poor boys', or 'boys will be boys';
Epstein et al., 1998) towards one of 'problem boys' (Francis and Skelton, 2005;
Mills et al., 2009).

However, towards the end of the Labour administration's period in to a coalition Conservative-Liberal government, the then Department of Children,
Schools and Families (DCSF) had somewhat developed their position on
gender and achievement to one which better recognized the complexities at
stake, and even feminist research findings highlighting such complexity, and
the implication of social constructions of gender, and school structures, in
patterns of gender and achievement. For example, the DCSF produced two
policy documents that challenged predominant ideas around boys as either
'victims' or 'problems' and girls as always academically successful and which
outlined the complexity of gender and achievement (DCSF 2009a,b). It has
yet to be seen how these documents fare under the coalition government and

whether the implications raised will be transformed into strategies implemented in schools.

Comparing policy on gender and achievement with that of countries such as Australia and the USA, some interesting points become apparent. Firstly, whilst the UK, North America and Australasia are all influenced by neoliberalism, it is the UK that places a specific focus on achievement and especially in relation to that of gender. Australia has educational policies on boys, and in these discourses focus on 'poor boys' or boys as victims of feminist agendas.

In the USA boys' education has yet to be the subject of policy but this does not mean to say that the kinds of concerns around 'failing boys' do not feature in discussions about education and schooling (Weaver-Hightower, 2009). Worries about what is happening to boys are not occupying a central place in debates around achievement and education, rather, as Weaver-Hightower (2009) points out, it is a group of best-selling books aimed at parents of boys and focusing on boys' mental health and well-being which have dominated the field (e.g. Pollack, 1998; Kindlon and Thompson, 2000; Dobson, 2005; Tyre, 2008). These are popularist, practice-based books. The absence of critical, theoretical interrogations of young masculinities has meant that teachers have turned to these books for advice and guidance as to how to respond to 'boys' needs' in schools. As Weaver-Hightower observes, this is potentially damaging and certainly detrimental to boys' (and girls') education as these books are, for the most part, based on outdated and simplistic psychological and biological explanations of gender and are also predominantly anti-feminist. The policy in the USA is then the same as that followed in the UK and some other Western countries. That is: first, 'gender' issues are regarded as shorthand for 'women's issues'; second, the focus is on neoconservative (rather than neoliberal) concerns around the setting of standards, accountability and testing (Weaver-Hightower, 2009). As such, gender takes a back seat although it has to be noted that the gaps in attainment based on 'race' feature significantly in policy discussions (see National Assessment of Educational Progress website for example). Given the specific focus on 'race' and attainment in the USA, Weaver Hightower warns of the racial implications that could follow an increased attention to boys' achievement similar to those that have prevailed in the UK (whereby certain groups of minority ethnic boys are pathologized, e.g. Black Caribbean boys). As is the situation in the UK and Australia, there are good reasons for looking at boys' achievement, not least in literacy, but lessons can be learnt from these countries in terms of how best to tackle gender under/achievement (Younger et al., 2005; Lingard et al., 2009).

Australia's response to gender and achievement in education has been more similar to that of the UK in that both have centred on boys' underachievement with little attention given to differences between groups of boys, as well as girls (Lingard et al., 2009). Unlike the UK, Australian educational policy documents have incorporated discourses around 'poor boys' and 'boys will be boys'. As we have shown above, in the UK, whilst such discourses co-existed with that of 'problem boys' and others, these were largely reflected in the professional educational literature, rather than in official government policy. In policy, 'boys' were constructed as biological/physiological bodies at the mercy of their instincts and socialized behaviours. Also, the UK never had the kinds of official policies on girls' education that were prevalent in Australia from the mid-1970s through to the 1990s which were aimed at addressing the injustices girls experienced in schooling (Mills, 2003). What has occurred in Australia is that these policies concerned with the education of girls 'have washed *girls* from the title and replaced it with the term gender' (Mills et al., 2009, p. 39). There is greater evidence of a backlash against feminism in the Australian policy context too as feminist contributions were more in evidence here than in the UK. To quote Pat Mahony, a leading British feminist (2003, p.75), 'One obvious difference between Australia and the UK is that we have had no tradition of a "femocracy" working with the central State.' There are two implications here: first, the involvement of feminists working on developing policy on girls' education indicates the commitment to social justice in Australia – something missing from UK educational policy (indeed there was no official policy on girls' education; Arnot et al., 1999). Second, justification of the re-focus on boys' needs demanded a vilification of previous approaches to show where it had all 'gone wrong'; and what was seen to have 'gone wrong' was girls' academic success, which was seen as having been bought at the expense of boys (Lingard et al., 2009). So there is clear evidence of an anti-feminist stance in Australian policy (Mills et al., 2009). This hegemony of the 'poor boys' perspective in Australia, in contrast to a variety of discourses in the UK, reflects: (a) the comparative strength and impact of feminist work in previous Australian policy (in relation to the UK), at which the backlash is targeted; and (b) the greater focus in UK policy with neoliberal standards, accountability and effectiveness.

Conclusion

What we have attempted to do in this chapter is provide a context for our findings on gender and high achieving pupils by setting out the social, economic and educational policy background of the UK. In looking at approaches to gender and achievement in other Western countries similarly influenced by neoliberalist agendas it has been possible to identify the nuances of gender and educational policy frameworks. If these students were at school in Australia, North America or continental Europe rather than the UK, the expectations, irrespective of the country, would be for them to do well and the education they received would be in anticipation of their future contribution to the economic market place. At the same time, these pupils are likely to be even more aware of the expectations of achievement as the quasi-market of the UK schooling system, with its emphasis on credentials and the individual's part in securing or failing to secure these, is located firmly within neoliberalist constructions of individual responsibility. Thus, as will be seen, young people in our study were fully aware that they were being provided with 'educational opportunities' and it was their responsibility to take these up. For example, homework has been shown in myriad research studies (see for example, Farrow et al., 1999; Hallam, 2004) to be disliked and regarded as inconsequential by school pupils. Nevertheless the students in our study were assiduous about homework, with most completing it the same day it was given, and only one or two pupils saying they left it to the weekend.

The schools attended by the pupils in our study all had gifted and talented registers and were all highly engaged with the achievement agenda. Indeed, many of the schools agreed to participate in the belief that being associated with a research study on 'high achievement' offered them a certain cachet. These schools were all in very different catchment areas ranging from inner-city to rural locations and the school populations varied accordingly. Understandably then, whilst all schools were 'signed up' to the achievement agenda, what being successful meant inevitably varied from school to school.

What we have also shown here is that 'achievement' tends, in policy terms, to be largely interpreted as attainment. And the attainment of credentials is about far more than the possession of superior cognitive skills or being more intelligent than everyone else (and we should note too that we do not believe that these exist unproblematically). As discussed earlier in this chapter, the intersectionality of gender, 'race' and social class is crucial to any understanding of achievement, and whilst some schools were populated predominantly by white, middle-class children others comprised a mixture of social class and ethnicity thus shaping the patterns of achievement in those schools. At the same time, we were not surprised to find that, even in schools with high minority ethnic populations, those pupils labelled as 'high achievers' were overwhelmingly white.

The rest of the chapters in this book turn attention to the findings of our study where we illustrate how being and becoming a 'high achiever' requires effort and demands attention to the production of a 'sociable self'. The extent to which these high achieving pupils were more, or less, successful in securing and maintaining a 'balance' between achieving in their academic work and being regarded as a sociable person provides a focus for discussion in the following chapters.

Notes

1   Although we acknowledge that such behaviours are not limited to middle-class girls.

2   *Accelerating Achievement and Ensuring Equity* (2010) US Department of Education; *Learning Together: Achievement through Choice and Opportunity* (2004) Australian Government: Department of Education, Science and Training. *Engaging Parents in Raising Achievement: Do Parents Know They Matter?* (2007a) UK Department for Children, Schools and Families.

3   In response to long-standing debates over whether men can be described as 'feminists', the term 'pro/feminist' is used to indicate both men and women who locate their research and writing within feminist theory.

2 Conceptualizing Gender and Achievement

Chapter Outline

Having introduced the key themes of this book and the education policy contextualizing them, we need now to explain the concepts underpinning our analysis. What do we mean by gender, and how are we analysing 'gender difference'? Our aim here is to explain our perspective and its origins, rather than to tease out the different ideological and/or theoretical approaches which have been applied to understanding about gender, behaviour and ability, and in debates concerning gender and achievement. Elsewhere two of us have attempted to map such diverse approaches, which include positions as diverse as sex role theory, functionalist theory, and evolutionary psychology (see Francis and Skelton, 2005). But here we attempt a much more straightforward task. We begin by providing a précis of developments in gender theory, finishing the section by explaining recent theoretical applications drawing on poststructuralist theories and the work of Mikhail Bakhtin, which we shall draw on in later chapters. Next we turn to the empirical study that provides the 'case' for this book. We explain the methodology of the study and describe the sample of schools and young people involved.

Gender Theory

Much public commentary on gender and achievement continues to distinguish between 'boys' and 'girls' as though these categories can be taken for granted, and to distinguish them is unproblematic. However, gender theory questions such assumptions and offers an account of why we tend to behave differently according to our socially ascribed 'sex'. Gender theory largely incorporates/overlaps with feminist theory. There are many feminist theoretical positions (including, for example, liberal feminism, radical feminism, Marxist feminism, black feminism, poststructuralist feminism and so on), and hence there are many different explanations and theories of gender. Fundamentally, contemporary feminist theory offers a highly developed political account of gender difference and the power inequalities resulting from, and contributing to, these differences. We focus here on those theories and perspectives which have informed the way we consider gender and education. Our aim is to briefly trace the debates from the 'second wave' feminist distinction and focus on 'nurture' rather 'nature' – when feminists such as Ann Oakley (UK) and Barbara Licht and Carol Dweck (US feminist psychologists) succeeded in driving forward the ideas of gender as socially constructed whilst 'sex roles' were located in physiology. Following theoretical development through to today we reach the postmodern stance adopted by third wave feminists[1] whereby 'sex' is itself seen as socially constructed (Butler, 1990; 1997; Halberstam, 1998).

Sex Role and Socialization Theories

Before elaborating 'sex role theory', it is important to contextualize these early cultural accounts of gender difference in the 'sexual politics' of second wave feminism. The various different feminist perspectives underpinning and developing in the period of 'second wave feminism' (the late 1960s, 1970s and early 1980s) have been well documented.[2] But these diverse feminist perspectives could generally be considered 'global feminisms', in that what united them was the idea that 'women' as a global group (albeit black women in the case of black feminism; or women of different social classes within Marxist feminism) were bound together by their common experiences of marginalization and oppression. Furthermore, these various feminist perspectives were united in the shared perception of feminism as a political and practical movement. Consequently second wave feminist perspectives subscribed to the notion that the goals were

- *Political*: a means of action, not simply theorizing
- *Critical*: not to accept that all knowledge is objective – because it was/is manufactured by those who were educated and had access to knowledge production (i.e. white upper/middle class men).
- *Praxis-oriented*: to change the way we did things (for educationalists, this included the way in which we researched problems and addressed teaching, and acknowledged the importance of subjectivity in those processes).

This 'globalism' can be particularly applied to the notion of 'patriarchy', adopted predominantly by radical feminism. Patriarchy (meaning literally 'rule by the father') formed one of the central tenets of second wave feminism: it was seen as oppressing *all* women (irrespective of 'race' and class). As two of us point out elsewhere (Skelton and Francis, 2009), where feminists might accept, modify or reject this explanation according to their theoretical position (e.g. whether patriarchy, white supremacy, capitalism, or a combination of these is primarily responsible for oppression), questions around power and control were key issues for most feminists.

Impacting on the development of sex role theory in feminist work was the increasing rejection of biological determinism among feminists, and the interest in cultural and sociological explanations for gender difference (or 'sex difference', as it was then termed). A body of work on the relationship between sex attribution and gender expectations, led by researchers such as Lake (1975) and Kessler and McKenna (1978) showed how people behaved very differently with infants depending on what they perceived the baby's sex to be. For example, in one frequently repeated study, mothers were handed the same baby at different times but told 'this is Adam' or 'this is Beth'. The mothers were far more likely to call them 'sweet', smile at them, and handle them more, when they believed they were holding a girl baby (Lake, 1975; Smith and Lloyd, 1978; Whyte, 1983). Meanwhile, anthropological studies were showing that 'sex roles' differ in different cultures (e.g. Hoffer, 1974). The idea that gender was a cultural construction and not a biological one was further refined by feminists through analysis of differences among various social groups (e.g. according to ethnicity and social class).

In fact, although seeking to demonstrate that gender was a cultural construction rather than a simple product of biology, a majority of second wave feminists did not reject outright the place of biology in explanations of gender (as has been later claimed by anti-feminists in the boys' underachievement debate, e.g. Moir and Moir, 1999). Leading British second wave theorist Ann Oakley (1981b, p. 53) mused on the 'relative importance of biology' but noted the interrelationship of how 'nurture affects nature' (p. 61). However, the key focus for second wave feminism was on rejecting biology ('sex') as determining roles. It was the need to distinguish between biological 'sex' (female/male) and the social construction resulting from such distinction (for example, dressing girl babies in pink and encouraging them to be gentle and decorous, while boys are dressed in blue and expected to be more boisterous) that lead to the coining of the term 'gender'. 'Gender' alluded to this social production and reproduction of gender difference, and the power inequalities inherent within it. So it was this that feminists attended to; that is they devoted their attention to identifying how gender was reproduced in traditional and stereotypical ways, and finding ways of challenging these notions.

In order to facilitate such analysis, then, the predominant explanation represented in the 1970s and early 1980s was that of *sex role* and *socialization* theories (Frazier and Sadker, 1973; Lobban, 1978, Delamont, 1980).[3] Sex role theories are an extension of role theories which say that children learn ways of relating to the world around them through observing how people act, and by being rewarded when they themselves demonstrate appropriate behaviour or punished when they display inappropriate behaviour (Gregory, 1969). Sex role socialization, the notion that girls and boys absorb social messages about their appropriate gender roles, was felt by many second wave feminists to be helpful, because it showed the ways in which gender differences were socially developed rather than being due to innate biological differences (Sutherland, 1981; Serbin, 1983). This was very much a 'top down' model which assumed that children observed and soaked up social information like sponges, emulating the behaviour of adults in the family, media and local community. For females it meant learning and internalizing such traits as caring, nurturing and selflessness, whilst males demonstrated characteristics such as aggression, independence and competitiveness (Oakley, 1972; Seidler, 1989). So, such theories suggest that young girls learn 'how to be a girl' by social messages such as receiving approval for feminine traits such as gentleness and helpfulness, whilst young boys are affirmed for being energetic and competitive (Oakley, 1972; Byrne, 1978; Seidler, 1989). These messages are conveyed to children (and adults) via social institutions including the family, local communities, education and childcare institutions, religious and cultural institutions, and the media. Hence these processes of gender socialization were seen to reproduce gender difference (distinct 'gender roles') through generations.

Within this theoretical approach, there have been two key accounts of how gender difference is perpetuated. Social learning theorists argued that gender identity was learned by children modelling their behaviour on the stereotypical behaviours of same-sex members of their family, peer group, local community and via the media (Sharpe, 1976). A different (albeit often overlapping) account was posited by cognitive-development theorists; here children's understanding of their gender identity was dependent upon their stage of cognitive development (see e.g. Kohlberg, 1966; Emmerich et al., 1977). It is such psychological theorizing of gender constructions which has been used to support the idea that sexism is at its peak in children aged 5–6 years (Sayers, 1984).

Socialization theories underpinned much second wave feminist research (both liberal and radical) in education. Feminist researchers focused on the role of educational institutions in the reproduction of gender difference, and the various ways in which this reproduction was achieved, via the curriculum, teacher expectations, peer regulation, school organizational practices and so on. Many feminist researchers, and especially radical feminists, argued that, like society as a whole, the education system reflected and elevated male values, and systematically demeaned and marginalized girls and women. Hence schools were seen as reproducing male domination of women by not only denying girls and women full access to existing knowledge and resources, but also failing to recognize female contributions to these areas. Furthermore, school organizational structures and procedures ignored (and hence were complicit in) the daily harassment of girls and women teachers by boys and men teachers (see e.g. Delamont, 1980; Spender, 1982; Mahony, 1985). Such research demonstrated how boys dominated teachers' time and attention, how they monopolized the classroom in terms of space and securing resources, how their interests dictated the curriculum and how they sexually harassed girls. Many of these practices on the part of the school – whereby gender difference was assumed and perpetuated, and girls systematically devalued – were seen by feminist researchers as comprising a 'hidden curriculum' via which female subordination was perpetuated.

Solutions proffered by feminist proponents of sex role and socialization perspectives differed according to the specific feminist views they espoused. For example, radical feminists tended to challenge the very structures and epistemological assumptions underpinning the education system, which they saw as patriarchal and perpetuating masculine values and power. Whereas liberal feminists tended to believe the then existing educational system could be altered to be more inclusive of girls and to better facilitate their opportunities. It was often argued that in order to combat gender stereotypical socialization, educationalists should encourage children to become involved in activities usually pursued by the opposite sex. For example, the booklet *Do You Provide Equal Educational Opportunities* (Equal Opportunities Commission, 1984) urges primary schools to ensure male and female dolls are available to boys and girls, and to encourage girls to engage with construction toys. Such logic underpinned the majority of 'equal opportunities' programmes in schools at this time (Myers, 2000). If children learned their gender identities through role modelling then it was thought all that was needed was to present them with non-stereotypical models and images. Reading books were vetted to ensure they provided girls (and boys) with a range of adult models; feminist teachers checked their language to avoid stereotypical allusions, and worked to ensure non-gender-discriminatory practice, and the 'Wendy House' became the 'Home Corner' (Skelton, 1989; Measor and Sikes, 1992). Of course, such approaches reflect belief in the possibility of social change, whereas, as we shall explain, a key criticism of sex role theories has been that they are unable to *account* for social change and resistance, as roles are viewed as fixed and continually reproduced by the 'agents of socialization'.

The implication of sex role/socialization perspectives was that a self-fulfilling prophesy was in operation – the processes of schooling undermined girls' confidence which resulted in them having lower expectations and not prioritizing exam success but seeing their futures primarily as wives and mothers. The nature of sex role theory, with its locus in the psyche, meant that initiatives were focused on the 'individual' and it was up to them to take the opportunities offered and develop less stereotyped behaviours and attitudes. Furthermore, such strategies tended to be focused on girls. As Madeleine Arnot (1991, p. 453) has argued, school-based strategies to support girls tended to be somewhat naive in their assumptions concerning the simplicity of the task, and tended to position girls as victims in need of remedy. But more than this, there was also a fundamental theoretical dilemma, in that socialization and sex role theories were unable to explain the very social changes that feminists espoused. By the mid-1980s, feminist education researchers were identifying the fluidity of gender roles among boys and girls in the classroom, thereby belying the view that gender roles were consistent/fixed, and drawing attention to agency in the construction of gender (e.g. Anyon, 1983; Riddell, 1989). Furthermore, society and its production of gender was changing, albeit often in unanticipated ways. It was those theories which located power relations as central which were found to be more relevant in understanding constructions of gender identity.

Accommodation and Resistance: Social Constructionist Accounts

Social constructionist feminists have contested the 'top down' view of socialization theories that regards institutions (e.g. family, friends, the media) as determining social behaviour. Instead they point out how people are not simply passive recipients of socialization but actively construct and impact upon the world, thus shaping their own lives and those of others. The general increase in girls' and women's educational participation and success – notable in the UK by the mid-1990s – is one example of the kind of social change which is difficult to explain from a 'sex role' perspective. Many girls are now achieving relative educational success *in spite of* the continued[4] male domination of the co-ed classroom which sex role theorists in the 1980s had previously postulated as explaining girls' apparent underachievement.

Such complexity, and the fluidity of 'gender roles', were increasingly recognized by feminist educational researchers studying the manifestation of gender in the classroom; these were theorized as 'accommodation and resistance' by researchers such as Anyon (1983) and Riddell (1989). Hence, the understanding of gender roles as fixed (so integral to sex role theory) grew increasingly problematic for feminists working in education. In the latter part of the 1980s, social constructionist accounts of gender began to emerge that addressed such challenges. Social constructionists see meaning, including identities, as socially situated and constructed through social interaction (e.g. Mead, 1934; Berger and Luckmann, 1966). Hence in this view gender is mutually constructed and developed due to the social expectations and perceptions perpetuated through interaction (so again, social constructionist perspectives see gendered behaviour as produced via social factors rather than as due to biological programming). Researchers drawing on these accounts were often particularly interested in the active part that young people themselves played in the construction of their gender identities, and the ways in which such constructions were achieved during interaction in educational environments. In contrast to the fixity and potential determinism of socialization theories, the social constructionist view is concerned with difference, contradiction and change – social constructionists attend to nuance and micro aspects of local interactions. So, for example, many feminist researchers have observed how particular constructions of gender and gender relations are produced in individual classroom environments, and the differences that aspects such as school culture, teacher approach and expectations, peer group dynamics (and so forth) can make to these productions. Educational researchers have shown how boys and girls endeavour to construct their gender identities in ways that are deemed most appropriate or desirable (and hence invested with status and power) to their peers and in the values of society at large.

One key contributor to social constructionist theory in gender and education was R.W. Connell, who contributed a strong analysis of gender and power, and famously drew on Gramsci's notion of hegemony to theorize how different constructions of gender (masculinity) are imbued with varying levels of social status (Connell, 1987, 1995). Connell (1995) terms the high status, socially accepted expression of masculinity 'hegemonic masculinity', identifying the way in which it excludes and subjugates other expressions of masculinity as well as femininity. This position was highly influential from the late 1980s on, triggering the trend towards a plural terminology for gender ('masculinities' and 'femininities'), and underpinning some of the key studies of masculinity in education.

Social constructionists have also commonly been concerned with the ways in which different aspects of social identity (for example, 'race', gender, social class, age, sexuality and so on) impact in interaction and on individual constructions of identity, and the various consequences for individuals. They have drawn attention to the way in which constructions of gender are relational: there can be no conception of masculinity without a femininity to compare and contrast it to. Such observations have underpinned subsequent theorizing around the performativity of gender (cf. Butler, 1990) – gender behaviours and aesthetics produced in relation to an 'other' and routinized via repetition to the extent that they often become unconscious.

Although there are elements of such concepts of performativity in classic social constructionist works such as that of Erving Goffman (1959), it is post-structuralist Judith Butler who most notably posited this approach within gender theory. And this marks a move away from what we might call 'partial' social constructionist positions. Although focusing on cultural aspects of gender construction, many social constructionists nevertheless see individuals as biologically sexed, with consequences flowing from this bodily difference in terms of the way others interact with them, hence perpetuating gender differences in behaviour and experience. In this view, men and women are physically (biologically) different, but gendered *behaviour* is socially produced. Hence the notion of *sex difference* is retained. However, other social constructionists go further (we might refer to them as 'complete' social constructionists), seeing biological sex itself as socially constructed. This is particularly the case for those influenced by poststructuralism.

Poststructuralist Theory

Poststructuralism is a particular strand of postmodernism, with its roots in literary criticism. It emerged in reaction to the structuralist movement in literary theory, which built on the work of Saussure to maintain that a universal structure of language exists and determines human thought (as we cannot think or speak outside the 'prison house of language'), and which can be scientifically analysed. Poststructuralists such as Barthes and Derrida set out to *deconstruct* these patterns of language, delighting in illustrating how the text can 'play' and be interpreted in multifarious ways, hence revealing that there are no fixed 'truths' of meaning. This work was situated within a wider movement in reaction to modernism's belief in the 'reason of science' and Enlightenment rationalism and universalism. Postmodernism, as this movement came to be called, rejected claims to reason and 'truth', maintaining the relativist position that there is no transcendent position from which 'the real' can be identified and tested – rather, 'truth' and 'reality' depend on perspective, and no perspective can claim to be more valid or 'true' than another.

The work of Michel Foucault has been particularly influential in gender theory, and in the social sciences more broadly. Foucault developed a critique of the subject and an analysis of power as operating through discourses rather than held by particular groups of people and lacked by others. He also developed the application of genealogical and discourse analytic methods. His work has in turn been built on by arguably the most famous poststructuralist feminist of contemporary times, Judith Butler, whom as we have seen, returned to early feminist preoccupations with 'sex' identification to argue that 'sex' as well as 'gender' is entirely socially constructed and perpetuated by acts of repetition via discourse. She and others have argued that, rather than just the behavioural aspects of gender being discursively produced, the apparent biological givens of sex difference are also discursively (socially) constructed, being actually far less consistent and immutable than we are lead to believe. For Butler, the human subject does not 'become' gendered;

rather gender animates the human subject (we cannot 'be' or be recognizable – 'intelligible', as Butler puts it – without gender). And whereas many feminists had previously studied sexuality as closely related to gender, Butler again explodes this differential, seeing (hetero)sexuality as an inseparable aspect of society's binarized sex/gender/sexuality production.

Poststructuralism has appealed to many feminists for a number of reasons, as one of us discusses elsewhere (Francis, 1999, 2001). Foucault's explanation of power as operating through discourses was able to explain the phenomena of resistance and contradiction which had proved so problematic for sex role theory (Foucault sees the self as passively positioned by certain discourses while simultaneously active in *positioning* in discourses). It was also able to explain some of the theoretical complexities that had challenged feminism in the 1980s: for example, the way in which power is constituted between women (and between men), as well as between women and men. This view of people as positioned in and produced by discourse can also explain the gendered nature of society as produced by gender discourses that position all selves as men or women, and present these categories as relational (Davies, 1989).

This work has, then, challenged previous feminist analysis that saw 'sex' as underpinning gender difference, and also notions of 'multiple masculinities and femininities'. Whereas such work has tended to veer towards typologies of different 'sorts' of masculinity or femininity, and to some extent apply fixity around these different 'types', poststructuralism sees gender as produced via discourse, and hence constantly and permanently in flux.

So how did these perspectives manifest in the field of gender and education? Bronwyn Davies' work made an early, influential contribution. She undertook a study exploring why gender performances remain so entrenched in spite of feminist efforts otherwise. Exploring young children's perceptions of various feminist fairy tales, she showed how 4- to 5-year-olds 'heard' the stories in particular ways – often very different to that presumably intended by the feminist author – due to gendered and age-specific discourses. The children employed 'category-maintenance work' to ensure they, and their peers, acted out the 'correct' gender: Davies (1989) showed how these practices were perpetuated between children in the classroom and playground, and the resulting impact on children's (gendered) power positions. A further early poststructuralist contributor in the field, Valerie Walkerdine (e.g. 1986, 1988, 1989, 1990, Walkerdine and Lucey, 1989), drew on both poststructuralist deconstructive and psychoanalytic accounts to reveal the ways in which girls are positioned in education policy and pedagogic discourses as lacking, attending to the gender discourses at work in social institutions. Some researchers have applied discourse analysis to the policy and media writing on 'boys' underachievement', identifying and examining the discourses producing these arguments. Since then, poststructuralist approaches have been taken up and applied to issues as diverse as girls and maths to children's productions of (hetero)sexuality in the classroom. It has been profoundly influential.

There are however a range of critiques of poststructuralist work on gender. Key early (and remaining) critiques of poststructuralism have been from those retaining elements of positivism/empiricism in their approach to research, and from those feminists retaining a universalist or emancipatory perspective. Postmodern theories, from a positivist perspective, amount to nothing more radical than a relativist view of life, with no more substance than storytelling (given poststructuralist rejection of traditional forms of evidence). Emancipatory theorists have accused postmodernist perspectives of advocating an apolitical agenda, deconstructing movements that seek to work for progressive social change. The feminist movement was born from Enlightenment, humanist premises of 'rights' and embraced what could be seen as a 'grand narrative' of emancipation and human betterment. As such, many feminists were concerned that poststructuralist deconstruction undermined the feminist political project (for examples of feminist scepticism about poststructuralism, see Balbus, 1986, or Hartsock, 1989). Moreover, as Jones (1997) and McNay (2000) discuss, poststructuralist theory revokes the agency required to further emancipatory projects due to its refutation of the coherent self which can make (rational or consistent) choices. Many theorists – feminist and otherwise – have been critical of postmodernism's tendency to deconstruct, criticize and even ridicule political/ideological 'grand narratives', without suggesting anything with which to replace these in order to address continuing social inequalities. This has led some to question whether poststructuralism is not simply an androcentric and/or reactionary position that upholds the status quo (e.g. Hartsock, 1990; Soper, 1990). More recently, concerns have been raised that an exclusive attention to 'text' (discourse) cannot account for the profound materiality of gender, as related to the sexed body (whether this is seen as sexed via discourse or biology). Theorists such as Cohen-Shabot (2007) and Paechter (2006) have maintained that the impact of what the former refers to as the 'meaty' body on gender performance and the reading of this performance is profound, and has not been adequately acknowledged in poststructuralist work.[5] This point concerning the importance of *bodies* in gender construction has been increasingly illustrated in empirical work in the gender and education field (Paechter, 2007; Francis, 2000; Jackson, 2006b; Francis et al., 2010).

As a result of these debates, the emphasis in some feminist research has shifted towards the possibility of redirecting rather than completely breaking with Enlightenment principles in order to retain the feminist project of emancipation (see Mouffe, 1996; Assiter, 1996; McNay, 2000). Others, including ourselves, have also begun to engage accounts that can arguably better address the role of the material (in addition to discourse) in analysis of gender constructions.

Other Recent Accounts of Gender

Feminists demanding what they consider to be a more hard-hitting, coherent account of inequality have sometimes turned back to structuralist theorists (or redefined and developed manifestations of key theorists' work) as the theoretical underpinning of their work. Neo-Marxist positions remain represented (see e.g. Mojab, 2006; Colley, 2007), but in particular, feminist educational researchers working in the field of social class and gender have often turned to Bourdieu's work to theorize their findings regarding social class inequality in education. Hence in work on gender and education, researchers have drawn on Bourdieu's concepts of capitals, habitus and distinction to analyse the production of class inequality in educational policy and settings, and the intersections of social class with gender and ethnicity (see e.g. Skeggs, 1997; Reay, 1998, 2004, 2006; Archer, 2003, Archer and Francis, 2007; Crozier et al., 2008).

Some feminists have found both poststructural and structural positions inadequate for explaining how inequalities and life experiences are not solely dependent on factors such as gender, class, ethnicity and so on. For example, even people sharing the same family and educational backgrounds may experience life very differently. Further, some see semiotic and poststructuralist accounts of experiences as constituted purely discursively (via language) as inadequate to explain such differences, or indeed to explain emotional experience more broadly. Such concerns have increasingly resulted in researchers turning to psychoanalysis. Psychoanalysis has been strongly represented in feminist theory since the emergence of second wave feminism, with the work of writers like Juliet Mitchell (1974) and Nancy Chodorow (1978) proving highly influential. And indeed, Lacan's poststructuralist psychoanalytic insights (and those of Juliet Kristeva, who was closely influenced by Lacan) have frequently been drawn on feminist poststructuralist theory. Yet in the 1980s and 1990s, with the notable exception of Valerie Walkerdine and Helen Lucey's work, these positions had rarely strongly informed feminist work in education. Now, however, some educational researchers are central to the body of work that sees itself as investigating the 'psycho-social', melding sociological and psychoanalytic theory and areas of exploration in order to explore individuals' experiences of social experience. Where poststructuralists such as Walkerdine (1990, 1997) see the psychic realm as discursively constituted, those drawing on the work of Klein in the 'psycho-social' movement include conceptions of selfhood and experience as pre-discursive experience. Researchers such as Helen Lucey have drawn on Kleinian concepts such as projection, splitting, demonization, ambivalence and so on in order to analyse the constructions of pupils in terms of their (gendered and socially classed) understandings of self and other in relation to educational achievement and 'standards' (2001, 2004; Lucey and Reay, 2002).

A Satisfactory Account of Gender?

So, theoretical positions represented in current research on gender and education remain as diverse as was the case 30 years ago. Many of the perspectives represented at that time remain, though some have fallen out of favour. Social learning theories have been widely critiqued, but remain represented both in government policy materials and in some liberal feminist accounts which for example recommend 'role modelling' and so on to address equality of opportunities. As we have seen, the influence of poststructuralism has been profound, both in terms of impact on many researchers and the reactions of others against it. Such reactions have resulted in new theoretical trajectories and developments.

What remains however, is – we would argue – something of an impasse in accounts of gender. As we shall elaborate, there are residual conundrums that characterize the field and that no single account has, as yet, been able to satisfactorily address. These include:

- Accounting for the fluidity of gender constructions, while recognizing the ongoing power and effect of the gender dualism

- Acknowledging the concentration of power according to social structures (gender/sexuality, 'race', class etc.) while simultaneously recognizing the fluidity and dispersal of power through discourse
- Acknowledging the role of the material in gender production, without returning to biological essentialism.

To explain, we need to draw together some of the key arguments emerging in the prior sections.

As we observed, the late 1980s saw a strong critique of sex role and socialization theories of gender, with growing attention to gender fluidity. The early 1990s also saw emergent sociological notions of a 'crisis of masculinity' due to apparently changed gender roles and expectations (often argued to be predicated on socio-economic shifts such as the decline of manufacturing and job stability). This analysis was in the UK and Australia strongly impacted by policy and media concerns regarding 'boys' underachievement'. These interests and anxieties precipitated a new focus on masculinity within educational research. A host of research and publications on masculinity in educational settings, especially focusing on boys' apparent underachievement, were produced during this period. The political perspectives of some of the authors concerned were controversial (some of this work contributed to the 'anti-feminist backlash' which was also manifest in some segments of the media and research during the mid- to late 1990s). However, much of this work on masculinity was undertaken by feminists and pro-feminists, who maintained that in order to properly understand gender power relations one needs to understand both femininity *and* masculinity, and their relation. As we have seen, the work of R.W. Connell in theorizing masculinity as multiple was highly influential. The concept of hegemonic masculinity (with other forms of masculinity – including 'subjugated masculinity' – existing below hegemonic masculinity in a hierarchy) underpinned many of the sociological educational studies in this period.

However, Connell's notion of different versions of masculinity has been criticized for two key reasons. Firstly, critics argue that the conception of 'multiple masculinities' expresses an underlying biological essentialism, because masculinity is positioned as always expressed by males. Various educational researchers in the late 1990s commented that these different 'sorts' of masculinity ('subjugated /complicit /hegemonic' in Connell's conception; or different 'types' in the accounts of some educational studies) appeared highly diverse, and yet often overlapping, with no criteria offered by which to distinguish them. As certain commentators mischievously observed, it was difficult not to conclude that all that these different 'masculinities' held in common (to identify them as masculine rather than feminine) was the possession of a penis (Hood-Williams, 1998; MacInnes, 1998). This conflation between sex and gender (whereby men always express masculinity and women femininity) indicated a problematic essentialism. And as critics asked, if gender is always directly related to the sexed body, what is the point of the concept of 'gender' at all – why not just talk sex (Hood-Williams, 1998; MacInnes, 1998)? The second key criticism was that the multiple masculinities approach tended to evoke typologies, with researchers identifying and categorizing apparently distinct 'types' of masculinity, often drawing on Connell's own categories. Yet as Connell has since pointed out, 'hegemonic', 'subjugated' masculinity and so on were only concepts, rather than intended to describe a specific fixed set of behaviours (Connell and Messerschmidt, 2005). Nevertheless, the ideas were often applied this way, leading to the creation (and thereby reification) of fixed 'types' not actually representative of the fluidity and overlap of gender constructions (Francis, 2000).

As we have explained, Judith Butler's work offered a radical alternative to such positions. Her early book, *Gender Trouble* (1990), articulated a strong poststructuralist account of sex/gender, arguing that in contrast to those who see sex representing the 'real' and gender as the performance of this sex distinction, sex as well as gender is a socially constructed distinction. As two of us have observed elsewhere (Skelton and Francis, 2009), Butler's arguments reawaken some themes present in early second wave feminist research, as researchers such as Garfinkel (1967) and Kessler and McKenna (1978) had similarly illustrated the social construction of dualistic perceptions of sex. Butler's work goes further in extending discussion of discursive dualisms to sexuality, and by providing an account of sex/gender as *performative* – constructed, normalized and maintained via the continual repetition of gendered acts which produce gender. These ideas, and those of other poststructuralist feminists working in the field of education, contribute theoretical tools by which to address the limitations of the 'multiple masculinities' approach discussed above. Not only are gender performances and reproductions seen as produced via discourse rather than 'chosen', but also sex difference itself is seen as discursively constructed (hence radically exploding essentialism).

An example of how such approaches can avoid essentialist links from gender to sex is provided by Judith Halberstam (1998). Taking up Butler's ideas about sex and gender as purely performative, Halberstam undertook analyses of *female masculinity* – as her subheading has it, 'Masculinity Without Men'. Here Halberstam's celebratory analysis of 'Drag King' masculinities as produced in non-gender traditional bodies (bodies socially ascribed female) takes the understanding of sex/gender as socially constructed to its logical conclusion. And her ideas have been applied in educational studies, both looking at 'female' performances of masculinity – for example Renold's (2007) examination of performances of 'TomBoyism' in the classroom; and Mendick's (2005) exploration of the constructions of excellence at maths – and 'male' teachers' performances of femininity (Francis, 2008). Yet in severing the link between biological sex and gender performance, Halberstam's analysis also precipitates a range of theoretical problems, including some of those highlighted at the beginning of this section – for example, how to analyse power inequalities (based on gender) and how to categorize masculinity and femininity for analytical purposes, if not via the sexed body?[6]

So, while these poststructuralist theoretical trajectories offer novel accounts of the phenomenon of gender, and fruitful avenues of analysis in educational research, the challenges of maintaining a forceful account of power that can adequately recognize wider, resilient patterns of gender inequality – and of other forms of inequality – remain. There has been, and continues to be, tension between structuralist and poststructuralist positions on power and (in) equality; between understandings of subjectivity as constituted by language or by the material world; and between emancipatory/activist and deconstructive poststructuralist approaches. We have engaged these debates in our research analyses and publications, and one of us (Becky Francis) has found the work of Mikhail Bakhtin useful in addressing some of these theoretical challenges.

The Contribution of Bakhtin to Gender Theory

Bakhtin was a theorist of language, interested in the fluidity and diversity of language use and creation of meaning. But fundamentally, he is interested in power – what he refers to as the centrifugal forces that broaden language and its meaning (e.g. local dialects, creole, etc. that challenge established, high status genres), and the centripetal forces of power and privilege that have asserted language norms and work to maintain them. The wider benefits of a Bakhtinian approach for feminist empirical research are detailed elsewhere (e.g. Francis, 2010, forthcoming). Like Foucault, Bakhtin sees language as never neutral, but rather reflecting and constructing power relations. But much more than Foucault, Bakhtin is interested in the impact of the material environment on the creation and interpretation of language. Francis (2008, 2010) has seen Bakhtin's concepts of *monoglossia* and *heteroglossia* (Bakhtin, 1981) as particularly useful in reference to gender. Bakhtin uses the term 'monoglossia' to refer to dominant forms of language, representing the world view/interests of dominant social groups, which are positioned or imposed as unitary and total. However, for Bakhtin, language is never static or fixed, but is instead diverse and inherently dialogic. Different meanings and readings constantly jostle in assertions or subversions as subjects use language in different ways. Hence while at the macro-linguistic level there may appear to be stability (monoglossia), at the micro level there is plasticity, contradiction and resistance: heteroglossia.

Francis (2008, 2010) argues that these concepts can be directly transposed to gender. She maintains that the dominant, binary account of sex/gender comprises gender monoglossia: integral to this binarized account of sex/gender is the animation of the Male/masculine as Subject, and the denigration of the Female/feminine as Other (de Beauvoir, 1973; Walkerdine, 1990). This binary account of gender bears power in that it authors itself as universal and 'the truth'/real, and it works to suppress and/or incorporate heteroglossia in order to maintain the monoglossic account. However, on even a cursory examination, this monoglossic account of gender duality can be demonstrated a fallacy – restless heteroglossia bubbles below the surface, and every gender dualistic claim or example can be provided with a counter-example that deconstructs or parodies it.

The gender binary which sits at the heart of the monoglossic account of gender is built on delineation of attributes as male/masculine and female/feminine. In the Western context, this delineation relates directly to Western Enlightenment (masculinized) values. Hence characteristics valorized within this value system are attributed to the male Subject, and denigrated antitheses to these values are projected to the female Other. Thus emerge the gender binaries identified and analysed in feminist literary criticism and other arenas: for example, masculinity as rational, strong, active; and femininity as emotional, weak, passive. Francis (2010; Francis et al., 2010) has used empirical data to illustrate that actually expression of such characteristics is heteroglossic and not closely linked to 'sex' assignment. Yet she also shows how specifically resonant tropes can be drawn on to signify gender monoglossia in interaction when otherwise behaviour might be read as heteroglossic. Elsewhere she elaborates her application of Bakhtin's concepts in mapping a monoglossic gender matrix (Francis, forthcoming) and its practices in disguising and suppressing gender heteroglossia. However, here we wish simply to outline our view that micro-level heteroglossia is promulgated both by those subjects that notably do not 'fit' the monoglossic gender-sexuality order (such as those who identify as gay, and transgendered and intersex individuals), but also within the contradictory productions that we maintain inevitably characterize *all* performances of gender.

Application of Bakhtinian concepts to gender addresses some of the theoretical conundrums raised above. For example, we are moved away from the problematic of choice/determinism by Bakhtin's attention to the role of audience and context in constructions of meaning. It is not enough to simply identify as a girl (or otherwise) – one must also be read as one by spectators, and the contextual reading may shift as much as the performance. Related to this point is the issue of the body. 'Bodies that matter' (Butler, 1993) are of fundamental importance in how the spectator reads gendered signs – and in the performance of gender. Hence bodies comprise a key aspect of the local terrain that Bakhtin insists we address in our analyses; and in informing productions and readings of gender. Our reading of bodies as 'sexed' informs in turn the signification of characteristics produced in interaction. For example, behaviour which might be read as 'strategic' in a boy/man might be construed as 'manipulative' in a girl/woman; and behaviours interpreted as 'aggressive' in a boy/man may be read instead as 'bitchy' if expressed by a woman (Francis, 2008b). Such readings are of course also infused by other social structures in which bodies are produced: behaviours performed by a white, middle-class male may be understood by spectators as 'assertive', where the same behaviours expressed by a black working-class male may be read instead as 'aggressive/confrontational' (Archer and Francis, 2007). Hence different signs in the gender matrix, even those which appear most clearly binarized as expressing masculinity or femininity, are prey to heteroglossic re-signification depending on the local discursive arena, and the discursive inscriptions applied to the bodies within it. Conversely, although less common, if 'sex' is unclear to the spectator, it is possible that gender may be ascribed according to the signification of the subject's behaviours as masculine or feminine. This illuminates the irreducible inter-relation between body and performance, and actor and spectator, in the production of gender.

So a Bakhtinian approach can help to address theoretical challenges that have perplexed feminists – agency/determinism, materiality/discourse. Application of the concepts of monoglossia and heteroglossia facilitates a nuance in analysis of the mercurial multiplicity of gender productions – something not possible for conceptions either of 'female masculinity/male femininity' or 'multiple masculinities/femininities' (see e.g. empirical analysis in Francis, 2010). Such analyses can, for example, recognize the ways in which individual productions of gender are shot through with contradiction, and incorporate both aspects of performance generally understood as 'masculine' and 'feminine'. Importantly, the approach also lends itself to a stronger account of structural power than in poststructuralist theories – for example, it facilitates analysis of how gender productions are performed within local socio-economic environments and to specific audiences to signify in particular ways within a binarized, 'monoglossic' gender system.

We do not focus strongly on the work of Bakhtin in our discussion of empirical data in this book, but do draw on this perspective,[7] and our analysis is strongly located within the broader poststructuralist approach outlined in this chapter. We hope that this brief account of gender theory as applied in the field of gender and education has provided adequate context to our theoretical approach.

The Study

So, having outlined the perspectives underpinning our approach and analyses in this book, we now want to tell you about the empirical research that provides the key 'case' for our analysis. This was an Economic and Social Research Council (ESRC)-funded[8] study that built on our previous qualitative work investigating pupils' constructions of social identity and learning.[9]

The research was set in secondary school (high school; the 11–16 age range), and focused on high achieving pupils, including those deemed popular in addition to being high academic achievers. In line with current educational policy, we defined 'high achievement' as expressed by educational credentials – albeit we do not ourselves subscribe to the view that achievement should be conceived so narrowly (see Chapter 1 of this book; also, Francis and Skelton, 2005). We identified 'high achieving' pupils via discussion with teachers: Heads of Year were asked to consult with colleagues to identify those pupils who achieve across a range of subjects from the top streams, and to provide evidence to support identification via details of pupils' Key Stage 2 SAT results (the exams for maths, English and science taken at the end of primary schooling) and their recent grades across subject areas. As we had expected, what was seen to consititute 'high achieving' differed from school to school, illustrating the relationality of conceptions of 'achievement' (see Chapter 1). However, in raising a sample our concern was simply to include pupils deemed among the highest academic achievers at their particular school. We also recognize that young people may be very high achieving in some subjects and low achieving in others, and that different subjects are accorded greater and lesser status in the curriculum. We resisted prioritizing certain subjects, but rather asked teachers to identify young people who tend to achieve very highly across subject areas. At each school, around one-third of pupils included were also identified as popular (and a gender balance ensured across the sample). This latter group was identified via this teacher consultation process concerning achievement, in conjunction with an exercise with young people to establish popularity.

'Popularity' is clearly a complex and slippery concept, both in its actual meaning (those most popular are not necessarily those most liked, as the concept incorporates aspects such as influence and admiration) and in perspective (those most popular with some groups may not be popular with others). We were interested in popularity among peers, rather than with teachers, as it is gendered peer-group power and status relations which are argued in the literature cited above to impact on gender and achievement (see the next chapter for elaboration). Hence all young people in identified top set classes were asked to complete a short survey comprising three questions: 'Which student do you most like in your class?'; 'Which student would other people say is most popular?'; and 'Which student would you most like to be like?' A holistic analysis of the results effectively indicated the most popular young people, as well as providing us with interesting data regarding overlaps and divergences between these different constructions of popularity. We had anticipated the possibility that few of those pupils identified as popular would be identified as in the highest achieving groups, but this was in fact not the case, as we shall elaborate later in the book.

Sample

In order to ensure a diverse sample the research was conducted across range of localities in England, including rural areas, small towns and the capital city. To ensure a tight focus, we limited our study to co-educational schools (as the inclusion of single-sex schools would have added an extra comparative aspect). We drew on Ofsted and school website reports to ensure diversity in our sample among schools in respect to social class, ethnic mix, and recorded achievement levels in individual schools. Nine schools were included in the sample, and in the largest school we worked in more than one class. The various schools are described in Table 2.4.

The study focused on high achieving pupils in Year 8 (12- to 13-year-olds). Researchers have found that disengagement with education accelerates at this age (Bleach et al., 1996; Myhill, 2002), which makes the cases of those who maintain their high achievement especially interesting. In each Year 8 class involved, between 6 and 8 pupils were identified, ensuring an even gender representation. The final sample included 71 pupils: 36 girls, 35 boys, of whom 62 are white and 9 are from other ethnic groups (the 5 pupils of African Caribbean heritage comprising the next most sizable group). In each case, around half of those included were also identified as popular. It is notable that minority ethnic pupils are somewhat under-represented in the total sample, especially given the London location of some sample schools. This is partly due to the particular demographic areas in which three of the four London schools were based (less ethnically mixed than in many areas of London). There were also some minority ethnic students who we would have liked to include in the study but who did not wish to participate. Nevertheless this under-representation is unexpected given the high rates of educational achievement among some minority ethnic groups and may also indicate teacher perceptions in identifying 'high achieving' pupils (see Brah and Minhas, 1985; Fordham, 1996; Archer and Francis, 2007).

Methods

Ethnographic observations were conducted in each school to document the interaction taking place in the classroom, focusing on the behaviours of those children identified as high achieving. This facilitated us in addressing our key research aims: to analyse the gender subjectivities of high achieving boys and girls (with attention to other aspects of subjectivity such as 'race' and social class) and to relate these to an analysis of their approach to, and achievement at, school work. Hence our observation focused on high achieving young people's work orientation, social behaviour/ interaction with teachers and peers, gender performance and the teacher's approaches to them, as well as documenting aspects of classroom organization and management practices which may have a bearing on these behaviours. Each class of children was tracked through different lessons for a full school day, with supplementary observation notes taken at break and lunchtimes: as demonstrated with some of our previous work, this approach is sufficient to supply a rich snapshot of classroom relationships and organization in each school (Skelton et al., 2009). At the majority of schools young people were subject to streaming as well as setting (the latter occured across the board), so those identified for observation remained with the same classmates through most of the day. However, at a minority of sample schools pupils returned to mixed ability groups when not lessons divided by set (e.g. such as maths, English and science).

As well as observing the identified young people in the classroom, we also conducted an individual, semi-structured interview with each of them. These lasted for approximately 30–40 minutes each. The schedule explored their opinions about school work; opinions about gender performance and gender in relation to school work; their subject preferences; their pastimes, hobbies and so on; their self-perceptions regarding their educational ability; and their self-perceptions concerning classroom dynamics and relationships.

In terms of the analysis, it was also a key intention to draw on the theories of poststructuralists such as Foucault and Butler, and Halberstam's ideas around disembodied gender, to inform our data analysis and develop our theorizations (see above, this chapter). While we draw out this analysis to some extent in this book, more detailed analysis of these issues can be found in other publications (see e.g. Francis, 2010). In addition to analysing young people's responses according to ethnicity, gender and social class, we also sought to be actively attuned to issues of embodiment and presentation in their performances. Hence we recorded aspects such as physical size, 'fashion-consciousness' and so on. This did not always feel comfortable (we were aware of the problematic potential to stereotype young people and/or to project our own preferences and tastes onto them, as well as our dubious degree of knowledge of contemporary teenage styles and subcultures!). However, we saw it as necessary in our aim to capture the role of material and aesthetic presentations on gender performance.

Categories According to Achievement and Popularity

All the pupils involved in the research were 'high achieving' within their schools (see above). However, using the information provided on different pupils we have also delineated between them to identify those who were more or less high achieving, and those who are more or less 'popular' (based on the pupil questionnaires, interviews and classroom observations). Hence within

Table 2.1 Achievement/Popularity categorization of pupils by gender

	Female	Male	Total
High Achieving and Popular (HAP)	10	12	22
Achieving and Popular (AP)	9	10	19
High Achieving (HA)	3	5	8
Achieving (A)	14	8	22
Total	**36**	**35**	**71**

Table 2.2 Achievement/Popularity categorization of pupils by social class

	Working-class	Middle-class	Unassigned	Total
High Achieving and Popular (HAP)	7	13	2	22
Achieving and Popular (AP)	6	8	5	19
High Achieving (HA)	9	10	3	22
Achieving (A)	2	6	0	8
Total	**24**	**37**	**10**	**71**

our sample of high achieving pupils we have distinguished between (very) 'high achieving' and 'achieving' pupils, and between popular and less popular pupils (see Tables 2.1–2.3).

The High Achieving and Popular (HAP) group comprise those pupils who are among the most high achieving in our sample of high achievers, and who are also identified as popular with classmates. Of the 71 pupils in our sample, 22 are identified as HAP (as opposed to 'achieving and popular' or 'high achieving')[10]. Of the 22 HAP pupils, 12 are boys and 10 are girls. Of the boys, 8 are middle-class and 3 are working-class, with one boy's social class unrecorded. Of the girls, 5 HAP girls are middle-class, 4 are working-class and one girl's social class was not recorded. Two of this group were from minority ethnic groups – an African Caribbean working-class boy and a British Chinese working-class girl: the rest of the group were white.

Secondly, we identified an 'Achieving and Popular' (AP) group – pupils who were identified as popular through the friendship questionnaire and who were achieving well, but would not rank as amongst the highest achieving in their class. There were 19 participants in this category: 9 were girls and 10 were boys. Of the 9 girls, 4 were middle-class and 2 were working-class, and we had no data from which to assign social class for 3 girls. Of the boys,

Table 2.3 Achievement/Popularity categorization of pupils by ethnicity

	African-Caribbean	Other minority ethnic groups	White	Total
High Achieving and Popular (HAP)	1	1	20	22
Achieving and Popular (AP)	0	1	18	19
High Achieving (HA)	3	3	16	22
Achieving (A)	1	0	7	8
Total	**5**	**5**	**61**	**71**

4 were middle-class, 4 were working-class and 2 boys' social class were not recorded. One boy in this group was of mixed heritage: a working-class boy from one of the small town schools. The rest of the group were white.

We also constructed two groups who did not appear to be popular from the questionnaire, again differentiated according to achievement: we labelled these 'High Achieving' (HA) and 'Achieving' (A).

The 'High Achieving' group comprised 22 pupils. Interestingly there were noticeably more girls than boys in this group, and more minority ethnic pupils than the other three groups. There were 14 girls and 8 boys. Of the girls, 5 were white working-class and 4 were white middle-class. There were 2 African Caribbean girls, one of whom was working-class and one middle-class. This group also included an Asian working-class girl and a South American middle-class girl: finally we were not given the data from which to assign the social class of a further white girl. Of the boys, 3 were white middle-class, one was white working-class; one boy was Turkish and middle-class; one boy African Caribbean working-class; and we were not given the data to assign a social class to two further white boys in this group.

Finally, the 'Achieving' group consisted of 8 pupils – 3 girls and 5 boys, the majority of whom were middle-class. One of this group was a North African working-class boy and the rest of the group were white. Of these there were three middle-class boys, 3 middle-class girls and a white working-class boy (Table 2.4).

Having provided an explanation of the epistemological underpinning of the book, and the methods of research undertaken in the empirical research on which the book is based, we can proceed to examine research findings on gender, popularity and high achievement.

Table 2.4: Description of the schools

Highgarden School is a large inner-London school. The catchment area is multi-ethnic and contains a mixture of both relatively affluent households and households renting housing association and council properties. The school itself contains a high number of students entitled to free school meals, with a relatively high proportion of students with learning difficulties and special educational needs. The largest groups of students are white British and black African Caribbean. The latest Ofsted report congratulates improvements at the school; nevertheless the atmosphere in the school is quite hectic and raucous, and the teaching staff need to deal with quite a high degree of behaviour management issues. A large number of lessons observed contained levels of disruption throughout.

Ironoaks School is a sizable comprehensive school in a residential suburb of London that contains a large proportion of white working-class households, but also borders on adjacent far more affluent areas. The school is situated near a large council estate from which a large proportion of the students are drawn. The school has a larger than average proportion of students eligible for free school meals, and with special educational needs. It has a larger than average intake of students from minority ethnic backgrounds, but this mix is low compared to many other areas in London. There is a good atmosphere at the school, and the students seemed relatively happy and engaged, although some of the lessons contained a degree of low-level disruption common to several of the London schools.

Kingswood School is a Church of England school located on the fringes of a small Cathedral city. Pupils are mainly white although there are a relatively high proportion of pupils from backgrounds other than white British (in line with national averages). The latest Ofsted report for the school notes that pupils arrive at the school with above average standards and from above average socio-economic backgrounds. The school organizes pupils into sets for all subjects. There is a friendly, calm atmosphere in the school and apparently few discipline problems. Pupils adhere to a strict school uniform policy.

Lannisport School is a comprehensive school in a rural English village. Most of the (predominantly white) students are drawn from the local rural community, or the nearest market town which is a few miles away. There is a mix of social class backgrounds. The atmosphere in the school seems happy and relaxed, and achievement results are higher than the national average. The students were markedly quiet and engaged in lessons.

Oldtown School is a comparatively very high attaining Roman Catholic school, situated in a relatively un-affluent, unfashionable area of suburban London. Pupils represent a wide mixture of social class backgrounds, and black and minority ethnic pupils comprise around 20 per cent of the school population (low for London). Pupils are streamed for the majority of subject areas. Staff pride themselves on the school's discipline and achievement, and a strict dress code is enforced, for both pupils and staff.

Queenswood School is a large comprehensive school, located on the outskirts of a small Cathedral city. It has a predominantly white population with a rapidly increasing number of pupils of Eastern European origin. There are no severely economically disadvantaged areas in this part of city and the pupils tend to come from middle and upper working-class backgrounds. Pupils are organized into sets for all subjects. There is a strict school uniform policy.

Saltcliffe School is located in a village in an affluent rural area of the East Midlands. The vast majority of the students are white British, with the number of students eligible for free school meals well below the national average. The proportion of students with learning difficulties or disabilities is also below average. The school has a reputation in the area for being an exceptionally good school that produces high achievement results.

Summerhall School is situated in a residential area a few miles outside a small Cathedral city. Pupils are predominantly white but with a significant minority from other ethnic groups. Pupils are placed into sets for all curriculum subjects. There is a rigidly enforced school uniform policy. There appear to be few discipline problems and there is a sense of warmth and good humour as pupils move around the school.

Winterfell School is a large comprehensive in a suburban area of London with a large proportion of white working-class families, and the student body reflects this: about two-thirds of the students are white, with one third coming from a wide range of minority ethnic backgrounds. There is a larger than average proportion of students eligible for free school meals. There is also a higher than average proportion of students with learning difficulties and disabilities. The latest Ofsted report notes that staff need to deal with various challenges, including a large 'highly mobile' student population. Lessons were often disrupted and staff needed to deal with quite a high degree of behaviour management issues.

Notes

1 An excellent and succinct articulation of 'third wave feminism' is given by Gaby Weiner (2006). Briefly, third wave feminism emerged around the 1990s and marked a shift away from second wave feminism's adherence to the notions of shared interests amongst women. It is feminism for a 'new generation' of academics who investigate and theorize gender and includes men as well as women researchers. It is 'more individual, complex and "imperfect" than previous waves. It is not as strictly defined or all-encompassing, … especially about personal choices' (Aapola et al., 2005, p. 205). Also, third wave feminism is less concerned about aligning activism with academic engagement, and 'seems more attached to the academy than previous waves' (Weiner, 2006, p. 82).

2 For elaboration for different 'types' of feminism in education, see e.g. Weiner, 1994; or Skelton and Francis, 2009.

3 Whilst theoretical frameworks based on the ways in which power shaped social and psychic investments in gender were in evidence in the early 1980s (Walden and Walkerdine, 1985), these took longer to become established within the field of education.

4 A large body of contemporary research, including findings from our own work, demonstrates that the gendered nature of classroom interaction, and the reflection of masculine values in curriculum and educational preoccupations, shows more continuity than change. See Chapter 3, or the introductory chapter to Skelton and Francis (2003) for elaboration.

5 An example is provided by the feminist keynote symposium entitled 'The Return of The Thing', and the content of the papers therein, presented at the British Educational Research Association Conference, 2007, and at the American Educational Research Association, New York, 2008, chaired by Helen Colley.

6 For further discussion of these dilemmas in relation to Judith Halberstam's work, see e.g. Paechter (2006); Francis (2008, 2010); Francis and Skelton (2008).

7 See especially Chapter 6

8 The project is titled 'The gender subjectivities of high achieving pupils', ESRC project number: (RES062230462).

9 See e.g. Francis, 2000; Francis and Archer, 2005; Skelton, 2001; Skelton and Francis, forthcoming; Skelton et al., 2010; Read et al., 2011).

10 In Chapter 6 we make a further distinction within this group of high achieving popular young people.

3 Facilitating High Achievement and the Issue of 'Balance'

If you type the words 'raising achievement in schools' into an internet search engine you will hit over 400,000 websites. Unsurprisingly, most of these websites are concerned with how schools and teachers can increase students' attainments on a year-by-year basis. You have to trawl through pages of websites to find those which headline what students can do to raise their own achievement and those that do seem oblivious to how coping with and getting through a school day is as much about the social as it is about the academic side of schooling. Biographies of famous people from sports stars to politicians to historical figures include memories of school days which seem to be all about how school work had to be managed alongside friendships with classmates and relationships with teachers. Even those who might today be regarded as academically successful such as Stephen Fry, and earlier, Charles Dickens, have all had their schooldays described in ways that indicated how the sociable aspect of schooling took priority over the educational side (Slater, 2009; Fry, 2010). The phrase we use throughout this book when referring to students' negotiations of the social and academic aspects of schooling is 'balance'. In order to explain what we mean when we talk about 'balance' it is helpful to consider how the term arises elsewhere. An example would be discussions in the media of how to manage and achieve a 'work–life balance'. It is quite a broad concept but one that is largely understood to mean that 'work' (i.e. employment and ambitions in that area) and 'life' (i.e. family, social, leisure, spiritual elements) are prioritized as and when appropriate. What it does not mean is that equal amounts of time have to be allocated to both on a daily basis. Employers have attempted to facilitate their employees' opportunities for securing a 'work–life balance' by introducing flexible working hours and maximizing the use of information technology. Whilst there are inevitable problems for both employers and employees in securing a practicable work–life balance the damages in failing to strive for this balance are severe: physiological and psychological stress to individuals, greater staff turnover and dissatisfaction, lower rates of creativity and production. However, achieving 'balance' in regard to 'work–life' is far from straightforward, as it is highly subjective because what suits one person does not suit another. An example of such differences was apparent in the disagreements made public in the media between the actors and mothers, Denise Van Outen and Natalie Cassidy, as to whether or when it was appropriate to return to work after having a child. Although it is impossible to come up with a scenario whereby the enactment of certain principles provides everyone with an effective 'work–life balance' there are certain characteristics that are associated with it. These include feeling a sense of achievement and enjoyment in terms of oneself, in the work one does, and in regard to relationships with family and friends. Some of these conceptualizations around a 'work–life balance' are evident in the discussions of the literature which shows how school students secure (or not) a 'balance' between successful academic achievement and good social relationships at school.

There are a substantial number of ethnographies of schools dating back to the 1960s that illustrate how many students – and boys in particular – fail to find a 'balance' between achieving at both schoolwork and social relations (Hargreaves, 1967; Ball, 1981; Abraham, 1995; Pollard, 2001). The concept of 'balance' was first used in educational work on gender by the likes of Valerie Walkerdine in the 1980s and has been increasingly elaborated by researchers of gender and achievement such as Carolyn Jackson (e.g. 2006a). The opposite to the 'disengaged student' is the 'swot' and, as we discuss elsewhere in the book, being ascribed as a 'boffin' is partly a consequence of failing to effectively navigate this balancing of academic work and peer relations. Furthermore, the significance of gendered subjectivities in the performance and production of a 'balanced' approach to academic and social relationships is frequently overlooked (for exceptions see Renold, 2001; Jackson, 2006a, 2010; Ringrose, 2007). One of the intentions of our research into high achieving students was to place gender and its inter-play with social class and ethnicity, alongside pupils' constructions of high achievement, in order to recognize what strategies were utilized by boys and girls who are actively performing academic success. For example, with all the emphasis in the media on 'boys' as 'underachievers' it would be easy to suppose that this is the case for all boys. Yet there is evidence that many boys, from differing ethnic and social class backgrounds, are doing well in class and enjoy their school experiences (Frosh et al., 2002; Martino and Pallotta Chiarolli, 2003).

Nevertheless, a raft of research maintains that 'laddish' performances of masculinity attract the highest social status in state secondary schooling envi-ronments (albeit this construction is 'raced' and classed, see e.g. Fordham, 1996; Connolly, 1998; Reay, 2002; Archer and Yamashita, 2003; Weis, 2004; Francis and Archer, 2005). 'Laddish' performances are, then, frequently aspired to and/or adopted by boys. Because 'laddish' constructions are based on performances of rebellion, irresponsibility and hedonism (Francis, 1999), they sit in opposition both to school practices (which demand obedience and conformity) and to learning (as learning requires diligence, care and reflec-tion). The characteristics associated with learning are those associated with femininity: hence those boys who are 'academically able' and are seen to work hard are frequently positioned as effeminate by other pupils and teachers (Forsey, 1990; Mac an Ghaill, 1994; Kehily and Nayak, 1996). Various studies have shown how constructions of 'laddish' masculinity as in opposition to academic learning discourage boys from achieving (a) because they do not wish to be seen as diligent or as achievers by their peers; and (b) because the classroom behaviours involved in 'laddish' performances of masculinity impede their learning (see, e.g. Epstein, 1997; Martino, 1999; Francis, 2000; Skelton, 2001; Jackson, 2002; Archer et al., 2007).

This body of research has focused on boys, particularly in the context of the focus on boys' achievement since the 1990s. However, such practices of resistance and peer pressure operating against high achievement have also been observed among some girls (Bettie, 2002; Jackson, 2006b). Indeed, many feminists have observed a specific tension for girls between social and academic success given the powerful association between female academic attainment and a-sexuality. This construction is produced by discursive bina-ries that locate reason, rationality and mind as masculine; and emotion, irra-tionality and body as feminine (Walkerdine, 1990). According to Walkerdine (1990), in taking up academic success, girls must identify with the Other, at the cost of their association with femininity. That 'braininess' is unfeminine is a strong cultural narrative (although examples of brainy female characters are increasing within popular culture, including for example Hermione Granger in the Harry Potter series, and Willow in Buffy the Vampire Slayer). Second wave feminist studies of schoolgirls found girls having to play down their academic prowess in order to maintain their heterosexual attractiveness (Gaskell, 1992). Evidence from some of our previous work shows that possible constructions of girlhood have broadened somewhat over time and, at least for many urban girls (often minority ethnic and/or middle-class girls, but sometimes working-class white girls too) incorporate higher ambitions and more positive views of academic attainment than has previously been the case (e.g. Francis, 2000). Nevertheless, we do not share the populist view of girls as 'having it all': a large body of research has demonstrated the continuing social restraints and tension for girls between heterosexual attractiveness and academic success (Hey, 1997; Renold, 2005; Renold and Allen, 2006; Mendick et al., 2008) – a tension which Mendick et al. (2008) maintain is not so acute for men.[i] There was some evidence to support these claims in our data, including the emphasis on 'looks' for girls, and statements such as that of Fred (white, middle-class, Ironoaks) who claims that at the prospect of a clever girl many boys would say 'eeugh! . . . [in disgusted voice] I don't want my girlfriend being smart and bodrick like'.

With this in mind then we might argue that the playing down of the performance of such gender differences through the deployment of strict uniform policies and strong management may comprise a vital first step in facilitating achievement, and broadening (rather than narrowing) pupils' horizons. Arguably this may also apply to social class distinction. However, support of these, almost military, approaches is highly challenging for us as 'liberal' researchers, committed to freedom of expression. One might also ask where schools ought to draw the line in any such 'dampening of difference' – for example, in relation to issues such as religious expression. That such 'strict' approaches also consistently represented high achieving, 'successful' schools in our sample points to the importance of such approaches in facilitating academic achievement, as well as mediating social distinction. Yet this arguably simply points to the ways in which the neoliberal policy context, with its preoccupation with 'standards' and achievement conceptualized as expressed via exam credentials frames and directs current school practice. For clearly such 'strict' approaches facilitate achievement, and yet as educationalists we may ask whether the educational 'ends' are legitimate as currently conceived, let alone whether they justify the means. These practices do of course also produce distinction in their own right, as for 'success' to be measured, failure must be identifiable as its relational Other. Such practices effectively Other particular groups of pupils, in patterns that reflect ethnicity and social class (Reay and Lucey, 2003).

Conversely, however, before dismissing 'strict' approaches as conservative attacks on freedom of expression, and indications of neoliberal excess, it is important that those of us interested in social justice reflect the implication of current differentiated practices among schools for social justice. Here we are drawing attention to the ways in which strict disciplinary approaches can dampen gender distinction, and this appears important. But further, within the current (neoliberal) system, with its focus on 'academic' selection and distinction, schools that maintain such 'strict' disciplinary approaches appear to be facilitating high achievement, as indicated by pupils' exam credentials (Sammons et al., 1995; Ofsted, 2002). And evidence clearly shows that working-class and minority ethnic pupils tend to be concentrated in less high achieving schools (Burgess et al., 2006; Cassen and Kingdon, 2007). If it is the case that, in applying lower expectations with regard to behaviour and discipline, schools in which particular pupil groups are concentrated are disadvantaging those pupils in terms of academic outcomes, this is an important social justice issue.

Much of this book is dedicated to consideration of the gendered nature of managing, or not, the 'balancing' of high achievement and social relationships. But before we address this issue further, the following section explores how high achieving boys and girls approach school and school work. We found that being recognized publicly by the school as 'high achieving' facilitated shared approaches to academic work amongst boys and girls that were irrespective of their gender, social class and ethnic background. These were: (1) being well regarded by the school which afforded them high status and which also encouraged their motivation and commitment to school work; (2) feeling part of a supportive group with many pupils talking of the importance of the class 'getting on' or 'bonding' as a whole; and (3) having effective relationships with teachers. Yet, as we elaborate here and in other chapters, individual performances of 'selfhood' differed considerably according to social class, ethnicity and gender. We explore here some of the general trends among the different groups of young people in our study. The detail, and often heteroglossic contradiction emerging within these trends, is unpicked in later chapters, especially chapters 5 and 6.

School–Student Relationships

Support for Education and Schooling

The students in our study were keenly aware of their privileged position within the organizational structures of their schools. Several of the schools 'set' the students for curriculum subjects and most often these were ability sets rather than mixed-ability groupings. The students in our study were in the top sets and many of them were on the 'gifted and talented' registers (see Chapter 1). Inevitably, some of the schools had greater discipline problems than others and some enjoyed sound academic reputations and were well known in their local areas to be 'good schools'. There were some common features of these schools including high expectations of pupils, and the enforcement of strict uniform and behavioural policies (see also Younger et al., 2005). One of our findings was that schools with a stronger attention to discipline, including strict uniform policies and strong classroom management, had the effect of dampening the performance of social distinction (gender, social class, and possibly ethnicity too). This was important and challenging in various respects which we go on to discuss after first illustrating how this 'dampening' was manifested.

The literature on gender and schooling has explored how, both independently and together, gender, ethnicity and social class provide groups of pupils with differential experiences of schooling. Studies have shown how girls continue to be seen as 'hard workers' in comparison to views of boys as 'naturally bright' (Maynard, 2002); and, black and working-class boys are more likely than other pupil groups to be regarded as disruptive and excluded from school (Sewell, 1997; Wright et al., 2000).

The boys and girls in this study, irrespective of social class and ethnicity, expressed very positive attitudes towards school and school work. It might seem to be obvious that such views were held, after all, they were successful 'products' of the school system in that they attained good grades in examinations, were seen by their teachers as academically able and, as a consequence, placed in ability groups or classes that reflected their high achievement. There has been ample evidence of how streaming or setting pupils into recognizable achievement groups produces positive attitudes from those deemed 'high performing' with the greater likelihood of disaffection and dissatisfaction from children placed in lower sets or classes (Hargreaves, 1967; Woods, 1979; Ball, 1981). However, it should be recognized that it has been shown elsewhere how social class, ethnicity and gender, independently and collectively, impacts differentially on pupils' perceptions of schooling. For example, studies by Lambart (1997) and Youdell (2004) (amongst others) have found middle-class girls and black working-class girls, respectively, were anti-school but pro-education. Similarly, research into masculinities and schooling have pointed to how some black middle- and working-class boys desire the opportunities education can provide whilst simultaneously rejecting schooling processes as 'the cost to their masculinity was too high' (Sewell, 1997: p. 103; see also Parry, 1996). There are also case studies that demonstrate how working-class boys who are pro-education and who attempt to accommodate the schooling system have to then produce an alternative, often conflicting self (masculinity) to their peers in order to 'fit in' (Power et al., 1998; Reay, 2002). The findings of our research showed that all high achieving pupils in our sample were pro-education and largely pro-school. In response to our enquiries about whether it was important to do well at school, minority ethnic, working-class students' comments included:

> *Louise*: Yeah . . . because it's going to help you later in life . . . like getting a job and becoming responsible and stuff. (Female, HA[1], African-Caribbean, working-class, Winterfell School)
>
> *Salima*: I think it is, 'cos if you mess about then you won't do well and get a good job. You can't go back to secondary school and repeat it, like you can do at college. (Female, HAP, Asian, working-class, Winterfell School)
>
> *Robbie*: Yeah, cos . . . my sister's in year 11 and at the moment she's like doing the mock exams and everything and she said that she wants to be a lawyer and you have to do really well to be a lawyer and you earn good money. So . . . school is quite important 'cos you need to learn to have a good job when you're older. (Male, AP, Mixed-heritage, working-class, Summerhall School)

Whilst such findings are interesting, these are not 'new', rather they contribute to those studies which have shown how the changing demands of the labour market, the position of women and the importance of credentialism have resulted in an increased value being placed by young people on school and the opportunities it provides to secure qualifications (Arnot et al., 1999; Francis, 2000; Ball et al., 2000). For example, while the young working-class men in Willis's (1977) and Corrigan's (1979) studies saw school as something that occupied time before starting work as an apprentice in one of the traditional masculine trades of steel, coal mining, the car industry or on the factory floor, the demise of these trades, the increase of 'female', i.e. people-related, occupations and the demand for paper qualifications have required them to broaden their outlooks. Now 'good grades' are expressly linked to 'good jobs':

> Carter: Um yeah. It's like if you don't get high grades, then you are limited to the amount of choice in jobs. (Male, HA, white, working-class, Queenswood School).
>
> Tom R.:   Um yeah because it's like say you get a good education and like get a good job yeah (Male, A, white, working-class, Summerhall School).
>
> Stuart: Yep, very important because uh . . . you have to you have to concentrate you have to focus . . . uh . . . later in life you need to, you need to say you've done well in school so you can go onto jobs and stuff. And yeah . . . (Male, A, white, working-class, Oldtown School).
>
> Matt: 'Cos then you can have like an easier life when you're older and because you have like, not an easier job, but if you're brainier then you'll get a better job and you'll have more money and stuff. (Male, AP, white, working-class, Kingswood School).

Of course the responses of these white, working-class boys did not mean they did not 'have a laugh' or 'mess about' as the observational data demonstrated that some of them did (see Chapter 6), but what was striking was why and where it was (un)acceptable to manifest pro- and anti-school behaviours. In some schools, 'backchatting' the teachers contributed towards the popularity of some high achieving pupils (particularly boys) whilst in others, such negative classroom behaviours would have undermined the popularity of the boy in the eyes of peers as well as teachers. It appears that the location and the environment/culture of the school was a compelling factor in understanding the behaviours of these high achieving pupils.

There were two more similarities than differences in attitudes towards school and subject preferences. Both boys and girls cited 'doing work' and 'liking subjects' as something they enjoyed most about school as frequently as they mentioned 'meeting friends'. Enjoyment of particular subjects was largely related to how good pupils were at them but importantly how effective the teachers were in delivering the subject. It was the expertise of the teacher in delivering a subject that impacted on whether pupils liked it or not – hence as many boys as girls disliked maths in a school or as many boys as girls enjoyed English[2] depending on how they perceived the abilities of the teacher. Certainly, gender stereotypical subject preferences were less evident than in earlier studies, although whether pupils were considered popular (or not) did seem to be influential. For example, English with its emphasis on emotion, communication and presentation is regarded as a 'girls' subject. Yet popular boys rated it as often as science and more than maths whilst none of the other (less/unpopular) boys listed it as a favourite subject. Subject choice has implications for career choices and more recently there has been a marked shift in girls' aspirations with studies showing that they are now more ambitious and that careers are seen as a significant part of their identities (Kenway et al., 1998; Francis, 2000; Tinklin et al., 2005). All the pupils in our study were looking towards professional occupations with both girls and boys identifying doctors, veterinary surgeons, architects, lawyers; running their own business; entering public service as police or fire officers; or entering media as a professional performer or journalist, yet there remained some gender trends. More emphasis was evident in girls' choices of 'caring' in their occupational futures ('working with the homeless'; 'doing something with kids') and the list provided by boys was both less wide ranging and, unlike the girls, identified work in the more masculine associated worlds of financial services and sports sciences.

Although specific questions about preferred ways of learning were not asked the responses of pupils to how they approached homework suggested that, for a majority of boys and girls, working alone – perhaps with the support of parents or older siblings – was the favoured means. All of the pupils were assiduous about homework with most completing it the same day it was given with only one or two pupils saying they left it to the weekend. However, the attitudes towards homework reflected those of other studies showing that they resented the school appropriating their leisure time and were particularly irritated by being set tasks they regarded as pointless such as designing a cover for a DVD (Hallam, 2004).

The point being made in this section is that pupils designated by schools as high achieving, irrespective of gender, ethnicity and social class, articulated clear commitment to the notion of education and valued the opportunities schools provided in enabling them to secure good qualifications. As such, both boys and girls actively participated in the requirements of their schools to attend school, engaged with the school work presented during the school day, and undertook and met deadlines for homework. At the same time, as we recognized above, a raft of research has demonstrated the impact of binarized gender constructions on academic achievement. Some of the nuances here, even among high achieving pupils, are examined later in the book.

Students' Feelings of Being Part of a Group

A second factor that high achieving pupils identified as facilitating their approach to school and school work was feeling they were part of a supportive, enabling group. The increasing significance in adolescence of the peer group and friendship has been well documented (Walker, 1988; Hey, 1997; Cook et al., 2007). Whilst the general tendency for children of all ages is a wish to 'fit in', in adolescence friendship and feeling part of a group becomes particularly important as young people adjust to the changes and challenges faced in moving to adulthood (Kiesner et al., 2002; Waldrip et al., 2008). Although classroom observations and interviews with children indicated there were specific friendship groups within the class and, to a lesser extent, across the year group, many commented on how they 'got on' as a (class) group:

> *Bethany*:   We're quite a good class we do bond quite well together. (Female, HA, white, working-class, Winterfell School).
>
> *Billy*:   Yeah there is (friendship groups) but most people, like me and my mates, we just mix in with everyone. It's like sometimes I'll be with my mates at lunch and sometimes with the girls and sometimes I'll be with the other ones, just mix around. We're all friends though. (Male, HAP, white, working-class, Winterfell School).
>
> *Peter:*   Um it's a lot like all the boys like all the boys and all the girls like all the girls really, generally. And occasionally some of the boys like some of the girls, and some of the girls like some of the boys, like sometimes the friendship groups change with like different groups of girls and boys but generally I don't think there are any, I don't think there's anybody in the class I don't like but there are people I like and people I just don't mind. (Male, HA, white, middle-class, Queenswood School).
>
> *Victoria*:   I just think it doesn't really matter what sort of music you listen to, if you just bond well together. (Female, AP, white, class-unknown, Saltcliffe School).

The notion of, and ability to, 'get on' with others is distinct from being seen as 'popular' (see Francis, 2009; Francis et al., 2010). It is reasonable to expect those 'popular' children to express an interest in liking and being liked by others. However, as can be seen from the comments above, pupils not deemed as popular also gave significance to good relationships amongst class members. The following remarks by Salima and Leo suggest, whoever they regarded as their 'real' friends, it was essential to the successful 'doing' of schooling and school work to 'get on' with everyone.

Salima: There are little cliques. Sometimes it's just girls or just boys but every-one still gets together – they still work together and talk. (Female, HA, Asian, working-class, Winterfell School)

Leo: I hang around with the 'bad breeds'[3] and I hang around with the 'neeks' but I more meet people who, like, are smart but they know how to interact with different people. (Male, HA, African-Carribean, working-class, Highgarden School).

At the same time, being able to 'get on' with others whilst also maintaining high educational achievement was more of a problem for some than for others. Whilst the majority of boys and girls said they felt 'ok', 'fine', 'good' or 'proud' of their academic success, the high achieving, not generally popular, girls demonstrated a level of discomfort and anxiety that was virtually absent in the comments of the other children we interviewed. This is something that will be taken up and discussed later in more detail in this chapter.

Teacher–Pupil Relationships

A third feature that facilitated high achievement which was articulated by both girls and boys was having effective relationships with teachers.

The attitudes and expectations of pupils in the UK towards, and of, their teachers have been of long-standing interest to researchers (Nash, 1978; Woods, 1990; Dubberley, 1993; Flutter and Ruddock, 2004; Whitehead and Clough, 2004). These studies have all identified similar lists of teacher skills and characteristics that pupils look for, e.g. teachers explaining work clearly, pitching their expectations of individual students at the right level, managing the class effectively, providing interesting lessons, utilizing practical approaches to teaching and learning, and engaging with pupils (Woods, 1990; Dorman and Adams, 2004; McIntyre et al., 2005). When it comes to the personal elements of pupil–teacher relations pupils regard 'good teachers' as those who are fair and just, are interested in them as individuals and maintain a balance between firm behaviour management and providing a relaxed classroom environment (Woods, 1990; Thornberg, 2008). Similarly, a major factor in shaping teachers' professional identities is their (successful) relationships with pupils (Day et al., 2007). There is, of course, a wide literature that has considered how acceptable classroom rules are negotiated by pupils and teachers together and how pupils 'suss out' new teachers (Pollard, 1987; Cooper and Hyland, 2000; Flutter and Rudduck, 2004). These studies have not sought to distinguish, nor have they identified, gender differences in the responses of boys and girls, however, there is evidence that suggests pupils do not hold differing expectations of teachers based on gender. For example, in one of our earlier studies, we found that primary age boys and girls think the gender of teachers is immaterial (Carrington et al., 2008) but there were some gendered patterns evident when it came to what they liked about their teachers. Whilst overall there was a broad similarity in the characteristics both boys and girls looked for in their teachers, boys focused more on aspects of the work teachers gave to them and girls on the supportive actions of the teachers (Hutchings et al., 2008).

The questions we asked pupils in interviews which elicited information about 'code talk' (that is, how pupils describe, for example, their experience of being a learner, how much control they have over their learning environments, how confident they are as learners: see Arnot and Reay, 2006, 2007) were:

- What do you enjoy most about school?[4]
- What don't you enjoy about school?
- Could you tell me about your favourite subjects at school?
- Could you tell me about your least favourite subjects at school?
- Do your friends in your class like/do well in the same subjects you like?
- How long do you spend on homework? Do you work on it with other classmates? Do you feel homework is important?
- How would your teachers say you're getting on with school work at the moment?
- Where would you put yourself in relation to others in your class, in terms of grades etc.? How does that make you feel?

What students said they liked and did not like about schools was frequently related to either their relationship with the teacher, or how effectively they felt the teacher was in doing the job of teaching. Of course this is not saying anything that is not already in the literature (e.g. Thiessen and Cook-Sather, 2007). However, as we have pointed out in Chapter 1, shifts in the educational system of the UK over the last two decades has placed more emphasis on the individual as the source of success (or failure), with successful schools seen as providing the springboard to academic achievement (with the assumption that they have effectively smoothed out potential social disadvantages created by social class or ethnic group differences (Chubb and Moe, 1997; Apple, 2004)). The evocation of neoliberalism's focus on individualism, effectiveness and efficiency (Pollitt, 1993; Giddens, 1998) can be found in the comments of pupils in recent studies of schooling where they view their success as down to 'effort' on their part, although teachers are seen as crucial in providing ready access to the curriculum (Hufton et al., 2002; Dunne and Gazeley, 2008). The pupils' code talk in our study indicated that their (high) ability, their gender and the context of the school interacted to inform how they perceived the function of and their relationships with teachers (see also Arnot and Reay, 2006).

There were two key elements noticeable in the students' code talk regarding teacher–pupil relationships: one was the significance of a stable teaching population; another was the gendered differences in the boys' and girls' expectations and perceptions of teachers.

Knowing the Teachers and Teachers' Familiarity with the School

It was important to the students that the teachers were familiar with the cultural and social context of the school in order to be able to provide a supportive learning climate:

> *Noah:* . . . with the more experienced teachers who have been at school longer they're a lot more laid back. I think you learn more with them than the new sort of teachers. (white, middle-class, Oldtown School)
>
> *Hamid:* Just probably her knowledge of the school, and she sort of doesn't know what she's doing. At the same time, she never explains the subject she just gives you work sheets and then she expects you to do it and I say 'what do I do?' and she says 'don't ask questions.' She's right in front of you . . .
>
> *Interviewer:* You said she doesn't know the school what do you mean by that?
>
> *Hamid:* Well like, cos some teachers are quite new some of them are like quite old but they still don't get the basics. (Turkish, middle-class, Highgarden School)
>
> *Kennedy:* Some of the teachers I don't like, the new ones who you can't really get used to. (white, middle-class, Highgarden School)

One of the most problematic consequences for high achieving pupils was in having to cope with apparent low levels of teacher commitment and morale. In these instances demands were placed on the resilience of individual pupils to maintain an investment in learning:

> *Bethany:* . . . I remember my maths teacher and she said that she don't even look at the homework she just throws it away afterwards . . . but I did always do my maths homework because I like maths. (white, working-class, Winterfell School)

> *Tristan*: Not that long (on homework), um most teachers will set me one, don't collect it and it's like really pointless homework so that stuff I don't do, but stuff that I do and I understand it's supposed to have been quite a bit of time.
>
> *Interviewer*: Ok so do you know which ones aren't going to get collected so you don't bother.
>
> *Tristan*: Yeah. (white, middle-class, Highgarden School)
>
> *Rose*: I don't really go to any clubs outside of school because the club I used to go to they stopped it because they said the teachers weren't getting paid enough. (African-Caribbean, middle-class, Highgarden School)

The function of teachers to provide pupils with supportive learning environments as well as in delivering the curriculum was then of key significance in facilitating high achieving pupils' approaches to their school work. Of similar note were the differing patterns in response of boys' and girls' to their articulation of professional skills and competencies.

Girls Are Judged By Teachers Whilst Boys Judge Teachers

Students' main concern with their teachers was their 'authority' either as 'knowledge experts' or as endorsers of their academic achievement. There were gender differences here as to which aspect of the teacher's role boys and girls gave emphasis to. For example, boys were most likely to be concerned with teachers' subject knowledge and pedagogical skills. Whilst girls tended to talk about boring *lessons* where they were just copying out of books, didn't find the content interesting or it was difficult, the overwhelming majority of girls did not focus on the teachers as the source of either boredom or interest in subjects. Although Victoria at Saltcliffe School did say that 'it depends what teacher you have 'cos, sort of a boring teacher than the lesson is sort of boring as well', it was predominantly boys who identified the teacher as a reason for liking or disliking a curriculum subject. In so doing, teachers were positioned as the gatekeepers of curriculum knowledge which, as far as these boys were concerned, they delivered more or less effectively:

> *Gareth*: Er I don't like the . . . er . . . some things in maths 'cos I find it tricky and I think like, I don't particularly like my teacher 'cos she, she talk, she goes over stuff that the teacher said yesterday, we already know but the stuff that we don't know she rushes it and then gives us the work and it's like a whole page of work but we [go through] about two questions then we have to stay in to do the rest, it's a bit unfair. (white, middle-class, Kingswood School)

> *Adam*: Well like I find Religious Moral Studies a bit boring because the teacher just goes on and on and I think we should do stuff like practical and stuff like that or watch videos which would make it a lot easier to understand and stuff like that. They just go on and on and you just get really bored and you want to talk to other people while they're doing it because it gets a bit boring after a while. (white, middle-class, Lannisport School)
>
> *Eric*: Well some, I don't really get on with some of the teachers, erm some of the lessons quite boring . . . I like to be a bit more active in lessons. (white, working-class, Kingswood School)
>
> *Sean*: I just I like the teacher and it's just quite fun. She's quite nice and we do like more interesting subjects. (white, social class unknown, Saltcliffe School)

In this sense boys tended to convey agency and authenticity in asserting evaluations of their teachers: their statements suggest an evaluative approach that implies boys' sense of authenticity as valid assessors of their teachers. Research has frequently highlighted such 'confident' authenticity in boys, showing for example how they tend to articulate higher perceptions of their abilities than girls, and to blame any low results on extrinsic factors such as teachers or examination practices, rather than on themselves (Stables and Stables, 1995; OECD, 2007; Weiten, 2008). Yet we would suggest beyond this that in their evaluation of their teachers, boys perform themselves as active, agentic 'consumers' of education, equipped to make such judgments in a neoliberal education (quasi) marketplace. Hence they perform themselves as active subjects in keeping with both enlightenment and neoliberal discourses that postulate an agentic, active individual acting rationally on the world/within economic markets.

In contrast, the girls were more likely to focus on teachers as authority figures who are in a position to legitimate their achievements. The literature on gender and education has pointed out how girls tend to have lower levels of self-confidence and articulate greater anxiety about performance at school than boys and that this can be said of both middle-class and working-class girls (Plummer, 2000; Walkerdine et al., 2001). Some girls referred directly to this, for example, Theresa (Saltcliffe School) said 'I don't have enough confidence in myself', going on to add that 'I think if I was a boy I'd do a bit better because I'd be able to, in a way, (perform) a bit better because I wouldn't be worried about getting stuff wrong, I'd have a go and ask the teacher if I wasn't sure and stuff like that'. For girls to be both academically successful and remain 'acceptably feminine' demands a careful negotiation of these competing demands (Jackson, 2006a; Francis et al., 2010) and, this may partly explain girls' concerns with 'pleasing the teacher' when it came to the teacher's role of 'gatekeepers of curriculum knowledge'. Whereas the boys cited above made judgements about teachers' abilities to deliver the curriculum, girls were more concerned with proving themselves to their teachers:

> Ruth: I did have a teacher say this morning that he (gave a) very good report for me 'cos I'd be doing excellent revision. So I was quite chuffed with that. (white, working-class, Lannisport School)

In replies to whether homework was important:

> Carrie: (Yes) . . . um because it gives, like, the teacher a chance to know what you can actually do on your own. (white, social class unknown, Kingswood School)
>
> Holly: Yes because it can show the teachers what you can do by yourself outside of school. (white, working-class, Queenswood School)
>
> Rowan: Yeah it is important really 'cos it just sort of it's like a sort of a check for the teachers just to make sure your understanding it at home as well as in the classroom. (white, middle-class, Oldtown School)

Those girls who talked about being 'annoyed' by some teachers went on to give explanations that suggested they were anxious about teachers treating them differently, if not unfairly:

> Michelle: . . . it's just when they have favourites . . . Sometimes if they're [pupils] particularly good at that subject or just you know a bit of a suck up.
>
> Interviewer: Right so do you think they'll be treated in a different way?
>
> Michelle: Um sometimes but sometimes they [teachers] make it obvious.
>
> Theresa: . . . and it's quite annoying because my brother he's like really good at everything and some of the teachers think I'll be like him, I always get called Matthew's little sister.

Hence in contrast to boys' performance of active authenticity in their (often critical) evaluations of teachers, girls tended to produce instead a more passive, self-critical construction. While this distinction supports previous research findings of girls' tendency to lower self-confidence and internalization of 'failure' (Jones and Jones, 1989; Sadker and Sadker, 1994) we would also want to draw attention to their 'failure' of positioning within neoliberal education discourses. Girls' apparent passivity and internalization of institutional problems produces them as failed consumers within the education quasi-market, as they do not produce themselves as agentic, or as authentic assessors of a 'product'. Such analysis further problematizes suggestions that (middle-class white) girls represent the ideal neoliberal self: flexible, achieving and 'having it all' (Ringrose, 2007; Skelton, 2010). Indeed, our findings lend further support to our previous critique of such positions, as failing to reflect constructions of authenticity and entrepreneuralism as profoundly masculine (Francis and Skelton, 2005).

We now want to turn our attention to the tensions between popularity and academic application and high achievement by looking at what pupils say about this. While much research has shown this tension to be an issue for groups of boys (and an impediment to their learning), in our study it was girls who articulated the greatest anxiety in this regard. What follows is a consideration of the pupils' conception of 'balance' between popularity and achievement. As we discuss more fully in Chapter 6, one means by which both girls and boys could manage their cleverness yet not be seen as a 'boffin' was to be regarded as popular by classmates. Those pupils nominated as 'popular' were (irrespective of social class and ethnicity) highly connected both socially and in terms of school work. This was made easier for them by their physical 'good looks', fashionable dress style and particular constructions of subjecthood, as will be elaborated in Chapters 5 and 6. However, not all the high achieving pupils had the abilities, skills or indeed 'good looks' that enabled them to maintain this balance, and many pupils – especially less popular girls – expressed anxiety in this regard.

High Achievement and 'Balance'

In her book, *Lads and Ladettes in School,* Carolyn Jackson (2006a) has a chapter entitled 'Balancing acts: Who can balance the books and a social life, and how?' in which she discusses the strategies pupils adopted in order to accommodate the (often conflicting) demands of school work and wanting to be seen as 'cool' and popular amongst classmates. These included appearing *not* to work, at least not too hard; ensuring there was time for chatting and 'hanging out' both in and out of class; for girls and boys, presenting an aesthetic image which for girls meant being fashionable, pretty and thin, whilst boys focused on being seen to be good at sport (see also Jackson, 2010 and Francis et al., 2010). But knowing the importance of 'balance' and being able to achieve it are very different things and many of the high achievers in our study struggled with the 'sociable' side of balance.

As was said earlier, adolescence is a key period for friendship and 'fitting in' and is of equal importance to girls and boys irrespective of whether they are seen as widely popular. For example, spending time with friends was important to all girls with over 50 per cent of the popular and not popular girls referring to it when talking about what they enjoyed doing outside school. However, the popular girls made greater mention of the significance of friends at school. Similarly, the high achieving and popular boys also stressed the importance of friendship at school. However, when it came to discussing what they enjoyed doing outside of the school environment less than 32 per cent of the popular boys mentioned spending time with friends as opposed to 79 per cent of those boys not deemed popular. Why might that be? When looking at their preferred activities the high achieving and popular boys talked about playing sports (which were wide ranging from football to running to rugby) and going to clubs – sporty and non-sporty – such as science and drama clubs. These are all active and competitive and tend to fit in with hegemonic constructions of masculinities (Martino and Pallotta Chiarolli, 2003). The high achieving less popular boys talked more about computer games and watching television (certainly television was not mentioned by HAP boys at all and only one mention of computer games). Generally the preferred activities of high achieving boys were more solitary such as drawing, playing guitar, listening to music or watching basketball. Shared activities were going to the cinema and bike rides. Perhaps the high achieving less popular boys felt the need to mention friends or perhaps the high achieving and popular boys either took them for granted and/or the male camaraderie that occurred through the sports and club activities facilitated friendship networks. Having said this, it was the responses of high achieving girls, who were not regarded as universally popular by others in the class, which indicated that they, more than any of the other high achieving pupils, struggled with their relationships with peers and teachers.

Being a High Achiever and 'Doing Girl'

The academic success of girls in schools as reported in the media does give the impression that girls are unproblematic academic achievers (Younger et al. 1999; Maynard, 2002; Ivinson and Murphy, 2007). However, far from 'having it all', many school girls, irrespective of social class and ethnicity, have problems coping with the expectations of academic success placed upon them by parents, teachers and, indeed, themselves (Lucey and Reay, 2000;

Walkerdine et al. 2001; Ali, 2003a; Osler and Vincent, 2003). Also these pressures are experienced as much by high achieving girls as by those who are struggling with school work (Allan, 2010). Indeed, in our study it was the most academically successful girls who found managing achievement alongside 'doing girl' particularly challenging. It should also be remembered that these girls came from both working- and middle-class backgrounds.

The ways in which social class and minority ethnic status shapes girls' educational experiences has been thoroughly documented. For example, the chances of getting into a 'good' school are far less likely for working-class girls, who tend to make the decision themselves as to the school they will go to whilst, in contrast, the parents of middle-class girls use their 'educational capital' to decide for them (Reay and Ball, 1998; O'Brien, 2003). Further obstacles are encountered when stereotypical social class expectations are used to provide career advice, sending working-class girls down conventional routes such as child-care and hairdressing (Francis et al., 2005). There are also problems for working-class and minority ethnic girls in their engagements with teachers whereby interactions are constrained by their different positionings which contrast with the shared language, understandings and experiences of teachers with middle-class girls (Osler and Vincent, 2003; George, 2007). Furthermore, some working-class girls in schools not regarded as 'good' (for example, those with high teacher turnover and poor test results) demonstrate low self-image, seeing themselves as 'rubbish' because they attend 'rubbish schools' (Lucey and Reay, 2000; see also Archer et al., 2003). This is not to say that middle-class girls have an easy time of it at school as the increasing emphasis on the individual as the source of success or failure at school (irrespective of social barriers) has placed enormous pressures on them; what may be regarded as achievement by a working-class girl and her family could be seen as failure by a middle-class girl and her family. For instance, Valerie Walkerdine and her colleagues illustrate how middle-class girls' successes are frequently seen as not 'good enough' by citing one middle-class mother's response to her daughter's news that she had obtained nine A grades at GCSE and one C grade as 'Oh well, congratulations on the A's anyway' (2001, p. 179). Indeed, increasingly, links are being made between middle-class girls' anxiety and stress in striving for high academic achievement and the increase in the level of self-harm and eating disorders reported amongst this group (Evans et al., 2004; Lundh et al., 2007). At the same time, not all middle-class girls self-harm, and there are working-class and minority ethnic girls who are as academically successful as their middle-class, white peers.

As mentioned earlier, one of the ways by which both girls and boys could manage their cleverness yet not be seen as a 'boffin' was to be regarded as popular by classmates. As we elaborate further in Chapters 5 and 6, being 'popular' was facilitated for such pupils via their gender constructions: being a 'proper girl' (interested in fashion and relationships) and a 'proper boy' (focused on sports) allowed their cleverness to be 'balanced out' (Jackson, 2006a). As Emma Renold and Alexandra Allen (2006) showed in their study, high achieving girls adopt varying approaches in treading a precarious line between 'doing girl' and 'doing success'; for example, this might involve devising ways in which their cleverness could be played down and expend efforts to ensure they fit in with the others, or, more rarely, rejecting conventional femininities and focusing on success. Whilst one approach involved being accepted, but at the cost of having to distance themselves from perceptions of themselves as 'high achievers', the other meant being isolated from girls' friendship groups. Thus, managing high achievement and femininities for girls requires the negotiation of productive/self-destructive attitudes and behaviours.

Such struggles involving anxiety, separation and rejection operating simultaneously with pride were evident in the explanations of the high achieving but not popular girls. These were girls who did not stand out for being particularly fashionable or unfashionable, particularly socially adept or inept, neither 'sparkling stars' nor 'serious swots'. Rather, they were girls who attempted to not stand out in any way (Hey, 1997). It was noticeable that the majority of the high achieving girls positioned themselves within the boundaries of conventional femininities which meant substantial investment in their relationships. In response to the question 'Where would you put yourself in relation to others in your class, in terms of grades etc.? How does that make you feel?', after correctly identifying themselves in the top rankings, Helen and Rebecca indicated that their 'feelings' about their position in class were experienced through their relationships with classmates, especially their female friends:

> Helen: . . . even my friend, well Jasmine says how she likes it that I don't boast about that I'm really smart even though she says that I am. Whereas like, whereas you have to kind of be, stay with everyone else. (white, working-class, Oldtown School)
>
> Rebecca: I'm a bit proud of myself but I wouldn't really like to move to set one, I don't know why but I wouldn't. I have some of my friends that sometimes talk behind my back or something and I don't really like them that much and they always moan and stuff and they're all in

set one so I don't want to go there. (white, middle-class, Highgarden School)

In a similar way, but with different responses to those girls who put their efforts into their peer/friendship groups, Lily and Bethany set up distinct barriers between 'people' on the one hand and 'school achievement' on the other:

> Lily: I wouldn't tend to worry about it too much . . . school isn't the main priority that I have anyway so I don't seem to worry about whether I'm doing well. (white, middle-class, Lannisport School)
>
> Bethany: I don't know I just kind of, when, with my work I just try my best and I don't really care what people think about me. (white, working-class, Winterfell School)

Whilst these high achieving girls articulated how they viewed their 'cleverness' through the eyes of their classmates, and particularly their friendships, they distinguished themselves from 'girly' femininities, whose ranks they either did not want, or could not aspire, to join.

> Louise: They're not posh but they're just girly. (African-Caribbean, working-class, Winterfell School)
>
> Bethany: My best friend we like nearly all the same stuff but my other friends they're, like, really girly all the time, so we're quite different. (white, working-class, Winterfell School)

Being 'girly' was defined in terms of 'other' to mode of femininity which the high achieving girls saw themselves as occupying:

> Helen: . . . they're ['emos' are] not very girly. They're all like, if something, like someone like tried to like act like girly, 'oh no, no, I can't do that'. But really, when you are a real girly person, like 'oh no that makes me feel ill' but then emos are kind of 'that's not bad' that kind of thing you know? (white, working-class, Oldtown School).

It was said earlier that relationships with teachers were of importance to both girls and boys and attention drawn to how girls were more likely than boys to describe these in terms of the authority of the teacher to 'judge' them. We also observed how girls tend to have lower levels of self-confidence and articulate greater anxiety about performance at school than boys. These girls were cognizant of their academic abilities but were often frustrated when their efforts were ignored or devalued by teachers. This frustration was evident in their comments as their 'good girlness' went unrewarded. We cited Bethany earlier who spoke of how her maths teacher failed to look at her homework and, in addition:

> *Zoe*: Sometimes it's really good to kind of know that you're good at it, if you know what I mean, but sometimes teachers, kind of, because you are so good . . . like in my maths class which I'm in at the moment they don't like, my teacher, she knows I can do it so she never bothers like asking me. So if I have my hand up she won't bother because she'll know I can do it and I think that's fair to ask other people. I'm not selfish but then eventually when you kind of go a few days and you think 'why hasn't she asked' it just gets a bit annoying. I just don't put my hand up and everyone's just turning around going '[shocked sound] she hasn't put her hand up!'. (white, middle-class, Winterfell School)
>
> *Helen*: Sometimes it's annoying when you're quite smart and you always try to do well 'cos the teachers expect so higher of you and sometimes when the people who are really naughty [are] one tiny little bit good they get massive praise but then the person who's been good, way better than them all the year, doesn't get anything and [girl] is on report so that's like really bad and she said that and then we've got this like [. . .] thing in our school and you get moved up if you do well and I've never been moved up because I've always done well so I've never done anything better than I normally do . . . It's just unfair really. (white, working-class, Oldtown School)

The pressure on girls to remain 'acceptably feminine' whilst also academically successful demands a careful negotiation of these competing demands (Francis et al., 2010; Jackson, 2010) and, this may partly explain these high achieving girls' efforts to not be seen to overly criticize teachers in the way that the boys in the study did. The high achieving boys took a critical, judgemental approach in noting what they perceived as teachers' shortcomings from 'being boring' to mishandling classroom management. When high achieving girls talked of teachers' inabilities to maintain discipline they continued within 'acceptably feminine' discourses by internalizing the problems of trying to learn in a disruptive environment, and withdrawing from the situation by 'letting things go' or 'being quiet':

> *Rose*: . . . it's hard sometimes when I'm not learning anything because teachers can't keep the class quiet half the time. I just tend to sit down in

> class and let things go as they do, 'cos me shouting won't make any
> difference. (African-Caribbean, middle-class, Highgarden School)
>
> Rebecca: . . . I know the teacher's really annoying but everybody was like . . .
> was shouting at her and she really shouldn't have done that 'cos after
> all she's a teacher and I was just like being quiet and everybody was
> laughing and I was thinking 'why are they laughing, they shouldn't do
> that'. (South American, middle-class, Highgarden School)

These high achieving, but not generally popular, girls were less able to draw on aesthetic embodied resources than their popular, academically successful female classmates (Francis et al., 2010) and so had to work hard in assessing how their cleverness could be made acceptable (or not) in order to allow them to get on with others. Similarly, they accommodated and even rationalized those teachers' approaches which lead to their learning needs being marginalized.

What we have shown in this chapter are the ways in which high achieving pupils perceive a successful balance between academic work and relationships with peers. For some, and high achieving girls in particular, this throws up a number of tensions. Although popularist discourses position boys as underachievers with girls having come to be seen as 'ideal pupils' then high achieving girls are regarded as adept at negotiating their way through the educational system. In current policy thinking, 'gender', when interpreted in neoliberalist concepts of performance, credentials and high standards, is no longer regarded as a constraint on girls' educational opportunities. Yet, what the high achieving girls in our study indicated is that 'gender', when understood in terms of identity, continues to act as a powerful force in engaging with, understanding and negotiating academic success with 'doing girl'.

In looking back at earlier studies of gender and schooling, it was shown how girls were seen to be, and felt themselves as, lacking confidence, desiring to please and expressing anxieties about their abilities, positioned them in ways that pushed them to the margins of the classroom (Stanworth, 1983; Sadker and Sadker, 1994). To be a 'proper school girl' demands that girls present as co-operative, diligent, conscientious with a care and concern for relationships with teachers and friends and a (heterosexual) interest in boys (Hey, 1997). It has been difficult for girls to effectively demonstrate their cleverness as displays of confidence which are often seen as 'pushy' or overly assertive (Renold and Allen, 2006). The tensions in adopting the masculine position of academic achiever in tangent with being a 'proper school girl' is revealed in the comments of the high achieving girls and, indeed, precedence is given to locating themselves within appropriate gendered subjectivities. It is from their gendered positions that these girls negotiate their cleverness with the consequence that they often fail to attract the attention of the teacher; and their relationships with girls are shaped by the extent to which they are willing to disguise their academic abilities. Far from 'having it all' high achieving girls, who are neither the 'sparkling stars' or the 'serious swots' of the class, experience school lives that continue to be circumscribed by gender.

So this chapter has highlighted the notion of 'balance', potential tensions between the diligence and application required for high achievement (and high attainment itself) and popularity, and the resulting challenge for young people to balance these aspects. We have also drawn out the different trends and concerns for the high achieving young people in our study in this regard, as well as the institutional points that they found important. In the next chapter we go on to look at those high achieving young people who are positioned as having 'failed' to balance.

Notes

1 HAP denotes a student seen as both high achieving and popular by classmates. HA refers to a pupil who was high achieving but not seen as popular amongst classmates (for a fuller explanation see Chapter 2).

2 Interestingly, it was only boys who were generally regarded as 'popular' that said English was a favourite subject. For these boys, English was cited as frequently as those subjects usually considered to be preferred more by males such as science and maths.

3 'Bad breeds' is a term applied in one inner-city, highly ethnically diverse school, and appeared to be an ethnicized term largely interpolating black and other minority ethnic pupils who engaged a 'gangster' aesthetic and resistant behaviour.

4 This is a brief outline of the questions. The interview schedule included sub-questions and/or prompts.

4

Boffins and Geeks: The Social Consequences for Young People Constructed as 'Too Hardworking'

The previous chapter explained the pressures on pupils to avoid appearing too academically inclined at the expense of sociability and their consequent concerns to 'balance' their sociability and academic achievement in schools. But what of young people who fail to achieve this balance? Those pupils who become preoccupied with their performances of 'cool school kid' or 'laddish' resistance at the expense of their academic attainment have been subjected to extensive research, as we saw in Chapter 3. It is the performances of these pupils that underpin the established hypothesis that laddish (and ladette) classroom behaviour impedes educational achievement (e.g. Francis, 1999; 2000; Jackson, 2002, 2006a). But scant research has attended to those failing to balance on the other side of the scales or see-saw (whichever visual metaphor you prefer) – those pupils perceived as excessively academically focused. This chapter seeks to address this lacuna, exploring the experiences of those pupils labelled for their compliance and academic orientation.

Etymology: From 'Swots' to 'Geeks'

The terms utilized to allude to such pupils vary over time and place, sometimes differing even between schools in the same area. However, they tend to be very effectively evocative, and their meaning to be immediately transparent even to academic researchers! Contemporary terms at the time of writing include 'boffin', or 'bof' for short (the terms used most frequently among pupils in our research project), 'geek', 'neek', 'keeno', 'keena', 'keenon', 'bodrick', 'nerd', and so on. In the USA, you would find references to 'dweebs' and 'nerds'. Traditionally, the label most British readers are likely to be familiar with is that of 'swot'. This term has probably been most established in British mainstream popular culture, especially in the post-war period of the twentieth century when 'the class swot' and 'teacher's pet' became a frequent figure in literature and comics. Indeed, today's pupils recognize this label, while no longer using it themselves. But it is important to point out that even in the second part of the twentieth century when the term 'swot' predominated, a range of other terminology was also used. For example, we have the 'ear 'oles' in Paul Willis' (1977) study *Learning to Labour*, and the 'Cyrils' in Connell et al.'s (1982)[1] study.

This proliferation of terms is significant, as the different terms invoke mildly different forms of subjecthood. For example, the notion of the 'swot' suggested a pupil who was not just highly academic and diligent, but also obsequious and oriented towards the teacher rather than peers. This construction is maintained in the contemporary terms 'keeno' and 'keena'/'keenon'. But it is somewhat distinct from the contemporary construction of the 'boffin' (or 'boff', 'bod', 'spod' or 'bodrick'), which evokes a bumbling professor type. And this is subtly different again to the terms 'geek' and 'nerd': these terms emanate from the USA, but have become commonly recognized and used among British young people due to the influence of US mediums of popular culture. Arguably, in their pop culture presentation (movies, and TV shows such as 'Glee' and 'The OC') the labels 'geek' and 'nerd' are more focused on (stigmatized) aesthetics, (poor) social skills and (unfashionable 'niche'/ genre) pastimes than on academic diligence. However, Figure 4.1 taken from Jill Harness (2009) 'Are you a Nerd, Dork, Geek or Dweeb?' illustrates the interplay of these factors.

Both the terms 'geek' and 'nerd' appear particularly associated with technical abilities and interests (computers, computer games and the internet, 'gadgets' and so on); number and/or word puzzles; and also a strong interest in fantasy/science fiction television, books and computer games. This point

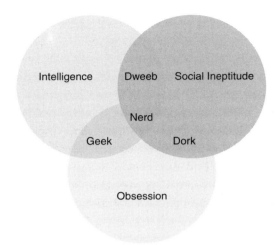

Figure 4.1 Are you a Nerd, Dork, Geek or Dweeb?
Source: (www.neatorama.com/2009/09/16/are-you-a-nerd-dork-geek-or-dweeb/)

already hints at the gendering of these terms, and a debate is developing about the extent to which representations of 'boffins and geeks' tend to be gendered (male), 'raced' (white or East Asian) and classed (middle-class) (see Mendick and Francis, forthcoming).

However, in all of these configurations it is arguable that academic achievement and low social skills and capital within the student peer group are conflated together: 'squareness' (unfashionability, lack of humour and fun), academic diligence and achievement, and poor social skills, are all hinted at in the various configurations, but are accentuated to greater or lesser extents in the various terms applied (Francis, 2009). In considering the application of these terms in the classroom we must remember that such constructions are not isolated to schools, or maintained solely by pupils. They exist in wider society too, and to some extent reflect the general social stigma of the 'clever dick' or 'know-all', which underpin these exacerbated school-based constructions.

It is important to note that these positionings, especially as represented by 'the geek' in popular US parlance, are gaining a new prominence in popular culture at the time of writing. Unlike the twentieth-century representations of 'the swot', who tended to be despised and ridiculed in the literature, the geek is increasingly represented in heroic narratives, from the male leads in Judd Apatow's movies, to the ex-school geek in *Romy and Michele's High School Reunion* (1997), or the assorted geeks and social outcasts in the internationally popular US TV series *Glee*. It may be argued that such narratives have been around a long time, for example as represented by *Spiderman* (wherein geek Peter Parker is transformed to superhero). Yet the current proliferation of such representations, especially of 'geeks' fighting back against the tyranny of the high-school 'jocks', has lead to the deployment of the term 'geek chic' (Mendick, 2005). US TV shows such as *Buffy the Vampire Slayer*, *The OC* and *Glee* have certainly put 'the geek' on the map, and assert geek non-conformity and intellectualism as desirable rather than risible. As such, it may be questioned as to how far the application of such labels is problematic for those at the receiving end. However, drawing on our research data we will show in this chapter that the application remains deeply problematic for those labelled as 'boffins'. This issue will be discussed more fully in reflection on the data presented, at the end of this chapter.

We begin by exploring the application of such labelling of certain high achieving pupils in schools, examining the impact of context, and then move on to look in more detail at the construction of, and experiences of, 'boffins' in schools.

Application of the 'Boffin' Label in Schools

The power of these labels applied to certain academically high achieving young people, and their strong effects, became quickly evident during our interviews, supporting wider research findings concerning pupils' fears of being labelled a 'boffin' or 'geek' (see e.g. Renold, 2001; Jackson, 2006a) for working hard at school. As we saw in Chapter 3, young people's talk about the often precarious balance between high achievement and popularity is saturated in anxiety about this label, with some expressing derision for 'boffins', and others articulating strong resentment of this label. What emerged undeniably was the power of spectre of the label 'boffin' (or similar) as one that might be conferred by peers should one be seen to 'overbalance' on the side of excessive academic application, at the expense of sociability. This clearly provoked anxiety, and acted as a deterrent, for many pupils (see also Francis, 2000; Jackson, 2006a).

What viscerally confirms the need to avoid receipt of such labelling for pupils is the practice of its application against others. Young people identified as 'boffins', 'geeks' etc. are a common feature of schools, albeit they necessarily comprise a small minority in any class or school (otherwise their behaviours could not be marked out as excessive – this relationality underpinning the 'boffin' label will be elaborated later in this chapter). Indeed, some of the high achieving pupils in our sample were already suffering the social consequences of this labelling. For example, Marie (white, HAP, working-class, Winterfell School) asserts that it is difficult for those achieving highly at school to be popular, because 'people think that they're geeks'; and elaborates with reference to her own case: 'people call me geek all the time 'cos like sometimes I wear glasses, somehow I'm a geek and like because like whenever like I put my hand up and I get a question right, everyone shouts out like "geek"'.

Hence our findings support previous research by Jackson (2002, 2006a), Francis and Archer (2005) and Renold (2006) showing that high achievement risks identification as a swot (as represented by any of the concept's contemporary terms). Of course, we have seen how these terms also invoke conformity (to the teacher and/or the school), and as Marie's words illustrate, it can be difficult to separate out the extent to which conformity is being problematized as well as, or rather than, high achievement. A number of studies have demonstrated that non-conformist and 'effortless' achievers may escape such labelling (see e.g. Mac an Ghaill, 1994; Jackson, 2006a); and indeed, we have evidence for this ourselves, which will be discussed when we explore the performances of high achieving and popular pupils in Chapters 5 and 6. Nevertheless, high achievement is clearly a key marker of 'boffinhood'; and as we shall show, such labelling can have a devastating impact on one's popularity at secondary school.

Context

Before we go on to look at pupils' experiences of being labelled 'boffins', it is worthwhile to reflect on the specific context of this positioning. Readers will note that our research took place in secondary schools. There is evidence that these labels are applied with strong effects in the primary school too (Renold, 2006; Renold and Allen, 2006); however, it is likely that the application of the 'boffin' label develops in the later years of primary schooling (elementary schooling to our non-UK readers); and especially in early secondary schooling (Key Stage 3 as it is currently labelled in the UK, covering 11- to 14-year-old pupils). As Mendick (2008) has documented, by sixth form (years 12–13) discursive space seems to be opened up for a potentially greater legitimization of intellect and academic application, allowing some young people to 'own' and even celebrate their 'geek' identities. This space cannot be guaranteed, even at undergraduate level: Reay et al. (2009) have shown that at some (non-elite post-1992) universities students still need to work to play down their academic application in order to be accepted by peers, where at other (indicatively elite) universities 'geek' identities are normalized and even celebrated. Hence age group, educational sector and type of institution all play a part in the extent to which these labels are applied and/or rendered problematic.

In addition to these variables, we found that school context has a significant impact on the drawing of boundaries around behaviours that may be positioned as 'swottish'. Behaviours derided as unacceptably conformist at some of the schools in our study appeared perfectly acceptable and normalized at others. For example, at rural, high achieving and predominantly middle-class Saltcliffe School, diligence and teacher approval were not penalized by peers:

> *German*: The teacher asks Michael some questions and he answers correctly in German. The teacher praises him by saying to the class 'So, Michael has done his assessment'. Michael smiles, no one laughs or takes the mickey in any way.
>
> *German*: Joel asks the teacher 'can we practise some more?' The teacher says yes. No one indicates Joel's wish is abnormal.

Similar practices were evident at Kingswood, a comparably positioned school in our study:

> *Maths*: The children are incredibly supportive of each other getting the right answers. When one boy answers a question correctly other boys said 'well done Jamil'. Another time a boy turns to another sitting behind who has got the right answer and claps him.
>
> *Science*: the teacher announces she has to leave the room for a few minutes in order to get some more worksheets. They [pupils] carry on exactly the same as they were when she was in the room – they all remain on task and the noise level does not increase.

Hence behaviour constructed as unremarkable at certain schools would likely have been problematized, or even rendered completely untenable, in others. These findings highlight the salience of the spatial in constructions of 'boffinhood'. Our sample of schools is small, rendering our findings about school context somewhat anecdotal, but it did appear that 'excessive' expressions of diligence and work orientation were more likely to be stigmatized at schools with higher proportions of working-class pupils (and in our sample these were also those schools in urban areas, tending to higher rates of ethnic diversity). This may be to do with school culture and teacher expectations as well as peer expectations, as schools in our study reflected the common UK trend wherein working-class pupils are concentrated in less high performing schools (Cassen and Kingdon, 2007). However, a relationship between social class and the constructions of what constitutes 'boffin' behaviour has been maintained in previous analysis by researchers such as Willis (1977), Mac an Ghaill (1994); Reay (2002); Bettie (2002); and Weis (2004). This various work recorded working-class oppositions to conformity to the school, and to performances of academic application and achievement within this context. Research, such as that of Diane Reay (e.g. 1998, 2002; Reay and Lucey, 2003) and Lois Weis (2004), has powerfully articulated the psycho-social motivations and explanations for such constructions, arguing that working-class children and their values are placed in deficit by the education system, causing many working class children to disengage, and to reassert an alternative value system which resists conformity to the school. Similarly, Fine et al. (2008) maintain that it is often schools as institutions themselves, via their ideologies and organizing strategies, that reproduce social class in the student body. They argue that such processes are read by students who are acutely attuned to the messages of distinction they receive, and their projected 'place' in this classed system; leading Fine et al. to brand this as 'schooling toward alienation' (p. 227).

To summarize our findings concerning school context, in recognizing the spatiality of constructions of 'boffinhood' we do not mean to argue that 'being a boffin' is more disparaged in some schools than others: the label (or its equivalent) was recognized and applied in all the schools in our study. Rather, the construction of The Boffin is a relational one, with boundaries of acceptable behaviour in relation to academic application drawn differently at different schools. The consequences and responses to such positioning are drawn out below.

The Boffin as Pariah

We have already noted the sort of spectral presence of The Boffin in schools. The label was rarely owned, or used by the 12- to 13-year-old students in our study in direct application to themselves. Rather, a lack of balance (in favour of excessive academic application) or 'boffin-ness' was often projected on to 'other' pupils in interview responses; or application of the label represented as 'what could happen' if one's classroom construction became unbalanced. Yet for all the pupils, the notion of The Boffin, and fear of being identified as one, clearly constituted an oppressive deterrent which functioned to constrain behaviour.

These efforts at maintaining 'balance' in social relations evoke Arendt's (1978) concepts of the pariah and the parvenu: The Boffin is a social pariah, signifying isolation and social rejection. Parvenus struggle to be accepted by dominant groups, always at risk of being revealed as inauthentic and reinscribed with the feared status of the pariah. These themes of social hierarchy, power, naming and (in)authenticity weave through all our findings around high achieving pupils' relations and experiences in school.

We saw in Chapter 3 how particular normative constructions of masculinity and femininity render the overt production of high academic attainment problematic for girls and boys, for different reasons. So gender is an important factor in the construction of the boffin label. In this section we explore the gendered discourses underpinning this construction, and the implications for those young people who fall prey to application of this label.

Only a few of the young people in our study (eight) could clearly be seen to 'fit' the stereotype of the boffin. Others in our sample who appeared to embody some aspects of this stereotype, or were identified as such by other pupils in interviews, did not encompass all aspects (for example, although not generally popular or gregarious, they might have close friends). And it was rarer still for young people to name themselves as boffins, although more discussed in interviews how they were stigmatized as such by other pupils. However, for those pupils that were stigmatized as boffins, Arendt's (1978) conception of the pariah seems highly applicable: these pupils tended to be isolated and excluded to the margins of the classroom. Some of these pupils did have a few close friends, but others appeared thrown together by default with other 'boffins' and a few appeared to lack friends entirely. Our observation notes record these pupils working quietly, either on their own or sometimes with a friend, apparently isolated (perhaps by choice) from the rest of the class and the often manic interaction around them. For example, we recorded the following in our observation notes:

> There are a few kids, including Winnie (Chinese heritage) and her short white friend on their table in the back corner, and Jeremy (white) at the front – who have not communicated with the other kids all lesson (Winterfell School, RE).

Winnie is sitting by herself in the corner (Winterfell School, RE).

Noah (white) is very quiet, seated by himself at the back. Looks a bit lost. (Oldtown School , French lesson).

Noah is still very much on his own. His body language is discrete and small, withdrawn. (Oldtown School, French lesson)

Noah is seen, first with Zeb coming down stairs together, and then in playground by himself. Later I see him again with Zeb and two other boys from a different class, all of whom might be described as 'a bit nerdy.' (Oldtown School, break time)

Teacher sets a task for kids to move around the class describing one another in Spanish. Again, Noah is a bit peripheral – has to wait for someone to become available. (Oldtown School, Spanish lesson)

In the intensely hierarchized and jostling social world of the school, wherein each class gaggles of parvenus eagerly pursue the favour of a few precariously 'popular' pupils, the presence of the boffin-pariah is salutary for the parvenu majority. This is what we meant when we discussed the materialization of the spectre earlier in the chapter: the presence of the boffin-pariah motivates other pupils to the necessary self-discipline to avoid such labelling themselves. As Arendt observes, the distinction between the parvenu and pariah is tenuous and precarious: pupils must carefully regulate their productions of self to avoid similar fates. So the sign of the boffin functions as a strong discursive control on pupils' classroom behaviour, and the threat of application is a deterrent from certain productions of pupilhood – including those that embrace academic application 'too far' or fail to achieve 'balance'.

Elsewhere one of us has drawn on Judith Butler's (1990) work to argue that boffins can be seen as abjected in classroom interaction, although this argument remains controversial given the evident capitals that these pupils possess (in their high achievement)[2] (Mendick and Francis, forthcoming). And indeed, Butler argues that the naming of abject groups in a sense gives life to these groups and a sense of identity and potential agency (although she remains attuned to the constraints and risks of such positions). Certainly Mendick's (2008) work with older 'geeks' demonstrates that this term can be positively owned and ironically embraced and celebrated. And although this was not the case for the younger students in our study, some 'boffins' did appear content in their small groups of similarly positioned peers, and it seemed from our interviews that 'boffins' were often less actively disliked compared to certain other pupils who offended gender and/or social norms in more direct ways. The position also appeared to offer potential freedom: in being positioned as 'outside' the social, 'boffins' were to some extent positioned beyond pressures to conform and balance. As Lily (white, HA, working-class, Lannisport School) considers,

> I mean you can be quite preoccupied if you're unpopular. But if you're unpopular then you have no reason to hold [back] because, because you haven't got any friends to impress or not. Might as well just do it. Because it doesn't matter what anybody thinks.

Likewise, in explaining how she is abused as a 'bodrick' by boys in her class, Mia (white, AP, middle-class, Ironoaks School) states defiantly, ' I'd rather be clever than not clever (. . .) some of my friends don't like it [being called bodricks] but I'm just sort of. In a way I take it as a compliment. Just good'.

Hence aspects of our interview and observation data suggest the possibility that for a few young people, the experience of being 'hailed' and discursively bracketed as a boffin brings a certain freedom in its articulation of pariah status, and consequent potential outsidership from social pressure. For pupils such as Mia, the ownership of her positioning as boffin allows a construction of agency and self-celebration of her school achievement, unfettered by the concerns of the parvenu who must strive for popularity.

Some discursive resistance to academic achievement as a negative construction was also evident in the talk of many high achieving pupils, including those identified as 'boffins'. These pupils countered discourses positioning them as boffins for their studiousness with a narrative of 'jealousy', arguing that those applying 'boffin' as a term of abuse were actually 'jealous' of the abusees' superior academic ability. This trope of jealousy occurred frequently in pupils' interviews: for example, Theresa (white, HA, social class unknown, Saltcliffe School) explains how a 'really clever' boy in her class 'always gets called really horrible names', 'because they're jealous: some of the people who aren't as clever as him are jealous so they call him things like Boffin and big head'. And Toby (white, AP, working-class, Ironoaks School) observes that 'cool' pupils are 'jealous' of high achievers, and consequently 'call them names, 'cos they're not as smart as them'.

Such narratives were also frequently coupled with moral discourses celebrating work ethic and deferred pleasure, in which underachieving 'jealous' pupils were positioned as lacking. Frank (white, AP, middle-class, Ironoaks School) asserts resentfully that he would 'rather be clever than stupid', and maintains that the abusers are 'usually the ones who try and be sort of all tough and which, if they want to do that's fine, but by the end of the day (. . .) they're all either going to have a really bad job or something'. Such stoic discourses valuing deferment of pleasure and work ethic clearly set up binaries of 'Us/Them' and were often directly or indirectly related to social class.

It is easy to presume that 'boffins' are middle-class, yet two of the eight pupils from our sample that fit the stereotype of the boffin are from working-class backgrounds (see also Reay, 2002; Renold and Allen, 2006). Nevertheless, it is noticeable that more of those pupil participants who partially fit the model, or complained about sometimes being called 'boffins' by peers, tended to be from middle-class backgrounds (in terms of ethnicity, there was more of a mix, perhaps demonstrating the overlap of different ethnic stereotypes with constructions of 'boffinhood'; for example of the Asian boffin [Francis and Archer, 2005], and indeed demanding reflection on Fordham's [1996] claims that for black students in white-dominated contexts, classroom conformity itself constitutes resistance). A binary of Us/Them constructed particularly frequently by our top-stream[3] interviewees in their defensive responses was between those in the top stream and those from lower 'ability' streams. And although many of our interviewees were themselves from a working-class background, the concentration of working-class pupils in lower streams meant that this dualism was strongly socially classed, as the language used by pupils indicated. So, for example, non-academically oriented/lower stream popular pupils were variously referred to by our top stream respondents as 'chavs', 'cool kids', and 'bad breeds'. 'Chav' denotes a person from a working-class/deprived social background who wears ostentatious designer clothes and sportswear. The term evokes the notion of 'common' attitudes and aesthetic expression, fundamentally producing an essentialization of poverty (see e.g. Skeggs, 2004); and it was particularly frequently applied among pupils in our study. 'Bad breed' was used in one inner-city, highly ethnically diverse school, and appeared to be an ethnicized term largely interpolating black and other minority ethnic pupils who engaged a 'gangster' aesthetic and resistant behaviour (for more details on these categorizations see Chapter 5). Hence achieving pupils, and particularly those ridiculed as 'boffins', were able to draw on moral discourses of work ethic, and those which construct the working classes as feckless, wanton and excessive (see Skeggs, 2004; Bauman, 2005) to reclaim subjecthood and reposition the abusers as Other.

Hence such practices illustrate the point that, although often quiet and apparently passive in the classroom, 'boffins' are not without power. The discursive resistance and retaliatory positioning discussed above draws on discourses of social class and morality dominant outside the world of the classroom, and such discourses may facilitate constructions of moral and intellectual superiority. And additionally, 'boffins'' diligent practices accrue capitals. Their conformity to the school does not necessarily guarantee their being liked or valued by teachers (see, e.g. Francis, 2000; Renold, 2005; Francis and Archer, 2005), yet their production of credentials, and practices of acquiescence to the (middle-class) institution, accrue capitals for higher education and the workplace.

Nevertheless, despite this, for those ascribed the pariah status of The Boffin, the possibility of celebratory ownership of this 'name' appeared extremely scant, and the consequences of such positioning were often painfully manifest in the interview data. Musing wistfully about those boys who appear able to incorporate high achievement and popularity, Noah (white, A, middle-class, Oldtown School) considers,

> I think it's harder to do that because of the name calling, everyone, as it spreads as a rumour then no one would really want to be friends with you, because at the moment everyone would think that you're um . . . like the names like you know. So um, it is harder um to be popular and um be intelligent but um, most people couldn't manage um if they. If the [curriculum] subject comes naturally to them then I think it makes it easier. But if the subject doesn't come naturally to them then they work extremely hard and other people will see that, and then you get the name calling.

Such painful articulations speak volumes for daily experience in schools where, as Holland et al. (1998) observe, social acceptance is of far more immediate import for most pupils than academic success.

The Gendered Boffin

Stigmatization of boffins is gendered. Stella (white, A, middle-class, Ironoaks School) echoes the views of many of her peers when she argues that bullying of 'boffins' is particularly targeted at, and practiced by, boys: 'I can't think of any boys in my whole year who don't kind of act bad some of the time [. . .] as a boy it's a lot harder to be sort of clever and things like that because you get bullied a lot more and you get called a wuss and things like that'. And as her comment hints, often, the abuse directed at male 'boffins' implicated sexuality. For example Frank (white, AP, middle-class, Ironoaks School) explains how, as well as being called a 'bod', he has been the target of 'quite homophobic stuff'. Jamie (white, HAP, middle-class, Highgarden School) considers of the pressure not to be seen as high achieving, 'I think it affects boys more than girls because the stereotype of girls is just um, sort of [. . .] a bit quiet. And if you don't sort of, *make a stand for yourself,* as a boy, then you're often sort of called gay or something.' Helen (white, HA, working-class, Oldtown School) concurs, remarking that boys 'can't get away with, really trying hard.[. . .] People'd just think you was a bit of a, gay, if you did, if you really tried'.

As discussed in Chapter 3, much research has analysed the way in which high-status 'laddish' performances of masculinity draw on gender discourses that construct academic application as feminine – and hence, those boys that pursue application as effete. It would appear that this construction leads to a discursive conflation between academic achievement and 'queer' sexuality in the case of boys. Stella (white, A, middle-class, Ironoaks School) recounts an example of the sort of homophobic bullying that a raft of studies[4] have shown to characterize everyday interactions in secondary schools:

> . . . there's a boy in the year above us who is like really camp and his name's Josh [. . .] and he, he got really badly bullied last year, people used to like beat him up in the changing rooms and throw away his clothes and stuff [. . .] But um yeah he used to like get bullied really bad, because he wasn't, because he was clever and he didn't, you know, sort of act all macho.

Her final sentence indicates that the boys' academic achievement ('cleverness') contributes to his being constructed as gay. And the example provides a powerful illustration of the potential consequences of being stigmatized as a pariah. One of our interviewees, Tristan (white, HA, middle-class, Highgarden School), was apparently subject to such bullying practices. He was constructed as a boffin by some of his peers, but had some close (similarly positioned) female friends, with whom he always sat in class. Observation notes record Tristan and these friends working away conscientiously amid chaotic scenes and very high volume created by their classmates. It was reported by one of his female friends in her interview that Tristan is the victim of homophobic bullying (and an apparent incident of this was observed in our classroom observations). However, to some extent, Tristan appeared to have accepted and embraced his interpellation as effete/feminine, engaging in friendships with girls and the friendship practices associated with girls; and hence providing an example of male femininity (see Halberstam, 1998; Francis, 2008). For example: 'Michelle is rocking around all over the place, while Tristan is working next to her. Now she's picking lint off Tristan's top' (Highgarden School, maths).

With regard to female boffins, and their imagined sexualities, Stella (white, A, middle-class, Ironoaks School) provides an interesting case. Stella gave a highly reflective interview in which she spoke very insightfully about the social constructedness of gender in the classroom, and her positioning as a female interpolated as boffin within this. For example, she recounts some of the (extremely hurtful) processes of exclusion from more popular groups of girls that she underwent on arrival at the school, and her lack of 'fit' because she is not prepared to compromise her high achievement and does not wear make-up or hyper-feminine fashionable clothing (for the links between popularity for girls and what McRobbie (2008) calls the 'fashion-beauty complex' see Chapter 5). She considers of herself and her friends that their achievement 'kind of stops us' from being popular: 'If we didn't do well in school and we wore more make-up or we wore mini skirts we might be able to join the gang'. Her words evoke the powerful heterosexualization of schools, and the observations by Walkerdine (1990) and others reported in Chapter 3 concerning the firm associations of female academic achievement with asexuality. Further, Stella's interview indicates the painful consequences of such positioning as asexual for girls, and the implications for pariah status. Girls/women must be sexually available for men within the normalizing heterosexual matrix, and perhaps the boffin's lack of 'balance', and prioritization of the academic over aesthetics, marks her as distinct and 'Other' in this regard. As Stella observes, 'I think there's a lot of pressure on girls to look, to wear make-up and be all grown up and you know have big boobs and stuff' (although she goes on to argue that boys are more likely than girls to be bullied for failure to produce gender norms).

The asexualization of the female 'boffins' reiterates tensions identified between academic attainment and sexuality and/or femininity for girls in previous studies (e.g. Walkerdine, 1990; Fine, 2003; Archer and Francis, 2005; Renold, 2006; Allan, 2010). Our analysis highlights how boffinhood is gendered, being associated with sexuality for boys (albeit subjugated, 'gay' sexuality) (see Epstein and Johnson, 1998); and with asexuality for girls. There are numerous historic precedents for the female construction – examples include the eighteenth- and nineteenth-century caricatures of the spinster school mistress or governess; the concerns that girls might be rendered infertile by scholarly work; and more recently, the early twentieth-century stereotype of the 'bluestocking', which was reinterpreted to mean women more interested in academic pursuits than in heterosexual marriage. Significantly, the discursive 'unsaid' (Foucault, 1980) of these stereotypes is lesbianism, which was occasionally hinted at in these demonizations, but rarely openly articulated (as too shocking a possibility to contend). Nayak and Kehily (2006) observe that secondary school boys often used the word 'lesbian' as a term of abuse to denote frigidity rather than actual same-sexual acts, as the latter appeared too radically unsettling a prospect to comprehend.[5] Taking our findings with respect to the positioning of boffins as 'sexually abnormal' and beyond the heterosexual matrix (boy boffins as 'gay' and girl boffins as 'asexual'), one of us has drawn on Judith Butler's work to argue that both male and female boffin-pariahs constitute 'queers' in the classroom – boys in their direct positioning as effete/gay and girls in their queer refusal of/outsiderness to the heterosexual matrix (see Francis, 2009).

Conclusions

We hope to have shown in this chapter how high academic achievement and popularity at school remains a problematic configuration for many pupils. Although there is evidence that 'geekdom' is higher profile and even celebrated in popular culture, with the new 'geek chic' making ownership of high academic achievement and diligence, and the resulting label 'boffin/ geek' more tenable for some, indicatively older, young people, this was not the case for the Year 8 pupils in our study. These young people talked frequently and openly of the need to achieve a 'balance' between their achievement and their sociability: that this balance was often experienced as precarious was highly evident in the data. Excess, or 'unbalance' in the favour of academic application, risked conferment of the boffin label, and marginalization as a pariah, a fate untenable/uncontemplatable for most pupils. Some of the 'boffins' in our study did indeed appear to be experiencing marginalization, isolation, disparagement and bullying, and those interpolated by the 'boffin' label were highly resentful and/or concerned at this labelling. We have, however, illustrated how such positioning does not render the boffin-pariah as powerless: their academic attainment and conformity to the institution facilitates the mobilization of particular, socially classed moral discourses around work ethic and deferred pleasure that may confer a sense of superiority. And the classroom practices of such pupils are likely to be rewarded by exam credentials and the post-school trajectories which these open up. Yet for many pupils the social costs of such positionings while locked in the intense social world of the compulsory school classroom are untenable (Holland et al., 1998).

This challenge of identity work to achieve balance, and the consequences for academic achievement, applies both to those discursively ascribed male and female. But the risks may be particularly acute for boys, to whom the 'naming' of boffin/queer appeared more readily applied, and for whom marginalization as boffin appears particularly risky (risking particularly pernicious forms of punishment in the form of homophobic verbal and physical bullying at the hands of other boys).

So, via their pathologized presence, boffins function as a symbol to motivate other pupils – especially those parvenus at risk of such Othering – to conform to the 'balanced', not excessively highly applied or achieving, production of pupilhood. That this identity work has a bearing on academic achievement in schools is obvious. And it is important in relation to this to keep in mind that boundaries delineating the constitution of 'boffin behaviour' are contextual and relational that shifts depending on the local discursive context of the school. We may hypothesize on the basis of this evidence, then, that at some, indicatively non-selective and working class/inner city schools, the boundaries of acceptable achievement are drawn lower than at others, with consequences for the academic performances of those pupils within them. Important questions for educationalists are raised by the implications of these findings, pertaining to social justice and the different levels of expectations and behaviours in different schools. And more broadly, educationalists need to attend carefully to the point that academic success is, for many secondary school pupils, constructed as incompatible with social popularity, and the consequences of such constructions both for those working to produce themselves as 'popular' and for those labelled as 'boffins'.

Notes

1 It is worth noting that these labels are gendered: both of these were applied solely to boys. Chris Griffin (1985) started her research 'expecting that I would find female equivalents to . . . "the earholes"', but found that no such female roles emerged. However, those writers of girls' 'school story' books (such as Enid Blyton) frequently drew attention to female characters who were highly studious and regarded by the other girls as unsociable by referring to them as 'snobs', 'sneaks' and 'creeps'.

2 Heather Mendick challenges the conception of Boffins as abject, and while Becky Francis defends the conception in relation to other groups who have been similarly conceived, she considers that

Homi Bhabha's notion of The Subaltern may be a more accurate evaluation of the Boffin's classroom position.

3   Streaming is the practice whereby pupils are split into different groups/classes for learning according to 'ability'.

4   A range of research shows the continuing homophobia practiced among pupils (most often boys) in schools, and the misogyny at root of much of this abuse (Epstein and Johnson, 1998; Kehily and Nayak, 1996, 2006; Martino and Pallotta-Chiarolli, 2003).

5   Presumably beyond the context of mainstream pornography!

High Achieving and Popular: The Ideal Neoliberal Subject

5

In the previous chapter we outlined the ways in which the 'balance' between achievement and popularity was seen as an issue for many of the high achieving pupils in our study, with the risk of being considered as the pariah figure of the 'boffin' an ever-present concern. Importantly, being 'clever', or at least being academically industrious, needs to be balanced with the appropriate degree of sociability amongst one's peers. We move now to focus in this chapter on what remains an over-riding preoccupation for the majority of school pupils – the development and maintenance of friendships and the complicated constructions of status and prestige associated with 'popularity'. Pratt and George's qualitative studies of first-year secondary school students found that for both boys and girls the greatest causes of anxiety were issues around friendship (2005; see also George, 2007). The transition from primary school to secondary school can be a daunting experience for many pupils, who have to adjust to unfamiliar – and usually much larger – surroundings, new systems and expectations, a loss of old friends and, crucially, a repositioning of status, from being the oldest members of an institution to being the youngest and least experienced.[1] Pratt and George note that this involves the need to 'learn to read, negotiate and adapt to a very different school culture'

(2005, p.16). It is these peer 'cultures' amongst secondary school pupils in our study that this chapter will be concerned, particularly in relation to friendship, status and popularity.

Over the last few decades a growing number of educationalists have explored the ways in which children's peer cultures work to influence and constrain children's constructions of meaning; their actions and communications with others; and the ways in which they conduct complex aspects of 'identity work' in relation to themselves and their peers.[2] One of the key arenas in which such work is carried out is in the area of friendship groups, and the ways in which such groups construct and maintain complex differential levels of status and prestige. Key to these constructions is the nebulous conception of 'popularity' (defined in this book as having a large number of friends and/or being widely 'known'[3]). As Currie et al. (2007) note, membership of a group (or exclusion from it) can greatly inform the construction of 'who you are' in terms of identity – both in relation to one's own self-identity and how others see you. Those who are accepted as friends with peers who are socially deemed to have high 'status' (either within a particular friendship group, or wider collectivities such as school year cohorts) can themselves acquire 'status' capital amongst their peer groups. As Adler et al. (1992) state, for such children '. . . having someone as a friend is a form of power, which those without close friendships do not have' (p. 162). Moreover, the consequences of finding yourself 'unpopular' can be severe, including the threat and the actuality of bullying and violence.

This concern with, and struggle for, popularity concerns both boys and girls. Although competition is a socially masculinized construction (Francis, 2000; Read, 2006), Merten (1997) and others have demonstrated that girls are equally as concerned with competing with their peers in terms of popularity and status, although they may face greater pressures to compete covertly for high status positions in order not to appear 'unfeminine' (Longino and Miner, 1987; Tracy, 1991, cited in Merten 1997). Discussing the pupils who comprised his sample, Merten argued that 'competition for popularity was a nearly ubiquitous concern for these junior high school girls' (ibid. p. 176).

This chapter is split into two sections. In part one we explore the nebulous concept of popularity, exploring the literature on the gendered, classed and 'racialized' ways in which popularity is constructed, and the views of our own participants on what makes – or at least contributes to – a pupil being perceived as popular or unpopular. We also look at the connections between popularity and celebrity culture, and the specific dynamic of 'authenticity' in relation to popularity. In part two we turn our attention to the varied array of friendship groups in the classes we studied, as described both by the participants and by our observations of their time at school. We take a look at some of the similarities and patterns involving friendship and 'sub-cultural' groupings in the schools in our study – particularly the (again, nebulously defined) groupings of the 'chavs' and the 'emos'.

Part One: The Concept of Popularity

What Makes You Popular?

The 'qualities' that are perceived to increase the chances of a pupil being 'popular' are themselves highly – and complexly – gendered. A key factor in achieving and maintaining popularity is through the ongoing performance of gender in what is seen to be 'appropriate' heterosexual ways – following here Butler's notion of the heterosexual matrix as a key 'grid of cultural intelligibility through which bodies, genders, and desires are naturalized. . .' (Butler, 1990, p.151). As we have heard, previous studies have shown that for boys (at both primary and secondary level) the desired qualities or abilities perceived to be important in order to gain popularity tend to centre around sport, physical prowess and/or intimidation (Adler et al., 1992; Renold, 2000; Pratt and George, 2005). Other important factors were interpersonal skills (Adler et al., 1992); wit and humour (Kehily and Nayak, 1997); 'doing' heterosexuality (Adler et al., 1992; Renold, 2000; Chambers et al., 2004) and being 'smart' or 'clever' (without being seen to try too hard in order to achieve this) (Mac an Ghaill, 1994; Renold, 2001; Francis, 2009; Skelton et al., 2009). For girls a similarly complex pattern has emerged from studies on the subject – stressing that, as with boys, social skills, 'effortless' achievement and the performance of heterosexuality are important, whilst also focusing greatly on girls' need to be perceived as pretty, fashionable and attractive (Bettis and Adams, 2003; Currie et al., 2007; George, 2007; Paechter and Clark, 2007) – and to balance being seen to 'do' heterosexuality without being seen to be too 'sexually forward' (Renold, 2000; Chambers et al., 2004; Currie et al., 2007).

Interestingly, as we shall see, in a number of cases characteristics traditionally associated as 'masculine' can also be successfully appropriated by popular girls – although it seems concessions need to be made, for example in balancing such characteristics with an overt interest in presenting as heterosexually attractive and/or valorizing aspects of hegemonic masculinity at the expense of characteristics associated with femininity. There is less emphasis on boys appropriating characteristics traditionally associated with femininity in order to be popular – although in our study both boys and girls equally cited kindness/niceness as a large factor in relation to popularity for both boys and girls, a characteristic often culturally associated with 'femininity'. However, this particularly related to kindness/niceness to one's *friends*, rather than the 'niceness' associated with the pro-school conformity of the culturally feminized 'good pupil' (Francis et al., 2010) (see below).

Being 'Clever'

As we have highlighted in Chapters 3 and 4, the degree to which one is judged as being 'clever' and/or high achieving often has an impact on a pupil's popularity. As this theme is central to the book as a whole, we will not repeat the discussion in detail here. However, it is important to reiterate here the degree to which 'cleverness' as a factor in being judged popular, and the degree of the necessity of 'balancing' high achievement with other perceived characteristics of popularity such as sociability, will often vary greatly according to factors such as gender, social class and ethnicity, and the peer culture of the class and school. For example, presentations of self as confidently or even arrogantly intellectual may contribute to one's popularity as a middle-class boy in certain streamed classes or schools predominantly populated by middle- or upper-class pupils (see Mac an Ghaill, 1994), whilst it would most likely contribute to being an unpopular outcast in classes or schools that consist predominantly of working-class pupils. In our study, focusing on a mixture of middle-class and working-class high achieving pupils mostly in top set classes, being seen as 'clever' and high achieving was not mentioned by itself as contributing to someone's popularity either positively or negatively. However, the necessity of 'balancing' high achievement or cleverness with sociability and having 'time for your friends' was mentioned by 8 girls and 5 boys, and ranked as one of the top cited descriptions of characteristics of 'unpopular' pupils.

Sports, Physicality and 'Toughness'

In our study nearly all of the high achieving popular (HAP) boys were interested in – and most were also noted as good at – some kind of sport. Moreover, boys especially brought up the issue of interest and ability in sport in answer to questions about what makes a person popular or unpopular – mentioned by 4 girls and 11 boys (see Table 5.1). A lack of interest/ability in sports was mentioned by 5 pupils, all boys, as a characteristic that might make someone unpopular (see Table 5.2). This supports previous literature which shows that interest/ability in physical sports has been shown to be a key issue in relation to popularity and status for boys, at both primary and secondary level. In Adler et al.'s study of elementary pupils in the USA 'those who were least proficient athletically were potential pariahs' (1992, p.172), and in Parker's (1996) study a group of boys known as the 'hard boys' would often bully and intimidate others for their perceived inadequacy at sport, utilizing homophobic language. Sporting ability is linked to dominant constructions of 'appropriate masculinity' in relation to physicality, aggression and competitiveness. In a UK study of 15-year-old white working-class boys, Smith (2007) states that a demonstrated skill in football/soccer 'represented the prestige resource in signifying "successful" masculinity' (Smith, 2007, p.186[4]). As two of us have noted elsewhere (Skelton and Francis, forthcoming), it is easier for middle-class boys to take up constructions of masculinity that are conducive to academic success, and indeed continuing social inequality makes it more likely for middle-class than working-class pupils to go on to succeed in occupational positions that require academic success. Thus the 'footballer' becomes an icon of the possibility for material success that is less likely to be found elsewhere. As Benjamin et al. (2003) note:

> For many working-class boys, the triumphant sportsman is a powerfully attractive emblem of how they could come to access the fortune, fame and power held out to them as possibilities by the football business and other gendered apparatuses of twenty-first century consumer capitalism (p. 551).

Connell, citing a 1990 US ethnography by Foley, describes how the sports enshrined in school culture works as a powerful legitimating tool for dominant discourses of masculinity:

> The game (American Football) directly defines a pattern of aggressive and dominating performance as the most admired form of masculinity; and indirectly, marginalizes others. The cheer-leaders become models of desirability among the girls; and their desirability further defines the hierarchy of masculinities among the boys, since only the most securely positioned boys will risk ridicule by asking them for a date (Connell, 2000, p.159.)

Interestingly, physicality is also valued in relation to popular girls (cheerleading, for example, is intensely physical); however, physical activities that are seen as the particular province of popular girls (cheerleading, dance, gymnastics) are often particularly constructed as 'feminine' pursuits and involve a degree of aesthetic 'display' and concern with appearance and dominant notions of heterosexual attractiveness that are absent from sports and activities more commonly associated with popular boys (Adler et al., 1992). Indeed Paechter and Head (1996) and others have discussed how 'sporty' girls are often seen negatively as transgressing appropriate norms of femininity. However, in a study of 15- to 16-year-old pupils in Sweden, Holm (2007) found that sports was linked to popularity for girls as well as boys, and the most popular group of girls in her study were seen as competing successfully against boys at football/soccer, which as we have noted is a highly masculinized sport outside of the USA and Canada. Interestingly, Holm found that these girls tended to admire qualities amongst other boys, for example their abilities in sport, their 'easy-going' interactions with each other (in contrast to the 'complexities' of girls' friendships), and viewing girls as more 'dull' and 'cautious'. Thus success in the masculinized arena of sports actually in this case paradoxically works to support traditional gender constructions: 'what might be seen as challenging traditional gender stereotypes thus goes along with a celebration of male activities and relations that might be taken to strengthen a (traditional) gender order' (Holm, 2007, p. 187).

Toughness, whether linked to sports or not, is also often linked to popularity in boys. For example, discussing boys in a study of elementary school children, Adler et al. noted:

> Toughness involved displays of physical prowess, athletic skill, and belligerency, especially in repartee with peers and adults. In the status hierarchy, boys who exhibited 'macho' behavioral patterns gained recognition from their peers for being tough. Often, boys in the high-status crowd were the 'class clowns' or 'troublemakers' in the school, thereby becoming the center of attention (Adler et al., 1992, p. 173).

Whilst not talked about as much as 'sportiness', a number of our participants did talk about the relationship between acting 'tough' in order to be popular – or at least popular in the sense of being 'well-known':

> *Albert*: um a lot of the time naughty people stand out don't they.
> *Interviewer*: right, they do.
> *Albert*: 'cos like you see someone doing something that they shouldn't then they . . . I wouldn't say look good, but [they] stand out from the rest.

Interviewer: sure, sure. So like would that make them more popular? Or sort of more . . .

Albert: yeah I think so, like if they're breaking the rules then, like people are going to think so did you hear about 'deedeedee' and what he did and stuff like that . . . their name's going to be going through people's heads.

(white, HAP, middle-class, Winterfell School)

Peter: Like sometimes the boys who are good at sport like show off about that . . . I've got a friend who always like comes up and like pretends to rugby tackle people to make himself look tough, and that's quite annoying.

(white, HA, middle-class, Queenswood School)

In an influential 1989 article, Connell discusses a number of possible identifications in relation to masculinity. Amongst these are 'alternative' forms of masculinity that emphasize sensitivity rather than toughness – one participant in Connell's study identified a group of boys named as the 'wimps', who along with the 'swots' were seen as alternative groupings to the dominant, most popular 'cool guys'. In another of Connell's studies – this time in an elite private school – a distinction was made amongst the pupils between the 'bloods' who were seen as 'hearty, sporting', and the 'Cyrils', who were constructed as 'wimpish, academic' (Connell 1989, p. 295). Whatever the permutations of ascribed meaning in these categorizations, toughness and physicality were valued more highly than softness and sensitivity, and these corresponded to the equivalent status of these groupings in the schools in which they operated. As Connell's categories imply, such 'hard' or 'macho' masculinities have also been linked to anti-school work positionings (as we have discussed throughout this book it is well documented that working hard academically has connotations of effeminate 'weakness'[5]). However, it is important to note that others such as Jackson (2006b) have argued that qualities of 'toughness' or 'hardness' are also valued characteristics amongst some groups of girls, particularly those girls adopting 'laddish' behaviours or dispositions.

Coolness

Another factor relating to popularity amongst both boys and girls is 'coolness' – another slippery concept that is not easy to define, but often relates to the sphere of impression management in terms of behaviour and appearance (Adler et al., 1992). For example, one aspect of 'coolness' relates to a perceived lack of concern or agitation over issues others might worry over (such as school performance, 'success' with relationships with the opposite gender), alongside a perceived 'effortless' success in these or other valued spheres. Another factor linked to 'coolness' is fashionability – being judged as having an appropriate aesthetic fashion sense that is again linked to perceived 'effortlessness'; one must not be seen as 'trying too hard' to achieve a certain look or risk being derided as a 'wannabe'. The importance of fashion in relation to popularity is highlighted in the following passage from our interviews with Leah, a white working-class HAP pupil from Queenswood School. Leah has just suggested someone who is popular in her class, Holly, and contrasted her with an unnamed less popular person.

> *Interviewer:* What's the difference between someone like Holly as you've just described, and this other person?
>
> *Leah:* Probably one of the things about them is probably fashion I'd say, like Holly, she wears quite fashionable clothes, and she likes to be up-to-date on certain things, but the other person in the class he doesn't wear particularly up-to-fashion clothes, he might wear something from like a couple of years ago or something.
>
> *Interviewer:* And that's quite interesting cos you know my automatic assumption when you were comparing the two, I was thinking it was two girls you were comparing.
>
> *Leah:* Yeah it's a girl and a boy.
>
> (white, HAP, working-class, Queenswood School)

Leah goes on to discuss what a 'fashionable boy' would look like: 'they have to be quite trendy and they have to look quite clean like in their haircut or something, erm instead of having like scraggly hair'. Whilst girls are more often discussed in the literature in relation to peer cultures around fashionability, as the quotation above shows, such cultures are also influential amongst boys (Frosh et al., 2002; Jackson, 2006a, 2006b).

Jokes and Humour

Playing the 'class clown' is another common aspect to popularity, particularly amongst boys. Interestingly, 'jokes' are also often used to 'police the boundaries' of friendship groups and delineate insiders and outsiders (Holm, 2007), whilst sexist and homophobic jokes and banter are routinely used by boys to construct and reinforce hegemonic heterosexual masculine presentations of self (Kenway and Fitzclarence, 1997; Kehily and Nayak, 1997; Smith, 2007). Laughing, joking and playfighting are just some of the ways in which, as Dalley-Trim (2007) puts it , boys' embodied performativities or 'bodywork' can run counter to school conceptions of the ideal 'good' conscientious pupil, positioning boys as 'troublemakers' – and thus also helping towards constructing ones' self as 'cool' (see above). In our study being 'funny' was one of the most commonly cited characteristics of popular pupils (mentioned by 5 girls and 8 boys). Finlay, the most popular boy in our Summerhall class, emphasizes the importance of being funny: 'most of my friends are funny and not afraid to embarrass themselves really', in contrast to less popular people who are 'just kind of boring and don't get involved in a lot of stuff' (white , HAP, middle-class, Summerhall School). His description of his friends as not being afraid to 'embarrass themselves' suggests the type of humour that involves what Goffman has described as 'loss of face' – exactly the type of 'class clown' behaviour where one is happy to risk the loss of one's own face, and which also often involves – although Finlay doesn't say it – the type of teasing and 'bantering' that involves the disruption of the 'face' of others, exactly the types of performance described by Dalley-Trim above.

Physical Attractiveness and Sexuality

Another characteristic associated with popularity is physical attractiveness (as perceived through dominant cultural norms) (see Holm, 2007). Whilst this can be important for boys (particularly in relation to fashionability and heterosexual 'success' in terms of appeal to girls), 'prettiness' and physical attractiveness in general are especially highly equated with the dominant image of the 'popular girl'. This was borne out in our study – as we discuss in Chapter 6 – it was very common for the HAP pupils in our study to be described in our notes as good-looking according to culturally dominant conceptions of the term. Heterosexuality is such a hegemonically dominant construction that sexuality was not actually mentioned by the pupils when articulating the characteristics of popular pupils, although there is an abundance of literature, supported by our study, detailing the ways in which heterosexuality is implicitly seen as the 'default' norm for all pupils, and 'otherness' assigned homophobically with homosexuality through jokes, bullying, and the casual equation of anything not meeting with approval as being 'gay' (Epstein and Johnson, 1998; Kehily, 2002). Performances of assertive and even aggressive heterosexuality were commonplace, especially amongst the 'alpha' pupils in our study, with heterosexuality acting as a cornerstone of the dominant forms of masculinity and femininity that are more or less essential to display in order to be popular (Francis et al., 2009).

Jackson (2006a, 2006b), Renold (2000), Currie et al. (2007), Pomerantz (2008) and others have detailed the huge investment of time, money and energy expended by girls in order to be judged heterosexually attractive and the power/status related to 'looking good'. This includes a certain amount of overt performance to demonstrate such effort to others, hinted at here by Jayne: 'it's just as important for boys to be pretty as girls, [as] good looking as girls, but girls have to always check in the mirror, put their lip gloss on, kind of make a big thing about it' (white, HAP, middle-class, Summerhall School).

Despite the popular cultural discourse of 'childhood as innocence', Francis (1998), Renold (2000) and others have persuasively documented the ways in which even primary school pupils' cultures are highly (hetero)sexualized. When undertaking research in this sector Renold recounts:

> From my first days in the field, I became increasingly aware of the ways in which girls were investing in the production of their bodies as heterosexually desirable commodities. This involved embodying heterosexual somatic (bodily) ideals. Typical daily rituals included checking and regulating arms, legs, hips and thighs, positioning their bodies and others' as 'too fat' or 'too thin' and advocating the need to diet. (2000, p. 310)

These pressures only increase during and after puberty. Such self-regulating behaviours and peer-policing was documented in our study (e.g. Francis et al. 2010), and has also been analysed in a range of other works (see e.g. Holland et al., 1998). In our sample, Stella told us she was bullied last year as her bullies thought her 'posh', clever, and 'fat' (actually our notes state that according to the interviewer she looks of average weight for her age group). For Stella it was the accusation of being 'fat' that hurt the most:

> *Stella*: Cos I'm not really from [the area in which the school is located] or anything and I don't talk like that, people call me 'posh'. And then cos I'm clever people call me 'bod'. And cos I'm a bit big they call me 'Oompa-loompa' [. . .]
>
> *Interviewer*: So does that, what does that make you feel like when they say that?
>
> *Stella*: when they say posh I just say well you know they're normal to themselves and I'm normal to me so it's just what you're like. When they say clever and 'bod', I am clever [so it doesn't matter to me]. But I don't really like it when they call me oompa loompa because you know I'm really sensitive about myself.
>
> (white, A, middle-class, Ironoaks School)

Stella went on to discuss how she was bullied last year (by one of the popular groups) and was attending counselling sessions as a consequence. Such pressures are not limited to girls. Another participant, Rebecca, discusses how a group of popular girls in her school would constantly bully a boy in relation to perceived bodily 'weaknesses':

> They said that his breath smelled and they got out Tic Tacs (a brand of peppermint lozenges) and they were like 'here here you should take some put them on' and they were making him eat it . . . and they start cussing him and they were like 'oh your lips are dry' and then they got this big tub of Vaseline out, and we're all like 'you're so mean!'
>
> (South American, HA, middle-class, Ironoaks School)

Ideals in relation to embodiment are also raced and classed. Adler et al. (1992) argue that socio-economic status matters more in relation to girls' popularity than boys because this determines the degree to which girls can access 'stylish' and 'fashionable' clothes and make-up (needless to say, as we have noted, these pressures increasingly affect boys too). Nevertheless, girls wearing 'too' revealing clothes or 'too much' make-up are often negatively ascribed by middle-class pupils as 'chavy', a common current (and most often pejorative) term ascribed to working-class femininities and masculinities (see later in this chapter). For teens/young women they can also be seen as indicative of the 'ladette', a highly classed construction (Jackson 2006a, 2006b), and/ or be judged to have 'crossed the line' in terms of acceptable performances of embodied sexuality and be labelled a 'slag' or a 'slut' – both highly classed constructions (see e.g. Kehily, 2004 for a discussion of the ways in which girls especially are continuously judged and 'policed', often by other girls, in relation to sexual 'reputation'; and Skeggs, 1997 for the cultural association of working-class femininity with stylistic and sexualized 'excess').

Weitz (2001) and others have also discussed how 'ideal' femininities are also dominantly constructed as white. In an interesting study of cheerleading culture in the USA (an activity consumately related to school popularity and status amongst girls), Bettis and Adams (2003) recount how the ideal of the white/'conventionally attractive' cheerleader could not be challenged even by formal measures designed to encourage minority ethnic pupils and those not 'conventionally attractive' to take cheerleading courses, and to ensure they were not formally discriminated against in trials. This was predominantly due to the association of cheerleaders with a high-status social group in the school known as the 'preps', who were predominantly white and from affluent backgrounds. The association of the 'cheerleading type' with 'cute', 'pretty', 'petite' – and white – femininity, along with a passive display of 'niceness' emphasized by the need for a constant smile, were ideals that many pupils in the school either could not, or refused to, adopt.

A growing body of feminist work has highlighted multiple ways in which discourses of femininity are inherently contradictory and insupportable:

> Dominant constructions of girlhood are constituted through a series of contradictions that operate to render the girl herself as an impossible subject. Girls and young women are generally represented as having (or being) too little or too much; as too fat or too thin; too clever or too stupid; too free or too restricted. The desiring subject is also a dissatisfied subject . . . and in the case of femininity, the primary focus of that dissatisfaction is constituted as within the self (Griffin, 2004).

McRobbie (2008), utilizing the Deleuzian notion of luminosity, has recently argued that one of a number of ways in which girls are made visible and culturally intelligible in 'post-feminist' Western society, is through the 'fashion and beauty complex'. From this springs the 'post-feminist masquerade', an impossible construction of femininity, stressing the ideal for women to be both successful in their working lives and also maintain an insupportably demanding standard of beauty and appearance. Drawing on Butler's influential work on the melancholic loss of same-sex desire and sociality made impossible by the pervasive dominance of the heterosexual matrix (1990), McRobbie posits a similar melancholic loss suffered by those whose selfhood is constructed through the postfeminist masquerade. Butler's conception of the 'illegible rage' emerging as a consequence of melancholic loss is in McRobbie's thesis shown, for example, through the increasing numbers of women who have eating disorders and who self-harm (2008).

Hey (2010) points out that the forms of ideal femininity expressed through the postfeminist masquerade are a middle-class ideal – working-class girls and women are less likely to have the material capital to maintain the insupportably high standards demanded by the 'fashion-beauty' complex, and are more structurally constrained from being able to realize the ideals of success in the world of education and work. Indeed, they are much more likely to be positioned as the 'other' to this ideal:

> Hyper-femininity used to be the analytic code which defined an earlier generation of working-class girls who 'went wrong'. . . Yet the hyper-femininity or immaculately groomed hetero-femininity now remarked upon in [McRobbie's work], has

become the propertized middle-class cultural and symbolic capital used to mark distinction against the bodies of white working- and lower middle-class women (Hey, 2010, p. 215).

Being 'Nice', Being 'Good'

For white middle-class girls especially, popularity is also often based on the need to be perceived as 'nice', or being the passive 'good girl' (Merten, 1997; Bettis and Adams, 2003; Currie et al., 2007). A number of studies have shown how popular girls have to balance trying to be 'nice' to everyone while simultaneously retaining the exclusivity of their friendship to those within the in-crowd, lest they lose their 'shine' by consorting too much with 'outsiders' (see Bettis and Adams, 2003; Merten, 1997). However in many studies being too nice, or too much of the 'good girl' – especially towards authority figures, can lead you to be categorized negatively as a 'goody-goody' (Renold, 2000).

Just as with the impossible standards required through the 'fashion-beauty complex' (see above), Walkerdine (1990) argued that dominant constructions of femininity, particularly the constructed valorization of feminine 'goodness' and 'selflessness', are impossible for girls and women to maintain. One way of trying to reconcile this impossibility is through the arena of friendship, where girls project anxieties over their own 'badness' onto other girls identified as different and excluded from the group.

The 'good girl' positioning is often challenged or rejected by working-class and some minority ethnic – especially African Caribbean – girls (Mirza, 1992; Reay, 2001). As well as being classed and 'race'-specific, it has also been increasingly challenged and replaced by the assertive, sexually active and 'knowing' construction of the ladette (Chambers et al., 2004; Jackson, 2006a). However, such constructions still retain contradictions that make impossible demands for girls (see Griffin, 2004; McRobbie, 2008).

What is interesting in our study is that being kind, friendly or helpful to your peers was the characteristic most commonly cited by our participants in relation to popular pupils, and it was cited by boys and girls virtually equally (see Table 5.1). It may be that being kind or helpful to your *peers* is not seen as a particularly feminized characteristic, whilst however being similarly helpful, docile and supportive to *teachers* – emblematic of the 'good girl' – is still devalued/feminized as being a 'suck-up'. Interestingly, being kind, helpful or just 'a good friend' is not a feature in existing studies about the characterization of popular boys, and boys in general are not generally perceived as placing as strong a value on friendship as girls (see discussion in Pratt

Table 5.1 Top perceived characteristics of 'popular' students by gender and popularity

Top Perceived Characteristics of 'Popular' Students [from the interview question 'What makes a person popular?']	Girls	Boys	Total	Not 'popular'	'Popular'	Total
Kind/friendly/helpful	18	20	38	10	28	38
Looks/appearance	22	9	31	20	11	31
Confidence/sociability	8	9	17	7	10	17
Sports/activities	4	11	15	6	9	15
Humour	5	8	13	7	6	13
Connectedness/'knowing' people	6	5	11	7	4	11

and George, 2005). Our study would suggest this is not necessarily the case, and supports Pratt and George's (2005) studies which showed boys developing stronger, supportive friendship links with other boys towards the end of primary school.

Sociability and Confidence

Finally, another important set of characteristics associated with popularity are the related qualities of sociability and confidence (Jackson, 2006a, 2006b). As we discuss in Chapter 6, the confidence and sociability of the HAP pupils in our study was highly noticeable in both interview and observation data. And interestingly, by far the most common characteristic linked to 'unpopular' pupils in our study was being 'shy' or 'quiet', and lacking social skills (see Table 5.2).

Like being described as kind or friendly, the stress on unpopular students' quietness or lack of interpersonal skills/sociability puts the emphasis on the *personality* of the student themselves as the primary factor for being seen as popular or unpopular – i.e. it is implied that it is the student's own 'fault' if they are not popular amongst their peers. However, as Scott's (2007) Goffmanian analysis of shyness shows, such seemingly individualized psychological characteristics are actually socially constructed, reflecting a wider social preoccupation with an often unattainable goal of being always 'poised, skilled and assertive' in our dealings with others (p. 2). Both social ease and social shyness become seen as essentialized personality traits that some individuals have and others do not – a stigmatized group of individuals who are deemed to be in need of 'help' in the form of self-help books or therapies (Scott, 2007).

Table 5.2 Top perceived characteristics of 'unpopular' students by gender and popularity

Top Perceived Characteristics of 'Unpopular' Students [from the interview question 'What makes a person unpopular?']	Girls	Boys	Total	Not 'popular'	'Popular'	Total
Shy/quiet/lack of social skills	14	16	30	10	20	30
Looks/appearance	7	9	16	5	11	16
Lack of niceness/friendliness	5	9	14	4	10	14
Cleverness/high achievement but not also sociable	8	5	13	4	9	13
Inauthenticity	7	1	8	0	8	8
No ability/interest in sports/ physical activities	0	5	5	2	3	5

Interestingly, these seemingly personality-linked characteristics were stressed far more often by students who are popular themselves (by approximately half of the participants deemed to be popular, as opposed to one-third of the other participants) – thus implicitly justifying their status as being by virtue of qualities inherent in their 'character', as part of a 'self' that is seemingly stable, authentic and linked to innate personality.

Pupils who were not deemed to be popular amongst their peers were in contrast much more likely to list external characteristics involving looks or appearance – in describing the attributes of popular pupils (approximately two-thirds of the less popular participants, compared with about a quarter of the popular participants). It is likely then that popular students feel most comfortable explaining, and possibly justifying, their own and others' popularity as caused by seemingly intrinsic qualities in relation to personality or character, whilst less popular students are much more likely to cite more 'shallow' (and implicitly less authentic) extrinsic characteristics such as looks and appearance as reasons for certain pupils' popularity (for a further exploration of the issue of appearance in relation to popularity see Francis et al., 2009). Indeed, the issue of 'authenticity' is a recurring theme in participants' discussions in relation to popularity and status amongst one's peers, which we will go on to explore next.

Authenticity

A number of writers have explored the relation between the current popularity of 'reality' shows such as Big Brother and the cultural valuing of the notion of personal authenticity in relation to contestants (see e.g. Hill, 2004).

Others such as Skeggs (2005a, 2005b) have discussed ways in which middle-class people appropriate and possess seemingly working-class signifiers (e.g. the 'mockney' accent) in order to align themselves more with a supposed working-class 'authenticity' and away from the pretensions associated with the middle class. Goffman (1959) has discussed at length the crucial importance in contemporary Western society of presenting a stable, coherent self to others, and the lengths to which other people will go to try and gauge the authenticity of a person's presentation of self, to try and disrupt a person's presentation, or alternatively collude with someone to maintain a presentation that has inadvertently 'slipped' (i.e. helping someone 'save face'). Crucially, for Goffman such presentations are not necessarily conscious calculations on the part of the 'actor', a conception taken further by poststructuralists such as Butler who sees the self existing not internally but constantly reiterated through performance. Scott (2007) has argued persuasively how shyness (which can be defined as a withdrawal from social interaction due to fears that your desired presentation of self will falter in some way, will not be consistently maintained) can be seen to be a highly rational reaction to the untenable social goal of constantly 'performing' a poised, stable, uncontradictory self.

Such instability may increase unconscious fears or anxieties about sustaining such a presentation of self to others – an unconscious form of 'stage fright'. We have already discussed how anxiety about the presentation of self in the form of *shyness* is socially stigmatized as a characteristic of 'unpopular' students, especially by those seen as 'popular'. We will be arguing here that a similar equation of *inauthenticity* with unpopularity by a number of girls in our study can be seen at least partly as a projection of fears/anxieties and ambivalence on the part of one's own inherently unstable presentation of self to others, unconsciously aggravated by the 'impossibilities' and contradictions of dominant constructions of femininity, which mitigate against the possibility of presenting a fictively stable authentic self.

As we have already noted, the seeming (in)authenticity of pupils was an explicitly addressed concern for a sizeable minority of pupils – in particular the high achieving and popular girls in our study. Seven girls and one boy – all deemed popular – discussed issues of authenticity in the representation of the self as linked to a pupil's potential popularity, and related concerns were expressed (mainly by girls) in other interview answers. Interestingly, the subject was mainly discussed in relation to the characteristics of (hypothetical) unpopular pupils. This, we would argue, lends support to the notion that a concern with (in)authenticity expressed by popular pupils in our study towards an 'other' – in this case hypothetical unpopular pupils – may involve a projection of anxieties concerning one's own authentic presentation of self.

The boy who explicitly mentioned authenticity in relation to what makes pupils unpopular was a white middle-class London-based participant, who mentioned how wearing brand name clothes that were found to actually be fake would be perceived negatively by pupils and might contribute to a person becoming unpopular. However, as we have discussed above, the ability to take part in the 'technologies of the self' that are encouraged by the 'fashion-beauty complex' are not equally available to all, and those from more financially comfortable backgrounds are more likely to succeed in 'passing' as fashionable (such as Russell, a middle-class boy who transformed his image due to constant teasing and successfully achieved a more popular status in Lacey's [1970] study). Those (often from working-class backgrounds) who are unwilling or unable to take part (and to be seemingly doing this authentically, rather than 'cheating' with fake brand goods) risk being identified with stigmatizing 'discourses of failure' (Hey, 2010), such as the (often) working-class women who are the objects of TV makeover shows (discussed in detail by McRobbie, 2008).

Apart from this example, the participants concerned with this issue in response to the question about what makes pupils unpopular were all themselves seen by peers as popular girls. This is not to say that boys are not also aware of and are concerned with the conception of fakeness/authenticity – for example, discussions of 'inauthentic wannabes' in school and university contexts were articulated by a number of male students in Jackson and Dempster (2009) study. However in our study this remained a particular topic of concern and interest for girls. These girls discussed primarily how 'trying too hard' to be somebody they 'were not', lying, boasting and 'not acting themselves' would make a student unpopular. For example, in this extract, Holly, a popular girl from Kingswood School, describes what she believed the characteristics of an unpopular person would be:

> Probably people who are really smart and they also, there's people who don't always act the way how you like to be acted towards, so for example me, Alison, Kate, *we just act like ourselves and stuff* but then there's Paul, I think it's Paul Phillips, he tries to like, I don't know how you put it, like *try and be more cool* but then *trying to do that he makes himself look a bit more stupid than what he may look already* . . .
>
> (white, AP, working-class, Kingswood School, our italics)

Holly above thus asserts (along with the conception that being 'smart' would make you unpopular) that there *is* an authentic self that can be unproblematically represented by herself and her friends to others – 'we just act like ourselves and stuff'. Interestingly she still uses the verb 'to act' here, suggesting an acknowledgment that the 'self', even if seen as lying authentically within a person, has to be 'performed' on the outside to others. Within this conception people can and *should* always perform an honest representation of one's 'internal' self. Holly arguably accredits herself and her friends as 'authentic', assuaging any anxieties over inauthenticity in her presentation of self by projecting this out to others beyond the constructed boundaries of her friendship group. To try to act inauthentically, to try and 'cheat' in your presentation of self, and to be 'caught' doing so, will engender the consequence of public shame and censure by one's peers ('makes himself look a bit more stupid than what he may look already').

Trying to be 'more cool' than you authentically 'really are' also suggests an implicit striving on the part of the pupil concerned to elevate their status in the peer hierarchy without actually being successfully judged by others as holding the necessary qualities. Such 'inauthentic' attempts at elevation are seen in very detrimental terms by students, who are labelled in the disdained category of the 'wannabe', the ultimate stigmatized projection of anxieties over authentic performance:

> *Kennedy:* um. . . well there's like four [friendship groups in the class], ok, well at the top is like um Clarys and Paulette and that lot and they're all at the top and then there's like the kind of chavy gangster people that aren't like the most popular but they're *there* [indicating a 'rung' lower down]. . . then there's like the pupils who are kind of like, I wouldn't call them neeky but like slightly more into school than anyone else and they're kind of like *there*, and then there's like the wannabes who are just at the bottom.
>
> *Interviewer:* Ok so is that like 'wannabe at the top'?
>
> *Kennedy:* Yeah wannabe, wannabe anything really.
>
> (white, HAP, middle-class, Highgarden School)

This supports other studies on girls and popularity that point to the central importance of 'being noticed and liked by the "right people" but not [being] a "social climber"' (Currie et al., 2007, p. 24) and girls' concerns with not wanting to be seen as a 'try-hard' (Baker, 2001, p. 367, borrowing the term from Bloustein, 1999). The social climber, the wannabe, the try-hard, all are nouns rather than verbs – like the 'shy person', inauthenticity becomes seen as an essentialized trait that some people 'have' whilst others do not. It becomes a label whose stigmatization is exacerbated through the 'illegible rage', the fears and anxieties of those girls trying to be 'popular', who are therefore those needing to invest most strongly in performing forms of femininity that as Walkerdine (1990) notes remain impossible to sustain.

The concept of the popular girl as needing to be authentic (or else risking falling into the category of the reviled 'wannabe') did not go unchallenged by participants. There was also a minority discourse articulated mainly by those not deemed as popular, that explicitly saw *popular* pupils as the inauthentic ones:

> *Paige:* When I came to school I . . . was kind of on the outside of the popular lot and you always have to be like make sure you didn't say anything wrong, make sure you didn't do anything wrong kind of thing. But it's just completely pointless cos it's like, well why pretend to be someone you're not?
>
> (white, HA, middle-class, Lannisport School)

So for people like Paige, who for a while was on the edge of the popular crowd in her school before opting out of this tiring liminal position, those who were *not* in the popular set were the authentic ones, free from the burden of pretending to be 'someone you're not' (see also Francis, 2009, on the freedom from social pressure felt by some participants constructed as outsiders due to their ascribed labels as 'boffins'). This alternative view on authenticity and popularity challenges who is perceived as authentic, but still crucially maintains the notion that it is possible to present an authentic, natural self to the outside world. This time, however, it is arguably a projection of anxieties over authentic performance of self from those who are not categorized as popular by their peers to those who are – again a projection outside the boundaries of one's friendship group (although participants did also sometimes question the authenticity of practices of those within as well as outside of their friendship circles).

Overall, then, a complicated picture emerges when we begin to try and tease out pupils' views as to the qualities linked to 'being popular'. Our study supports previous literature on the subject which suggests that such qualities are highly gendered, 'raced' and 'classed'. Characteristics will often be cited as commonly linked to popular pupils in general – for example confidence, sociability, being 'hard' or 'cool', being a 'good friend'. However they will often vary in the extent to which they are deemed important at any one time for particular pupils, for particular friendship groups and in particular schools and localities, according to structural relations of power related to, for example, gender, race, and class, sexuality and (dis)ability. Moreover, social inequalities of power in relation to these facets of identity impact on the degree to which particular pupils will easily be able to, or want to, access and adopt certain characteristics linked to being 'popular'. For example, we have seen how conceptions of 'prettiness' associated with being a cheerleader in US schools are highly classed and raced, and often resisted and challenged by girls from working-class and minority ethnic backgrounds. Similarly, the degree to which being seen as 'clever' and expending effort on academic tasks will work for or against a pupil in terms of popularity and will often vary greatly according to the interplay of factors relating to social class, gender and 'race' in that friendship group, class or school. Overall we can see that the pressures to present an appropriate 'presentation of self' – and to have it successfully judged by peers as 'authentic' – are enormous and intricately complicated. So how was this game of popularity played out by the participants in our study?

Part Two: The Structure and Dynamics of Particular Friendship Groups: The Pupils in Our Study

As can be seen with the case of Paige in the preceding section, many pupils either are unwilling or unable to expend the energy necessary to compete for a place in the school's 'popular' crowd. However, although studies generally document the existence of an accepted overall elite 'popular' group, or series of groups, within a particular educational setting, nevertheless many alternative groupings exist at any one time, and pupils will often find themselves negotiating hierarchies of status within these groupings as well. What follows is a discussion of the friendship groupings in the classes we studied, based on our interpretations of pupil interviews and our observations. As such these sketches are a partial, subjective sketch of a 'snapshot in time' – the way we as researchers viewed the complex, shifting patterns of friendship between pupils, or the ways in which they were described to us, as strangers, by our participants. We met these pupils for only a few days at a certain point in their lives, and of course their allegiances and interactions with others in their school will have shifted and changed innumerable times since that point. We also only have data on social class for those pupils who were identified as high achieving and were therefore part of the interview sample – the only information we have of the other pupils are through descriptions in observation notes and mentions in the interviews of our interview participants. With these caveats in mind, we move on now to describe the friendship groups we perceived within each of our 'target' classes.

The Small Town Schools

Kingswood School

At Kingswood (a 'small town' school) we identified one main popular girls group and one main popular boys group in our target class, who were characterized by one of its members as 'sporty'. The girls' group included Natalie (an HAP pupil in our study, and Caitlin and Gemma, both AP pupils). The 'popular' boys included Laurence (HAP), and Gareth, Eric and Matt (all AP pupils). Kingswood is a predominantly white school and all the pupils mentioned here were white. Natalie, Caitlin and Gemma are all middle-class, whilst the boys in the popular group came from a mixture of middle-class and working-class backgrounds. In field notes the researcher noted that Natalie especially stood out as confident, mature, fashion-conscious, wearing make-up and having dyed hair, in contrast to Caitlin and Gemma who wore no make-up and who had 'mousey' brown hair tied back in ponytails. Natalie also mentions in her interview that she has a male best friend, Peter, and enjoys lessons with him the most (he is not part of the class studied).

Two other groups were identified that seemed to occupy a place in the hierarchy below the popular groups but not deemed to contain 'unpopular pupils', including a 'mosher' group (into 'heavy rock', in status terms similar to indie kids), containing mainly boys and a couple of girls, and a separate group of girls (identified only by Eric) who mainly 'sit in the back and argue'.

Queenswood School

Queenswood is again a predominantly white school based in a small town, and all the pupils mentioned here are white. Like many other classes the Queenswood class also contained a popular girls group and a (middling) popular boys group. The girls included Jayne (HAP, middle-class), Holly (AP, working-class) and Leah (HAP, working-class). These girls were notable in their 'fashionable' appearance, particularly Holly, described by Leah as a particular example of a fashionable 'cool' popular pupil, and our observation notes describe her as 'undoubtedly one of the fashion leaders of the class'. She has a layered very modern haircut, wears a short skirt, tights and round-toed shoes' (Queenswood observation notes). Interestingly, Holly also plays for a local girl's football team – a partial challenge to dominant valued forms of femininity that value forms of physicality such as dance or gymnastics more highly than sports such as football.

The most popular boy in the class, Will (HAP, middle-class), is not actually identified with the main group of boys in the class. This group is described by one of its members, Carter (HA, working-class), as being in the 'middle' in terms of status – he believes a common interest in sport keeps them from being unpopular. There is also a less popular boys group identified – including Scott (A) and Peter (HA), both middle-class. Scott says that some members of the group are more academic than others, but they share common interests including a shared taste in music (he doesn't state which type). Like many participants in our study, Holly describes two main groups of pupils within the school – 'chavs' and 'emos' (these categorizations are discussed in detail below), with the chavs having higher status. However she insists that the popular girls in her class do not belong to either group but are 'individuals'.

Summerhall School

Summerhall was our third school set in a small town location and was again predominantly white – all of our participants from this school were white apart from Robbie, a mixed heritage, working-class AP pupil. In his interview Robbie states that there are no 'chavs' in the maths class that was the focus of our study, although Sonya (white, HA, middle-class) describes the most popular girl group in the class as being a 'bit chavy'. This group included Kelly (a white, HAP, middle-class pupil) and two other popular girls, Melissa and Cher, who were not included in the study. This class was also notable for having a single boy, Finlay (white, HAP, middle-class), who was noticeably 'top dog' in terms of popularity amongst the boys in his class. Finlay was noted by the observer as being 'followed around' by a number of other boys in the class who were also somewhat of a 'fan club' for the dominant central character of Finlay. Unlike most other classes there did not seem to be a single 'popular' group of boys in Summerhall – numerous participants talked of the boys in the class all getting on well with each other. Boys who were perhaps more centrally connected to Finlay than others included Robbie (discussed above) as well as Patrick (white, HAP, middle–class) and Paul (white, AP, middle-class). Finlay gives as reasons for their friendship the fact that the group is all achieving at the same level (well but not *too* well, and not at the expense of other activities), and that they are all interested in sport (indeed Robbie carried around a bag with the name of his school's football team on). Also in this class were a 'middling popular' girls group including Sonya (white, HA, middle-class) who were characterized by Sonya herself as 'quite loud' and who like 'having a laugh', and a less popular quiet studious girls group including Danielle (white, HA, working-class).

The Urban Schools

Winterfell School (Class 1)

In contrast to the small town schools discussed so far, Winterfell is a multi-ethnic urban school. Again with this class there are a 'popular' boys group and a popular girls group. The girls include two of our participants – Marie (white, HAP, working-class) and Bethany (white, HA, working-class) – the girls discussed above as having an ambiguous connection with 'emo' culture, as well as Roxanne (African Caribbean) and Andrea (Mediterranean, possibly Turkish origin), who were not achieving highly enough to be targeted as participants in the study. Unlike the popular groups in the other class at Winterfell, this group comprises pupils of various ethnicities. However, within the group, Marie and Bethany, both white, described themselves as best friends. The popular boys group was also multi-ethnic in character and included Albert (white, HAP, middle-class) Ned (white) and Bobby (African Caribbean). Two other, less popular groups of pupils were also identified – again one group of boys and one of girls. The girls group described one of its members, Salima (Asian, HA, working-class), as 'girly', often talking about 'music tracks, fashion stuff, nails, movies'. Interestingly Salima, like Holly at Queenswood School, was a 'girly girl' who was also interested in football.

In the second Winterfell class there were two popular groups of girls strongly demarcated according to ethnicity – one group comprising black girls and one comprising white girls. The group containing black girls included Louise (HA, working-class) and Shelley. The white girl group included Zoe (HA, middle-class), Tara, and Mallory (HAP, working-class). Mallory and Tara are described as 'best friends' and seem to be the elite 'core' within the group, with Zoe describing herself as more on the periphery of the group (and indeed these girls had just had a 'falling out' at the time of interview, which seemed to be due to the jostling of more peripheral members in trying to get closer to the central core of Tara and Mallory). Louise describes the differences between the two girls groups firstly by saying that Mallory and Tara's group are 'like the posh ones and like they carry handbags and stuff', before correcting herself and saying she means 'girly' rather than posh. In contrast she describes her group as 'funny and loud'. The 'emphasized femininity' implied by the term 'girly' seems to concord with the observer's notes on the appearance of the girls in Tara's group – for example Tara herself is described as 'very pretty, slim, bubbly, articulate and analytical. Some make-up but not loads. Wears bright blonde hair tied back, and jewellery. Wears mini-skirt and pumps, and jumper pulled over her hands. Has white nail extensions'. Nevertheless Louise and her group are also described as wearing fashionable clothes and accessories – Louise is described as 'hair tied back, a bit gawky, but fashionable (Alice band, hair slides, bling earrings, trendy skirt and pumps)'. Other participants describe the difference between the groups explicitly in terms of 'race', often preceded by variations of the phrase 'I'm not being racist, but. . .' (see below).

The class also had a popular group of boys – including Mark and Billy, both white working-class HAP pupils. Louise describes this group, and Mark and Billy in particular, as 'the funny boys'. Another slightly less popular group of girls was identified by one of this group, Nina (white, HA, working-class), who are into indie/metal music. Interestingly, the Nina group included Marie, Bethany and Roxanne from the popular girl group in Class 1 as part of this group.

Highgarden School

Like Winterfell, Highgarden was a multi-ethnic urban school. In our Highgarden class, a number of 'popular' groups could be loosely identified – a white boys group, a white girls group, and a black mixed boys and girls group who are loosely connected to a wider school-based popular group nicknamed the 'Bad Breeds'. This included Paul, Jensen and Michelle (of these only Paul was noted as popular in the class questionnaire, although Jensen and Michelle were cited by others as being members of this wider school-based popular group). According to Leo, an African Caribbean, HA, boy in our study, the Bad Breeds consisted mainly of year 10 pupils, characterized as engaging in 'bad' behaviour such as stealing pupils' mobile phones and bullying some of the younger pupils. Leo describes himself as having friends both amongst the 'Bad Breeds' and the 'Neeks'. Interestingly, Leo uses the term 'neeks' here (another term for 'geek' or 'boffin'; see Chapter 4) to describe the white popular groups in the study – suggesting that the white popular groups in this high achieving class were seen as having *less* status and negatively described as 'Neeks' according to broader school-wide hierarchies. The popular white boys group included Jamie, a middle-class HAP pupil in the study, and a boy we have identified elsewhere in the book as Joel. The white girls group included Kennedy, a middle-class HAP pupil, and friends Kelly and Karen. Jamie, Kimberley, Kelly and Karen also formed an intersecting friendship group and had formed a band together. These pupils, especially Jamie, had a slightly 'indie' fashion style in terms of hair and accessories, and were described somewhat affectionately as 'hippies' by Rebecca, another girl in the class (see below). This group could be compared to the popular girls group in Winterfell 1 and the indie group in Saltcliffe (below) containing mostly white, middle-class pupils, having some interest in 'indie' or 'metal' music/fashion and who are seen as having slightly less status in terms of overall school hierarchies outside their own particular class.

Finally, our Highgarden class had two notable 'less popular' groups. One of these contained a group of three friends: Jennifer (an African Caribbean girl not one of our participants), Tristan (a white, HA, middle-class boy) and Rebecca (South American, HA, middle-class girl). Another group of African Caribbean, South Asian and white 'quiet' girls formed an identifiable group in the class – a group which included Rose (an African Caribbean, HA, middle-class girl).

Oldtown School

Friendship groupings in the setted English class where we observed seemed to contain crystallizations of wider groups contained in the year group as a whole; therefore this outline focuses on these wider friendship groups.

Firstly, two distinct popular girls groups could be identified across the year group. One group of girls did not have any representatives in the English class; the other group contained three girls that were part of this English class – Amy, Jenna and Shannon, the latter a white middle-class HAP participant in our study. There were also two popular boys groups – a 'nice' boys group that likes working (according to one of our participants, Helen), which included Richard (white, HAP, middle-class), Simon (a white, AP, middle-class student) and a boy who wasn't described as popular in the questionnaire but was nevertheless described as part of the group – Stuart (a North African, A, working-class student). Despite being characterized as 'nice guys' who like working, according to Helen (a white, HA, working-class pupil), another participant, Amanda (white, AP, middle-class), singled out two boys in this group as achieving popularity (in the sense of being 'known') because they were often in trouble with the teacher. Helen also defined an 'ugly, hate work' popular boys group as existing in the year group, none of whom apparently were in the class we studied. Finally, one of the 'nice' boys, Simon, also singled out two different boys in the year, again not part of our class, and who we did not observe, who were apparently part of a popular group that were into R&B music.

After these there were a number of friendship groups described as 'the lower ranks' by Helen – Helen situated her own friendship group of girls at this level, as well as another girls group who 'try to be good' but are actually 'quite wild'. Another 'lower ranking' group was described as containing 'skater dudes', thus loosely falling under the indie-alternative banner, as did a further 'emo' group described by Helen. A girl in this latter group, Lauren, was trying to initiate her friend Petra into the gang, a move Helen believed was doomed to failure as Petra was 'too girly'.

One of our participants, Amanda (white, AP, middle-class), can be seen as a kind of 'wild card'; she described herself as mixing with all of these variously described mid-popular groups, as well as some of the less popular groups. These less popular groups included a 'geeky' girls group to which Rowan (white, A, middle-class, pupil) belonged and several 'geeky' boys groups, one of which included Noah (white, A, middle-class).

Ironoaks School

Participants at Ironoaks School also talked of two main groups that dominated school peer culture – the 'Chavs' and the 'Indies' (as will be discussed further below, 'indie' is loosely defined as an alternative, slightly hippy/punky style that is considered less extreme than emo or goth). Most of our description of this school's friendship groups comes from one of the participants, Stella (white, A, middle-class), who aligns herself with the 'indie' style. She described how the 'Chavs' were the dominant grouping in school (she had been bullied by members of this group the year before). In her interview she discusses that within this overall group a number of smaller sub-groups existed, for example a group consisting mainly of Somalian boys, and a girl group and a further mixed gender group of unstated ethnicities. She describes most of these groups as living on a very large working-class housing estate near the school. Second in status to these groups are the 'Indies', who seem to be more middle-class, and who don't generally come from the estate. Within this nebulous grouping are the 'proper emos' – more extreme in their alternative style and are mainly in higher years or mix with higher age year groups, according to Stella.

Within the class a number of popular girls were visibly into mainstream fashion and emphasized femininity. This included two pretty blonde girls called Cheryl and Shannon (the latter explicitly called a 'chav' by Stella) and Gail, a British Chinese, HAP, girl. Seemingly next in terms of status, and containing pupils of quite varying popularity according to the questionnaire, were a mixed gender, predominantly white and middle-class group that Stella called 'The Weirdos', which included Stella herself, Fred (white, A, middle-class), Frank (white, AP, middle-class), Toby (white, AP, working-class) and Mia (white, AP, middle-class). In her interview Grace described herself as feeling on the edge of this group rather than centrally placed, a role possibly shared by Amber (a white, AP, working-class,). Like many schools, the less popular pupils seemed to form smaller pair friendships or sit alone rather than forming a tangible grouping (at least one that was discussed in participant interviews or observed by researchers).

The Rural Schools

Saltcliffe School

Like our 'small town' schools, both of the rural schools in our study had a predominantly white student body. As with Winterfell and Highgarden above, Saltcliffe School contained a popular 'indie' group (characterized here as into 'skinny' jeans and Converse sneakers) who were considered to have slightly less status outside their own class. This 'indie' group included Michelle (white, HAP), Denise (white, AP) and Victoria (white, AP) and a number of boys who were not participants in the study (unfortunately we were not allowed data from Saltcliffe School that might indicate social class positioning). Also popular were a group of 'sporty' white boys including Michael (HAP), Sean (AP) and Mark (AP), as well as a very popular boy called Jake, a 'class clown' who did not achieve high enough grades to be included as an interview participant. As with a number of other schools the highest status group school-wide were described as the 'chavs' (a group associated by participants with wearing tracksuits and 'hoodies' and listening to R&B and rap music). It is not clear whether the sporty white boys in our class were also associated with the 'chavs' or whether (as seemed to be the case in most of our schools) this school-wide popular group seemed to have less of a group presence inside these top sets – or possibly pupils were more hesitant to associate their own classmates with a label that contains paradoxical high status (within the school) and pejorative connotations (in the wider social world).

Lannisport School

Our last school, Lannisport, is also a rurally based school and again predominantly white. Unlike most of our classes which were top sets, our target class at Lannisport was a mixed ability English class. The friendship groups described in the data were less defined by the class itself and had stronger connections with a number of clearly defined friendship groups that existed across the year group. These groups were associated with particular spatial locations – a popular boys group and a popular girls group would always socialize by the canteen; a 'middling/less popular' group, predominantly girls, would congregate around the 'F Block', and another group of girls of similar status, the 'Benchies', would hang around the benches in the playground. The popular girls group had a number of status variations within the group – at the top were two girls, named Janine and Clara, not included in the study. Also quite central to the group were two white pupils, Anita and Rachel, who were part of the mixed ability English class but whose grades precluded them from the study. About five other pupils, again not included in the study, could be ascertained as belonging on the periphery of this central group. The popular boys group included the core figure of Adam, again a white, HAP, middle-class pupil who was most centrally placed in his group, without however the total domination displayed by Finlay at Summerhall School. Other figures on the fringes of this group included Warren (white, HA, unassigned in terms of social class). The 'F Block' group, described by Paige as being 'less pretty and popular, more clever', included Paige herself (white, HA, middle-class), and Ruth (white, HA, working-class), whilst the 'Benchies' included Lily (white, HA, middle-class), who stated that she would also sit with 'F Blockers' in classes where fellow Benchies were not present.

Commonalities: Gender, Class and Ethnicity

As we can see, within the classes we studied – often amongst the top sets of the school – there was considerable variation amongst friendship groups, as well as some strong commonalities.

Firstly, there was ample evidence of groups being defined or described in relation to characteristics associated with popularity discussed in Part One, and in highly gendered ways. The girls who belong to the 'popular' groupings are most often described in our notes as good-looking, fashion-conscious and having dyed hair and or wearing make-up – supporting previous literature on the relationship between popularity and the demonstration of 'emphasized femininity'. A good proportion of the popular boys were also noted as good-looking and/or fashionable, or were described as 'funny'. As would be expected from the discussion in Part One, sport and physical activity also seemed to play a tangible role in relation to boys' friendship groupings and the status held by these groups. For example, Gareth at Kingswood described himself as belonging to the 'sporty boys kind of group' in his class, and like most of the popular boys interviewed described an interest in football or other sports, and played for the school's football team. There were some subtle variations to the prescriptions for popularity described in Part One: for example, Holly, a very popular girl at Queenswood School, seems to be both an overtly 'girly girl', with the associated trappings of dominant 'emphasized femininity' and also a keen football player. However, as we have noted above, having popular status sanctions a certain degree of flexibility in terms of presentation of self not afforded to those who are less popular – and in general the degree of coherence to accepted 'norms' of appropriate masculinity and femininity was (dishearteningly) uniform and widespread.

Another noticeable pattern is the tendency for pupils of the same gender, and to a slightly lesser extent ethnicity and social class, to group together. In most classes there was an identifiable 'popular' boys group and a popular girls group, and most of the other groups in the classes were formed on gender lines. As we have seen there were occasional mixed gender friendship groups, and some members of same-gender friendship groups also had friendship bonds with pupils of a different gender – for example Natalie and her friend Charlie in Kingswood School. Moreover, there are occasions where a particular pupil may describe both boys and girls as belonging to an over-arching 'popular' group – for example Laurence at Kingswood stated that his friendship group included both boys and girls (identified by others as belonging to separate groups), although boys and girls would often do different things at breaktimes – the boys playing football and the girls 'just chatting'.

In terms of ethnicity, most of the schools in the sample had predominantly white classes, and any divisions according to white ethnicities were not immediately noticeable to us as observers, or commented on by pupils. In the urban-based schools in our study, with a much more ethnically diverse pupil body, we observed some noticeable divisions of friendship groupings in relation to ethnicity. In the second Winterfell class, for example, there was an identifiable popular 'black girls' group and popular 'white girls' group.

This is remarked on by a number of the participants, such as Mallory below, a prominent member of the white girls group, who was keen to stress that the difference was not due to racism:

> I think just, just uh, without sounding like a bit like it's not racist but colour. Definitely between the girls. Like in that corner that's all like the black girls and then in these two there's all the white girls and it's not racist because we don't class it as that because we still speak to each other but it's who we, they prefer to hang around to hang around with them and we prefer, nothing to do with our colour just our likeness to each other. (white, HAP, working-class)

Here Mallory paradoxically states that the friendship groups are nothing to do with 'colour' but 'just our likeness to each other' – a distinction presumably in relation to common tastes, interests in clothes, music and so on, which she does not perceive to be racialized. However, as we shall see in the next section, such tastes and interests are often indeed racialized, as well as gendered and classed. The construction of particular friendship groups in relation to class were harder to ascertain, often because we would only have social class data for pupils if we had actually interviewed them for the study. However, as we shall see, many friendship groups were associated with the sub-cultural styles described as 'chav' or 'emo', both of which have social class connotations, the former strongly so.

Commonalities: the 'Emos' and the 'Chavs'

In terms of status hierarchies, it seems common for two overall 'sub-cultures' to be discussed by participants as existing within their schools – the 'chavs' (sometimes referred to as 'gangster' or 'gangster chav') and the 'emos' (or sometimes the 'indie' or 'metal' kids). As we shall see, both groups are seen to have a certain degree of status – the 'chavs' are often equated with the most popular kids in school, with 'emos' occupying a secondary but still elevated status. However, interestingly, being labelled as a 'chav' or an 'emo' is something that most pupils seem to want to avoid, as the labels also have derogatory associations.

The 'chav' is a stereotypical term used for classist ridicule in popular culture, loosely describing a style of dress that prefers brand-name clothing, and associated negatively with working-class pupils. Skeggs (1997) argues that the middle classes often define and construct value against that which is seen as working-class, and due to social inequalities of power styles of presentation of self that are deemed as 'working-class' will often be linked negatively according to dominant norms of social 'taste', and those deemed 'middle-class' constructed as the aspirational standard against which everything else must be judged (see Bourdieu, 1986b). Such gendered and classed discourses of 'taste' and 'style' are picked up, reproduced and reinforced through the peer culture of the school.

There is substantial literature on white appropriation of black cultural forms such as R&B, rap and hip-hop, and some pupils described the predominantly white 'chav' groups in their school as adopting music and fashion tastes and styles associated with R&B and rap. Moreover, in ethnically diverse schools such as Highgarden we found a combining of the 'chav' with 'gangster/gangsta' – a form of culture associated with African Caribbean pupils/young people and connected with a quite strongly masculinized hypersexuality, resistance or rebelliousness in relation to figures of authority and a music/fashion taste relating to rap and R&B (see e.g. Nayak and Kehily, 2006). Participants tended to state that 'chavs' were not commonly represented amongst the higher sets – Holly at Queenswood School for example states 'most of the chavs at our school don't have the most largest ability of . . . learning' (white, AP, working class). This could be related to a 'too cool for school' discourse that is associated with 'chav' subculture, and, as 'chav' is culturally more associated with working-class pupils, reflects continuing inequalities relating to social class and achievement at school. Despite much literature linking popularity with those with middle-class cultural capital, at some schools pupils in our study described the 'chavs' as belonging to the most popular groups at school – emphasizing the complicated and ambiguous status of such categories. However, as we shall see, the very denotation of the name 'chav' holds within it a derogatory classed connotation that works to subtly undermine the tenuous high status generated by popularity within school peer culture, reaffirming wider socio-cultural hierarchies where the higher status of 'middle-classness' is reasserted.

As with all forms of identification, the signifiers for 'chav'-ness seem to be a little ambiguous. Sonya (white, HA, middle-class) at Summerhall School, for example, describes the most popular girl group in the class as 'a bit chavy'. This group includes the most popular girl in class, Kelley (white, HAP, middle-class). Kelley is described in our notes as:

> tall, slim, long blonde hair, probably very fashionable (difficult to tell given the
> very strict school uniform policy) but her hair is about as elaborate as it can be

> within the restrictions. Gets in 'pink' wherever possible e.g. pink socks, pencil
> case, pens/pencils, bag. Her pencil case had the word 'golddigga' embossed on it
> (Summerhall observation notes).

As discussed above, the 'chav' stereotype is linked to an interest in brand-name mainstream fashion (seen to be utilized 'too much' and in a 'garish' manner according to 'normal' middle-class tastes) and dominant cultural forms of (emphasized) femininity. It is possible that Kelley may be seen as fitting this look with her fashionability, her liking for pink and her long blonde hair. However, the picture is – as is usually the case – more complicated. Kelley, like Sonya, comes from a middle-class background (one of her parents is an accountant and the other owns a building company). Also, Sonya herself makes use of hair accessories (she has 'mouse-brown hair which was slightly curly and pulled back in a sparkly hairband'; observation notes). Sonya's glasses were brand name ('Red or Dead') and she had the same 'Golddigga' (another popular fashion brand) pencil case as Kelley. There are some implications here of both pupils wishing to in some way be associated with signifiers of mainstream fashionability and possibly the status of 'chav', although Sonya does not label herself as such.

Of course this is just the researcher's interpretation of Kelley and Sonya's appearance, but from this point of view the only difference seems to be long blonde hair! Both have a 'Golddigga' pencil case and Sonya also shows some awareness of/interest in brand name fashion by wearing Red or Dead glasses. Moreover, both girls come from solidly middle-class backgrounds with professional parents.

In another instance, Stella talks more specifically about what a 'chav' signifies, at least to her. In the following extract she recounts the efforts of one of her 'emo' (see below) friends to gain inclusion to popular groups in the following way:

> Stella: My best friend Launa she, she acts a lot more grown up than her
> own age and she's a proper emo and then she decided she was
> going to get a pink 'Just Do It'[6] bag and I was like 'no you're an
> emo, *pink*? You know, emos don't get pink 'Just Do It' bags and she
> got one, and then she decided she wanted to go out with four dif-
> ferent people who are in the chavvy group so, these two boys um,
> (. . .) they're like some of the heads of the chavvy boys – they took
> her out to [a district in London relatively near the school] to try turn
> her into a normal person which is, like, a chav. Unfortunately all the
> money had been stolen off their card.

Interviewer: oh no

Stella: yeah but she didn't get turned into one, but she did want to be one, so that she could kind of be in the popular group and then go out with these people. I don't know, she's kind of gradually turning chav, but I don't want to say it to her 'cos she'd get really annoyed. (white, A, middle-class, Ironoaks School)

This dense extract contains numerous interwoven themes of in/authenticity, remaking, betrayal, 'balance', social class, gender production and heterosexuality. It is notable that in the context of their largely working-class school, what Stella constructs as 'chavvy' is the established social (popular) subject – the 'normal person', as she puts it. Middle-class Stella positions herself as outside such normality, as the pariah, and yet her use of the word 'chav' serves also to undermine this working-class subjecthood and reposition it as Other, drawing on the middle-class snobbery and pathologization of working-class embodiment from the world outside the school that the term 'chav' reflects (see Skeggs, 2004).

Interestingly, Stella describes her friend Launa as attempting to 'transition' from one notable peer group to another – she is seeking to raise her status by constructing herself as a 'chav', leaving her current 'emo' identity behind. Emos (sometimes called 'goths' – the most common name for this style in the 1980s and 1990s) are characterized in popular culture by a liking for indie alternative music, and a preference for black clothes, dyed black hair and piercings (note Stella's shock at emo Launa choosing a pink bag) – although like all groups of this sort this characterization is a loose construction containing much stereotypical baggage. Whilst less overtly classed than the epithet of 'chav', there are some indications from our study that an 'emo' (or more often a less extreme 'indie') style was more commonly adopted or associated with middle-class students. Girls and boys who construct themselves and/or are viewed as belonging to this subculture are usually not seen as belonging to the *most* popular groups in school (although neither are they deemed to be unpopular), due in part to their presentation of alternative constructions of masculinity and femininity that challenge or sit uneasily with dominant constructions. As we have seen, one characteristic of the most 'popular' boys and girls is often seen to be conformity to mainstream fashionability, and emo dress styles challenge this. For boys and especially girls the particular styles of dress and make-up can challenge dominant mainstream notions of 'prettiness' and attractiveness. 'Emo kids' are also often characterized – whether this is actually the case or not – as not being interested in or excelling at the types of physical sports and activities that are important in terms of popularity. They are also characterized as being interested in music with an emotionally sensitive/'depressing' tone or lyrics ('emo' being short for 'emotional') – all of which tends to challenge dominant constructions of masculinity especially (Smith, 2007). In Smith's study the popular boys asserted their dominance in terms of social status over 'goth' pupils in their class by taunting them that they take up such an identity only because they are bad at football and know they wouldn't get into the team:

> Subordinated masculine identities such as those exhibited by 'goths', in defiantly deviating from the 'norm', are felt as a challenging alternative and consequently are ruthlessly pathologized and positioned as 'other' for preferring pursuits that, in their absence of physical aggression, categorically locate them as 'feminine'.
> (Smith, 2007, p. 187)

Therefore a certain challenge to dominant conceptions of masculinity and femininity is associated with the 'emo' style – and it could be argued that the comfort of higher social or economic capital makes it a little easier for middle-class pupils to risk challenging such conceptions in this way, hence the connection between 'emo' style and 'middle-classness'.

None of the participants in the study talked about identifying themselves as a 'chav' or an 'emo'. We have discussed how the derogatory classed connotations inherent in the former term would act against pupils choosing to explicitly 'own' the identity. Moreover, as we have mentioned, being explicitly labelled, or labelling yourself, as a member of *any* explicit group can be seen as 'uncool'. As is the case with many 'sub-cultural' forms of identity, students who could be perceived as a particular sub-cultural style do not wish to be explicitly identified as such, as they would prefer to see their style as something individual to them. Kennedy (white, HAP, middle-class), for example, is at pains to state her and friends are *not* emo: 'well everyone calls our group like the the um . . . emos, grungers, rockers, anything they like, but we're really not like that at all'. However she then goes on to discuss how her friends dress in subtle ways (often relating to the way things are worn than the actual items themselves) that can indeed be equated with indie/emo style:

> Interviewer: So do you have things that you are more likely to wear in your group that other people are less likely to wear, and that sort of thing?
>
> Kennedy: um I suppose I mean our styles are quite the same but like they're different. If you were to . . . get an item of clothing then you could dress it our way or you could dress it their way, but in the end we're wearing the same things.

Interviewer: I find that really interesting. How is 'dressing it your way'? How would that be?

Kennedy: well say like you're wearing a pair of skinny jeans and Converse [trainers] . . . they can wear it exactly the same but . . . ours might be a bit more like dressed down, kind of grubbier. [with] jeans [that are] kind of ripped . . . Their's might be like . . . you see their Converse and they're like completely pristine and really new and fresh and ours just look like completely battered. But it's like yeah there's a style to it . . . two people can wear exactly the same thing and it can mean *so* much and be so different. (white, HAP, middle-class, Highgarden School)

Despite a certain status attached to these groups, being explicitly labelled as a member of such groups is a form of peer sanctioning. The teasing and ridicule connected with the term 'emo', for example, can be easily seen in the following incident related by Marie, a white, HAP, working-class pupil at Winterfell School. She recounts how an 'experiment' with dying her hair black caused Marie and her best friend Bethany to be mockingly referred to as emo:

Marie: Like um people say that I'm an emo and stuff just cause I dyed my hair black, no one really knows the truth, but they just say all this stuff. So they start something but I know it's not true so I ignore it, but it gets quite irritating because people come up to me and say 'are you an emo?' and I'm just like 'go away'.

Interviewer: So what does an emo mean?

Marie: In this school it means you slit you wrists and everything so like, really annoying. And people go like 'can you show me your wrists,' and I'm like 'no go away, I don't need to show you anything' [. . .] Me and my best friend, Bethany [. . .] just 'cos we're like best friends and we both dyed our hair like something to experiment, and everyone like says 'oh they're the emos.' It's just like, oh well. (white, HAP, working-class, Winterfell School)

Marie, at this point in her life anyway, seems not keen to be associated too strongly with a sub-cultural style that has certain pejorative associations amongst her peers, even whilst the style wins paradoxical status for being 'different'. Marie's group of friends in the class were the most popular in the class, and included her best friend Bethany (a white girl who has a slightly 'indie'/emo style, who was wearing 'emo' style thick black eyeliner on one day and blue eyeliner the next day), Kesha (an African Caribbean girl who wore mid-length plaited hair and small pearl earrings, and was quite 'mainstream' in her fashion style), Roxanne (a mixed heritage white and African Caribbean girl deemed most popular in the class, who wore her hair pulled severely into a short puffy ponytail on top of her head) and Andrea (a girl with a skin tone that suggests a Mediterranean ethnicity, and who had a slightly 'tomboy' style, with long straight hair, trousers and 1980s style black pump shoes). We can see Marie's keenness to assert that dying her hair was an 'experiment' rather than aiming to authentically 'become' something different. As we have seen above, changing your presentation of self in terms of fashion and appearance is a risky strategy for many pupils, as it opens one up to the risk of being labelled an inauthentic 'wannabe'. However, elsewhere in the interview Marie discusses the style of fashion that she prefers, and states that she and her friends like wearing 'odd' things occasionally:

> Marie: I like wearing, well all of us really like wearing really colourful stuff and stuff, like some of us wear really odd stuff. Cos we – like sometimes we like people looking at us, like 'what are they wearing?' Cos like everyone's looking at us but we just like wearing anything that suits us, we don't really care what people think.
>
> Interviewer: Sure sure and did you say it's more kind of alternative stuff or more sort of fashion, like labels?
>
> Marie: yeah like probably both. Like sometimes we wear labels but sometimes we just anything really.
>
> Interviewer: what sort of labels do you. . .?
>
> Marie: um . . . probably I like a lot of like River Island and New Look stuff so yeah.
>
> (white, HAP, working-class, Winterfell School)

So we can see that Marie actually enjoys challenging pupils' expectations as to her presentation of self – 'sometimes we like people looking at us', whilst she also tries to resist being tied too firmly into a sub-cultural style, stating that her and her friend's clothing preferences are geared around individual taste – 'we just like wearing anything that suits us'. Whilst she does not have the comfort of classed social capital, there is a degree of security that Marie's popularity at least temporarily affords her in being able to push the boundaries of presentation of self to a certain degree, away from what is conventionally expected in mainstream fashion (just as Andrea's popularity allows her to present a slightly – but not too strongly – 'tomboy' style, preferring in our observations to wear trousers rather than a skirt, and minimal make-up). However, if Marie is judged by her peers to have strayed too far in this 'experimenting', she may be teased or mocked – as with the case of the dyed hair experiment above. This then leads to Marie's attempts to distance herself from the alternative category posited for her – 'emo', with her assurances that the hair dye was a temporary experiment, and that she and her friends like 'really colourful stuff' as opposed to the dark colours preferred by emo fashion.

There seems to be a subtle dynamic at work whereby if a person is seen to align themselves *too* closely with a particular style such as 'chav' or 'emo' then it can be seen as someone trying to make 'too much of themselves', trying to gain status by being 'different'. Such a person will then be 'brought down to size' paradoxically in part by being *labelled* as a member of this particular subculture, and therefore possibly being derided for being part of a homogenous group rather than someone who is different and individual. This, in addition to the reassertion of the higher cultural status of white 'middle-classness' and white middle-class masculinity and femininity (when name-calling someone a 'chav') and/or the reassertion of 'appropriate' masculinity and femininity (when name-calling someone an 'emo'), can work as a very powerful sanction. We can see this dynamic at work with the following discussion by Holly:

> Holly: I don't want to like rate myself too high because some people would like class yourself as big headed or something.
> Interviewer: Really?
> Holly: Yeah some people are very, like, if you wear one kind of thing people will call you like a chav or emo or something.
> Interviewer: And that would happen amongst your group you think?
> Holly: Not always, it's like other people around you and then word gets spread around until you actually hear it and then.
> (white, AP, working class, Queenswood School)

In this example, Holly has just been asked to rank herself in the class according to achievement. She had placed herself somewhere in the middle, as it transpires she didn't want to seem bigheaded. She then interestingly gives an example of being seen as bigheaded as 'wear[ing] one kind of thing' – aligning themselves with a particular sub-cultural style. This will immediately be sanctioned by peers through being *labelled* as a member of the particular group you were aligning yourself towards. The punishment you receive by being labelled in this way works to counteract any status you might have been wishing to acquire by being distinctive and 'different'. We have seen elsewhere in this book that being high achieving is not necessarily a problem in terms of popularity so long as you do not *advertise* this distinctiveness too much. The same dynamic is at play with sub-cultural style. At a certain subtle point your peers will decide you have 'crossed the line' and become too distinctive in a certain way, or have tried too openly to acquire status and cachet (in ways that may challenge dominant social notions of appropriate gendered and classed aspirational style), and this will be negatively sanctioned by peers through name-calling. In terms of achievement you may be derided as a boffin or a nerd, in terms of sub-cultural style you may be derided as an 'emo' or a 'chav'. Whilst being clever, or being 'emo' or 'chav' might have a certain (complicated, ambiguous) status or value amongst peers, you will be sanctioned if you are seen to be consciously striving too much to attain such status for yourself.

Conclusions

In this chapter we have focused on the ways in which children's 'peer cultures' and friendship group dynamics influence and constrain the complex and fluid 'identity work' of secondary school pupils. In particular the notion of 'popularity', and the ongoing, constantly shifting (re-)construction of differential boundaries of status and prestige amongst different individuals and groupings have been explored. Pupils' own (often ambivalent and/or contradictory) conceptions of 'popularity' were outlined, including: the degree to which popularity relates to 'good looks' and being 'fashionable'; their constructions of and (dis)identifications with the nebulous, differentially statused 'sub-cultural' groupings identified within schools (such as the 'emos' and the 'chavs'); the contradictory desires of many pupils to both 'belong' to a group and to be seen as a unique 'individual' in charge of her/his own neoliberal 'project of the self'; and the 'policing' of boundaries and the complex internal dynamics of pupil friendship groups. What we have shown is how such performances of identity (and their interpretation by others) are infused with culturally dominant discourses relating to gender, class, and 'race', whilst sometimes also working to disrupt such discourses.

Notes

1 See Measor and Woods, 1984; Delamont and Galton, 1986; Hargreaves and Galton, 2002; Pratt and George, 2005.

2 See e.g. Lacey, 1970; Willis, 1977; Measor and Woods, 1984; Delamont and Galton, 1986; Best, 1989; Connell, 1989; Adler et al., 1992; Hey, 1997; Renold, 2000, 2001.

3 See Best, 1989; Adler et al., 1992; Hey, 1997; Bettis and Adams, 2003; Currie et al., 2007; George, 2007

4 See also Renold, 1997, Connelly, 1998, Skelton, 2000; Swain, 2000.

5 See also e.g. Mac an Ghail, 1994; Epstein, 1997; Francis, 2000; Mills, 2001, Frosh et al., 2002.

6 A style of bag by the sportswear brand Nike.

6 High Achieving and Popular: How Do They Do It

So, we have seen how gender plays a crucial part in constructions of popularity, and the ways in which these manifest in classroom peer dynamics. But how do these young people manage their high attainment, alongside their popularity – especially as this 'balance' has been shown to be so difficult? As we saw in Chapters 3 and 4, lack of balance has been an explanation (a) for underachievement, in the case of those who prioritize their popularity and sociability at the expense of their academic focus and (b) for lack of popularity, among those who jeopardize their sociability with peers by their diligence in the classroom. We established in the previous chapter that high achieving popular pupils maintain their 'balance' between sociability and their high attainment outcomes partly via their sociability in the classroom – sociability being one of the key characteristics seen as essential in order to be popular. But how, then, do they avoid this sociability mitigating against their academic success? This chapter will address the specific strategies via which high achieving popular pupils manage to maintain their school work, and avoid alienating the teacher, in spite of their sociability with peers. Their gender subjectivities, and the ways in which they used gender performance to maintain their popularity, will remain a key focus.

What we will argue is that two key aspects enabled this balance for the high achieving popular pupils in our study – one is their gendered 'modes of being', including their embodied, aesthetic presentations, and their interactive performances of self (both aspects strongly gendered). The other is the specific classroom strategies they adopted in relation to the academic tasks set by the teacher. As we shall see, these two key aspects overlap somewhat and there are multiple factors to examine within each aspect.

This chapter is divided into two sections. We begin by looking in the first section at high achieving and popular young people's 'modes of being', with attention to their embodied, gendered subjectivities. The second section explores the specific classroom strategies that HAP young people adopted to manage their engagement with pedagogy and production of attainment.

Beyond our references to HAP pupils, in this chapter we also refer to 'alpha' pupils. As we explained in Chapter 2, HAP pupils are distinguished from those young people in our study sample who were simply achieving well (i.e. HAP pupils have exceptionally high attainment within their school), and from those who were less popular. However, pupils' school relationships are often so overtly stratified that it was also possible for us to identify that this group of 22 HAP pupils included 14 who stand out as being one of the most popular pupils in their class or year group – and these we have dubbed 'alpha' pupils.[1] Of the 12 HAP boys, 5 are categorized as 'alpha': 3 middle-class white boys, one white working-class boy and one Caribbean-heritage working-class boy (the only minority ethnic boy included in the HAP sample). Of the 10 HAP girls, 9 are noted as 'alpha', including 4 middle-class white girls, 3 working-class white girls, one working-class girl of Chinese heritage (the only minority ethnic girl included in the HAP sample), and one white girl whose social class was not recorded.[2]

Part One: Gendered 'Modes of Being'

Appearance

Aware of the impact of aesthetics on peer dynamics in school (see e.g. Hey, 1997; Jackson, 2006a; George, 2007), we sought to record the appearance of young people in our study as an aspect of data collection. A striking finding that emerged from this approach was the strong connection of physical appearance to popularity. Although this may be seen as stating the obvious (albeit a rather bleak statement), in fact very little sociological research has attended closely to 'looks' as an aspect of classroom relations (or arguably to relationships generally) – perhaps precisely because of the 'bleak' and essentialist connotations of such conclusions (by which we mean, the implication that one's physical embodiment – beyond structures such as gender and 'race' – might fundamentally impact on one's life chances). Within this study, a particularly significant finding was the overwhelming tendency for HAP young people to be noted as both fashionable and 'good-looking'[3] (see Chapter 5). Indeed, all of the 'alpha' pupils barring one were specifically noted as physically attractive (the exception, a boy, was described as relatively nondescript). Indicative examples include the following descriptions of various 'alpha' HAP pupils:

> *Kennedy*: (white, middle-class, Highgarden)
> Tall, slender, white, long blondie-brown hair in a feathery cut. Middle-class accent. Pretty. Fashionable. Wearing braces. Is wearing a short pleated skirt and black tights, and lots of thin silver bangles.
>
> *Gail*: (British Chinese, working-class, Ironoaks)
> Long black hair, pretty face, quite chubby, wears make-up and has customized her uniform jumper with several badges. She wears ¾ length black trousers, black tights and girlie pointed shoes.
>
> *Billy*: (white, working-class, Winterfell)
> Tall white boy with gelled up dark hair, quite good-looking, cocky, loose tie.
>
> *Adam*: (white, middle-class, Lannisport)
> By far the most popular boy. Quite slight and small with short brown hair. He's quite good-looking and has a sort of quiet maturity/presence.

This strong tendency for HAP pupils to conform to dominant social constructions in terms of both fashionable styling and 'physical attractiveness' supports Carolyn Jackson's (2006a) analysis of the importance of these aspects in classroom relations, and their strong contribution in enabling pupils to 'balance' achievement and popularity. While applying particularly to the 'alpha' pupils, a majority in the broader HAP sample were also described as fashionable and/or good-looking. As we have discussed in Chapter 5, it is notable that for those who were *not*, descriptions sometimes referred to *other* aspects which might explain their relative popularity. For example, of two HAP boys who were noted as physically attractive, Mark (Winterfell) is identified as 'the Class Clown' and Richard (Oldtown) is observed to be notably cheerful and funny – and both boys are noted as good at sport.

Clearly, what counts as 'good looking' is a cultural construction – attributes considered attractive in some cultures and environments are not always in others. Moreover, we are often reminded that 'beauty is in the eye of the beholder' and although findings such as ours suggest constructions of beauty may be somewhat less diverse and individual than this phrase suggests, clearly there is diversity in aesthetic/sexual attraction. Nevertheless, within a particular socio-historic environment (in this case, the West in the early twenty-first century) particular 'versions' of attractiveness, perpetuated through traditional and contemporary social institutions and discourses, become hegemonic. Although dominant conceptions of what 'counts' as attractive and fashionable are produced by discourses of gender, class and 'race', it was notable that these conceptions were not exclusive according to these social variables: there is diversity across the descriptions of pupils identified as 'attractive' (including for example different social classes, ethnicities, stylistic differences, height differences, etc.).

But within this, the binarized gender order dictates that what is considered attractive for a boy is somewhat different for a girl. This means that what might be attractive in a girl is not necessarily an asset for a boy (long eyelashes, for example, or pouting lips, let alone expectations around height, musculature, etc.). Moreover, these distinct expectations also impact on aesthetic expressions (e.g. restrictive, tight-fitting clothes for girls to emphasize desired 'slim curvaceousness' and restricted movement; make-up to heighten colourful ornateness and to achieve desired accentuation of eyes and mouth; sporty/non-restrictive clothes for boys to accentuate/facilitate activity, and short hair to emphasize utility or long hair to evoke rebellion). So, for example, the vast majority of 'alpha' girls in our study had long straight(ened) hair (fashionable at the time of research). And these girls also tended to wear make-up and accessories such as jewellery, hair accessories and so on: copiously in schools where this was tolerated, subtly in schools where it was not. 'Alpha' boys in contrast sometimes had styled and/or gelled shorter hair, ties and collars worn in certain 'jaunty' or casual ways and 'masculine' accessories such as dark coloured sportswear branded bags, pencil cases and so on[4]. Hence these pupils' 'good looks' were strongly gendered and involved the processes of 'boying' and 'girling' which underpin subjectivity (Butler, 1993; Nayak and Kehily, 2006). These findings also support previous work that shows how the production of hyper-femininity is integrally bound up with heterosexuality (Renold, 2005), and with the (re)production of male subject and female Other perpetuated by the heterosexual matrix (see Butler, 1990) – we explore this angle further below. So our findings indicate that aesthetic practices of 'doing girl' continue to be both more overtly sexualized and more arduous in comparison with 'doing boy' (Renold, 2005). But for both HAP girls and boys, embodied, aesthetic aspects such as 'good looks' and fashionability appeared important elements in their production of 'intelligible' gender: these aspects facilitated the 'balance' to ensure that their gender performances are read as intelligible in spite of their high academic attainment.

Sociability and Confidence

Another arresting point to emerge from our analysis of the behaviour of high achieving popular young people within our study of high achievers is their sociability, reflected in both observation and interview data. We would suggest that this sociability (and social confidence, as we shall see below), closely interrelated with their 'good looks', comprises a further factor in enabling HAP young people to maintain their high achievement without jeopardizing their popularity.

Chapter 5 examined the ways in which HAP pupils interacted in peer networks to secure popularity, and the gendered nature of peer interaction. This sociability also emerged strongly from HAP young people's interview responses. For example, HAP girls consistently talked about friends being the most enjoyable aspect of school, and prioritized communication and relationships with friends. Interestingly, this distinguished the HAP girls from less popular female participants, as well as male participants (Skelton et al., 2010). HAP boys were less consistent in foregrounding friends as a positive aspect of school: around half mentioned enjoyable lessons first instead – the majority of these citing sport. Indeed, as we have seen in the previous chapter, their prioritization of sport as a preferred activity distinguished HAP boys from less popular boys, hence supporting findings from numerous other studies that ability and enthusiasm for sport is an important aspect in producing the successfully masculine, and hence potentially popular, boy (e.g. Connolly, 1998; Martino, 1999; Skelton, 2001; Jackson, 2006a).

Despite the HAP boys mentioning friendships less frequently in their interviews in comparison to HAP girls, classroom observations, nevertheless, consistently record these boys as sociable in class. This was the case for HAP boys and girls alike, and they were often (especially for the 'alpha' pupils) at the centre of classroom interaction. Perhaps this confirmation of sociability is unsurprising given the HAP pupils' identification as 'popular'. But in the context of the body of research reported in Chapter 3 (including some of our own work) that high achievement is problematic to balance with popularity, our findings regarding the sociability of HAP pupils provides an important reminder that high attainment does not necessarily result in classroom isolation and unpopularity. This is particularly underlined by the point that 14 of the 22 pupils identified as high achieving and popular were further identified as the *most* popular ('alpha') pupils in their classes. The sociability of these pupils may indicate that strong social skills contribute to this outcome (see also Jackson, 2006a). On the other hand, it may be that this sociability is also facilitated by other aspects of embodied subjectivity, notably their 'good looks' and fashionability, as we saw above.

Closely related to this finding of the HAP pupils' sociability (and perhaps to their 'good looks' too) is their apparently high levels of confidence. We found that the HAP young people expressed confidence both during their interviews, and in their productions of self in classroom interaction – and this was the case for girls and boys, irrespective of social class. They tended to be highly aware of their high academic achievement: as we have noted elsewhere, it is notable that the current preoccupation with achievement and delineation of 'giftedness' in schools has manifested in an acute and detailed awareness among pupils of their positioning in hierarchies of achievement (Francis et al., 2010). Far from being embarrassed by, or uncomfortable with, their achievement however, the HAP pupils (again, girls *and* boys, and across social groups) tended to appear comfortable with their perceived high ability; albeit girls seemed somewhat more likely than boys to underestimate their achievement in relation to their peers. We have already seen in the previous chapter that, in addition to this confidence about their academic achievement, these young people were also generally confident of their own authenticity, perceiving their popularity as based on intrinsic merit (kindness, friendliness and so on), rather than extrinsic aspects.

This confident subjectivity was extremely evident in HAP pupils' – and especially the 'alpha' pupils' – production of selfhood in the classroom. They tended to be loud, assertive and at the centre of events. Again, this was the case for HAP pupils across social groups, irrespective of gender, social class and ethnicity. However, individual performances of selfhood and modes of interaction did vary according to these factors, most notably gender.

Gender-sexuality

As we outlined in Chapter 2, we see gender as discursively produced, and therefore have in our analysis sought to avoid the automatic conflation of gender with sex (e.g. that productions of gender by those discursively ascribed 'male' are automatically 'masculine'; or that those by selves ascribed 'female' are necessarily 'feminine'). However, it was notable that, unlike some other young people in our wider sample, all the HAP pupils produced performances of gender that were relatively monological in their conformity to monoglossic, binarized, societal productions of gender (Francis et al., 2010). (Albeit, as with all gender productions, there were inconsistencies and transgressions, as we come to discuss.) From a Butlerian perspective we would say that these gender performances were clearly 'intelligible', and we would suggest that this finding is significant for the HAP pupils' popularity. We have seen how reproduction of such apparently monological binary gender distinctions apply especially to the 'alpha' pupils' physical appearance, which conformed to dominant social expectations of what it is to be an attractive girl, or boy, respectively. In this section we want to explore these young people's practices of 'doing girl' and 'doing boy' in the classroom, identifying any apparently distinctive features of such performance.

Doing Girl

There are many examples in our data of girls 'doing girl' in the classroom. Given HAP pupils' tendency to be at the centre of attention it is not surprising that their behaviours in this regard are recorded particularly frequently. But perhaps beyond this, these HAP girls may have been among those especially invested in 'girling'. 'Girling' often involved overt demonstration of stereotypical feminine interests, such as fashion, celebrities, popular music and so on. Indicative examples include:

> When I enter the drama hall, the teacher hasn't yet arrived . . . Shannon and Chantelle are doing a dance routine on the stage, watched appreciatively by a few other girls (Winterfell, Drama).

> Kennedy says, 'I want to change my name to Kennedy Sykes. Oh my god that sounds *amazing*. Don't you think it sounds like a model?' (Highgarden, Spanish)

Many feminist educational studies have remarked on the propensity for girls to apply make-up in the classroom (e.g. Riddell, 1992; Holland et al., 1998; Francis, 2000), and how such acts constitute both an ostentatious production of femininity (what Davies [1989] would term 'gender category maintenance') and resistance to the school. Butler (1993) has drawn attention to the way such behaviours comprise the very ingredients for the production of feminine selfhood: in her discussion of 'girling', she uses the example of the application of lipstick to illustrate how it is not the (sexed) subject that chooses to highlight their gender via applying lipstick, but rather the act of applying lipstick which makes the (integrally gendered) subject intelligible. It seems pertinent, then, to consider the numerous episodes in which this specific method of 'girling' was adopted within our study. Make-up was banned, and this rule rigorously upheld, at a few of the (notably high-achieving) schools in which we researched; but at other schools such prohibitions, if existent in official policy, were not closely enforced. In these schools many girls wore copious and highly visible make-up, and extrovert application in class was frequent. Observation notes from one school include:

> Mallory and Zoe have nail polish out and Mallory is painting Tara's nails. The teacher notices and tells them 'It's not the time for that, girls' (Winterfell, RE).
>
> . . .
>
> The teacher quietens them down. Roisin (small white girl with long yellow wavy hair) is applying mascara in her mirror very ostentatiously and right in front of the teacher, who eventually takes it from her and tells her to put it in her bag. In taking the mascara he causes Roisin to put a blob on her nose, which causes consternation from Sharon and much giggling between her and the other white girls nearby as she wipes it off.
>
> . . .
>
> Mallory is applying lip-gloss while Zoe holds the mirror for her (Winterfell, RE). Maisie (sitting next to Zoe) is checking her mobile and is told by the teacher to put it away. Mallory and Tara are applying lip-gloss (and Mallory continues to do so as she asks the teacher a question) (Winterfell, History).

As other studies have demonstrated, girls' apparent preoccupation with make-up and 'superficial' interests allows girls to be positioned by boys and by teachers as vain and superficial themselves. Such disparagement is of course ironic given that these ways of 'performing girl' reflect girls' production of themselves as objects of the 'male gaze' which is expected and demanded within the heterosexual matrix (see e.g. Holland et al., 1998; Francis, 2000; Renold, 2006). Such processes are illustrated when we see a teacher say to Gail ('alpha' HAP British Chinese girl) and her table mates, 'Listen – this is quite complicated – [don't think about] hair and all that sort of stuff, cos this is complicated' (Ironoaks, Music). Such statements explicitly Other femininity as deficient in its superficiality (Walkerdine, 1990).

But, does the application of such tropes of 'ditzy'/'bimbo' work to help HAP girls underplay their academic application/ability, and hence better 'balance' their achievement with their gendered sociability? This certainly appeared to be the case. McRobbie (2008) argues that within a contemporary social contract regarding gender relations and (in)equality, girls are compelled to engage a 'post-feminist masquerade'. This involves young women performing hyper-femininity and submissiveness if they are to simultaneously take up traditionally masculine aspects of performance that denote 'success' in education and career, without jeopardizing their 'heterosexual desirability' (2007, p. 726) or risk being positioned as inappropriately aggressive or competitive. What McRobbie is describing, of course, is a further example of 'balancing'. It may be that HAP girls' performances as preoccupied with (hetero) sexualized aesthetics play a role in such precarious productions of balance to maintain this 'masquerade'.

Although these episodes of 'girling' were recorded particularly frequently among the HAP pupils in our observation notes, it is arguable that they were not necessarily distinct from the practices adopted by some other girls beyond the HAP sample. Indeed, our data might be seen simply to confirm previous research findings highlighting the arduousness of 'doing girl', and the integral role of aesthetics and (hetero)sexuality within these productions. Therefore we were especially interested in *different* constructions of femininity emergent through the data, and the distinctions between some of the 'alpha' girls' productions of femininity and those of other pupils. To illustrate such distinctions we offer an extract from a drama class at Oldtown school, where the young people had organized themselves into groups to work on a task. 'Alpha' HAP white middle-class girl Shannon, and her friends Samantha (white, also 'alpha' but not so high achieving as Shannon, and therefore not an interview participant) and Amy (white, also not a participant), had formed a separate group from the other group of girls:

> Shannon, Samantha and Amy sit together apart from the other girls, who are crowded together comparing work.
>
> Amanda and Felicity sing lines of a pop song. Samantha, Shannon and Amy are quietly chatting together on the separate table – they are much more aloofly 'mature' and 'femme' than the other girls who are all working together on one table and are very squealy, loud and animated. Of the 'popular' girls, Samantha particularly is more 'teen' in her posture. The other girls are very animated, as are Richard, Simon, Mark and Stuart – not much gender distinction here [between the bigger group of girls and the boys]. Simon and Mark

start shouting and high five-ing Rahim – and are told to quieten down by the teacher. Helen walks about looking superior, with her hands behind her back. She's very interactive with the teacher, asking lots of questions; 'I thought you said –' etc. The bigger group of girls start screeching at a nude picture they've found in the magazine – Helen: 'Sir, sir, it's inappropriate!' Other girls on the table – Jo, Ella and Felicity – are all screeching, laughing and making noises of disgust. Amanda remains seated, and declares in humorous exasperation, 'It's only a man's bottom. I thought it was *dead* people!' There's much hilarity and 'eurrghing', especially from Felicity. Other (cool) girls on the other table noticeably *don't* bother to come over to look.

And under these notes the observer has added,

(Interesting to note that the two quiet tables here are the cool girls and the least cool boys.)

Various themes emerge here. One is the way in which embodiment shapes performance: Samantha's slim, elegant body seems particularly suited to, or productive of, the nonchalant, elegant and self-contained pose she habitually adopts when seated. So again, we see the impact of the physical body in facilitating (or potentially, constraining) particular performances of gender.

A further emergent production is a relational construction of maturity/immaturity. The 'alpha' girls described are invested in a production of femininity as mature and aloof, which can only work as a relational construction produced against the behaviour of boys and the less 'cool' group of girls. In their interviews various HAP girls from different schools alluded to the 'immaturity' of other pupils (frequently boys), hence perpetuating the relational positioning of themselves as mature (Francis, 2000). Interestingly, their 'mature' behaviour and decorum renders them far quieter in this class than the other girls, who might be seen to some extent to be doing masculinity in their demanding and raucous behaviour. Nevertheless, these non-alpha girls are also simultaneously 'doing girl' via their identification with heterosexuality, as illustrated by Helen's rather flirtatious engagement with the male teacher; and via the girls' ostentatious attention to the picture of the naked man. Their performance of prudish, 'innocent' femininity in their affected disgust marks them out as 'immature' in relation to the HAP and HAP/alpha girls' responses. For example, HAP Amanda remarks in 'mature' exasperation 'It's only a man's bottom!', and the 'alpha' group do not even deign to show interest, again performing their total disdain for such juvenility, and in so doing leaving spectators to infer their own sexual knowingness.

Hence these different performances of femininity (and masculinity) draw on quite different discourses, and hence in some ways contradict each other; yet they also interweave and support one another. It is important to reflect on how different constructions of femininity can operate relationally to one another (as well as to masculinity) and to reiterate that some constructions of gender are more imbued with social status than others.

'Precocious Femininity'

Building on these findings concerning the social status of a mature, sexually knowing (though not necessarily sexually active), hyper-feminine production of femininity, we found that such constructions were sometimes used by HAP (especially 'alpha') pupils simultaneous to quite masculine productions of behaviour. The 'alpha' HAP girls in our sample tended to adopt classroom behaviours that involved traditionally masculine traits such as confidence, assertion and resistance. As we have said, they tended to be at the centre of classroom events, and relatively 'loud' – in less strongly disciplined classes, frequently engaging in banter with the teacher and/or peers. However, these girls managed to produce such (masculine) behaviours within a production of 'girling' – in other words, in spite of the masculine elements in their behaviours, they still signified strongly as 'feminine'. This signification could be achieved via the performance of what we have termed *precocious femininity*, a production that all the HAP 'alpha' girls in our sample produced at various times during our observations.[5] Arguably some of the data shown above comprise examples of 'precocious' performances. For example, Mallory's application of make-up as she calls for the teacher's attention (see data presented on pages 151). But the harsh manner in which Mallory repeatedly roars 'SIR!' at the top of her voice to gain his attention later in the lesson illustrates the way in which such constructions can contain behaviour which otherwise might be read as masculine.

To illustrate further what we mean by this term, we include an example from our data – it involves other girls from the HAP girls in our sample, but comprises a particularly vivid illustration, as follows:

> A couple of black girls near the back ask the [good looking, black male] teacher his first name. He won't tell them. One asks, 'Is it Mikey?' Reiss [white, 'alpha', not an interview participant] says 'Mickey Mouse'. The teacher quietens them down (Winterfell, RE).
>
> . . .

Louise [black African Caribbean, middle-class, HA] and Latifah [black 'alpha', not an interview participant] are giggling together [about the teacher]. The dual-heritage girl with ringlets asks the teacher his first name. She bursts out giggling at him as he hesitates, she's very flirtatious and he and she have lots of eye contact in this exchange. She asks 'Is it Marcus?' causing more giggles (Winterfell, RE).

The overt flirtatiousness of the girls involved in these exchanges and the male teacher's evident embarrassment to some extent reverse traditional hetero-sexual constructions of male as active pursuer and female as passive object, the girls' behaviour involving characteristics such as confidence, assertion and rebelliousness which would usually be ascribed as masculine. However, here within the girls' embodied construction of 'precocious' girlhood, such traits become translated within the heterosexualized notion of the female 'tease'. To read this from a semiotic perspective (see Chapter 2), there is a gen-dering process between the sign (in this case the girls' speech/behaviour as delineated in the above data extract), signifiers (the embodiment of this text) and signified (the reading of the interaction by those concerned – including by the observer).[6]

So precocious femininity may be seen as a means of 'balancing' within McRobbie's (2008) post-feminist masquerade in the secondary school context. We would argue that it does so both by accentuating heterosexual femininity, and also (in so doing) by distracting from or masking aspects of production which would otherwise be constructed as masculine, thus maintaining the illusion of a monoglossic gender dualism (Francis et al. 2010).

Having discussed some of the methods and expression of performances of high status femininity adopted by HAP girls in our sample, we turn now to the HAP boys' gendered subjectivities.

'Doing Boy'

The trends in distinction between boys' and girls' classroom behaviours according to constructions of masculinity and femininity have been widely documented in feminist educational research. One of the key findings in this body of work is that boys' productions of masculinity in the classroom tend to involve far more physicality, including a huge range of actions from throw-ing things at one another, to fighting (e.g. Epstein, 1997; Francis, 2000; Mills, 2001; Skelton, 2001; Martino and Pallotta-Chiorelli, 2003; Renold, 2005; Jackson, 2006a), and indeed, as we have seen in Chapter 5, this resonates with the importance of a degree of 'toughness' and physicality in order to be popular. Examples from the current study include:

> Billy [white working-class HAP and an alpha] and Larry are laughing and thumping one another (quite hard) (Winterfell, History)
>
> . . .
>
> Jamil, Billy and Larry are playing a hand smacking game across their desk. The teacher calls their attention but they carry on. The smacks are hard! (Winterfell, History)

However, there was some evidence of the impact of social class on these constructions: some of the HAP boys in our study invested in more 'mature' and calmer performances of masculinity. Although the small size of our sample of HAP pupils means that analysis regarding social class will inevitably be somewhat impressionistic, it did appear that productions of masculinity as assertive and assured but also 'rational' and calm were particularly indicative of middle-class boys. As we have mentioned in the previous chapter, Mac an Ghaill (1994; Redman and Mac an Ghaill, 1997) identifies how some middle-class boys perform masculinity via productions of confident, even arrogant, 'intellect', playing up their apparently 'effortless' achievement, and investing in an enlightenment model of rationality and authenticity. Our findings support this to some extent, as such behaviours were observed among boys in our HAP sample. Crucially however, our findings suggest that certain embodied and aesthetic aspects such as 'good looks', ability at sport and fashionability may have enabled 'balance' between such productions of rationality and peer-oriented popularity.

Especially, our finding that nearly all the HAP boys were recorded to centralize, and usually were noted to be good at, sport, highlights an additional element constituting embodied 'authenticity' of masculinity. As with their physicality and domination of space in the classroom, a raft of international research has established the importance of ability at sport as an aspect of establishing masculinity for schoolboys (see Chapter 5). Our findings confirm its centrality in establishing and maintaining 'popular masculinity' (including among high achieving boys). However, beyond this, our findings suggest that 'being good at sport' can provide an important cornerstone of authentic masculinity that allows HAP boys to incorporate other, potentially 'feminine' constructions into their subjectivities (e.g. orientation to school work; reflexivity; articulate communication, and so on), without the overall masculine construction being disturbed. As in the converse case of 'precocious femininity', the accentuation of particular, resonant, signifiers of gender (here masculinity) help to mask or distract from other aspects of production which might otherwise disrupt the monoglossic façade.

Although a few of the HAP boys did construct themselves as 'class clowns', or irrepressible rogues, in contrast to many other boys these constructions did not tend to involve confrontation with the teacher. Of those in our sample, HAP 'alpha' boy Billy (white, working class) was one of those who produced himself most overtly in traditionally 'laddish' ways. His 'clowning' often involved aspects of sexuality, for example:

> Billy is 'masturbating' his drink bottle (Winterfell, History).
>
> Billy is asked what he thought of the scenario in the film, and responds, 'Quite perverted, cos you never know what they're gonna be doing to the children' (class groans [as though used to Billy's sexual preoccupations]) (Winterfell, English).

It was noticeable that observations did not record girls feigning masturbation, or any of the other overtly sexual expressions recorded among boys in our sample: as has been documented in previous work, girls and boys have different ways of performing heterosexuality in the classroom (e.g. Lees, 1992; Fine, 2003; Epstein and Johnson, 1998; Holland et al., 1998; Nayak and Kehily, 2006; Renold, 2006; Youdell, 2006). Such casualized, 'knowing' and humorous/devalued sexual references are integral to successful performances of masculinity in which the masculine subject is produced as actively heterosexual. Hence such tropes again provide key indicators of monoglossic masculinity for boys, which may help HAP boys to achieve 'balance'. We shall elaborate the role of heterosexuality in such constructions further below.

Heterosexuality

The production of heterosexual subjectivities appeared notably central to the classroom productions of all the 'alpha' pupils in our sample. We have seen above examples of the particular performances of sexuality that high achieving popular pupils produce to construct their gender. However, it was also notable that these pupils – and popular pupils generally – frequently mixed and interacted with pupils of the opposite sex, and were seemingly at ease with mixed-sex interaction. This was in contrast to many other young people in the classes observed, many of whom rarely appeared to engage members of the opposite sex, and performed reluctance or awkwardness if, for example, asked to sit next to a member of the opposite sex by a teacher. Arguably such mixed interaction on the part of popular pupils is simply indicative of their popularity (i.e. they are popular with girls and boys alike). However, the level of confidence in their mixed-sex interaction, and the sometimes flirtatious content of these, emerged strongly in the data. As such, we deduce that 'alpha' boys' and girls' frequent engagement in interaction by members of the opposite sex comprised a mark of their high status.

This, coupled with the point that heterosexual relationships were a relatively frequent topic of conversation among 'alpha' pupils in this 12- to 13-year-old age-group,[7] highlights how the 'alpha' pupils are constantly 'doing' heterosexuality in the classroom.

To sum up this section, we have outlined the tendencies for HAP pupils to hold 'embodied capital' – or what Jackson (2006a) terms 'physical resources' – via their physical appearance and attention to aesthetics. And we have observed how such embodiment is mobilized in, and integral to, the HAP pupils' productions of gendered subjectivity within the classroom context. But what of their productions of high academic achievement? We turn now to findings regarding the HAP pupils' engagement with the academic tasks set by the teacher, and other aspects of classroom behaviour.

Part Two: High Achieving Popular Young People's Engagement with Pedagogy

In Chapter 3 we discuss how high achieving boys and girls approach school and school work. Here we expand on this discussion and give examples of the ways in which high achieving and popular students connected with and negotiated classroom teaching and learning. For instance, as noted in this chapter earlier, perhaps unsurprisingly the HAP students were highly engaged with the teachers' pedagogy. These students consistently worked hard and finished on time the assignments they were given and in the ways asked for by the teacher. This was not always easy as the conditions in some of the schools were indeed very challenging. For example, some classes were observed that verged on chaos yet, despite this, HAP pupils were seen to be 'getting on' with their work. More notable was that some of these HAP students were simultaneously taking a part in the ensuing turmoil! These HAP pupils were publicly keen participants in teaching and learning events, showing themselves eager to answer the teacher's questions. These were the pupils who were the main contributors to lessons, often raising their hands and engaging with the teacher. Those (albeit few) HAP students who also tended to act as a 'clown' in class were still eager to take part and showed themselves centrally involved in the learning activities of the classroom. The following offer a few illustrations of this behaviour:

> Albert [white, middle-class, HAP, alpha] puts up his hand and gets the answer right . . .
>
> Albert has his hand up quite a lot, but the teacher is ignoring him – I think she's trying to get other people to have a go.
>
> The teacher puts up some sample work on the board, and asks the class how they would mark it. Albert gives very clear, articulate answers (Winterfell, Geography)
>
> Richard [white, middle-class, HAP], has hand up a lot – very 'applied.'
>
> Richard's hand up again as Martha tries to answer. Shannon [white, middle-class, HAP, alpha] volunteers answer. Amanda [white, middle-class, AP] and Richard both have hands up. Other kids start sticking up hands too. Chantelle volunteers answer calmly. Then Richard (who's had hand up) is asked and gives very extended example. (Oldtown, English)

As was said earlier, finding that high achieving pupils apply themselves in class is hardly revelatory. However, what is intriguing is that these pupils manage to be both evidently hardworking yet remain popular with their classmates. This is surprising given that there is research, including some of our own, that suggests that public displays in the classroom of hard work is likely to position those pupils as less likely to be popular and more likely to be regarded by classmates as a 'boffin' or 'keeno' (see, e.g. Epstein et al, 1998; Francis, 2000, 2009; Skelton, 2001; Jackson, 2002, 2006a; Renold and Allen, 2006). In spite of that, a majority of the HAP pupils did not appear to be remotely concerned, never mind put off, by having their academic success paraded before classmates through teacher praise. For instance, in a Spanish lesson at Highgarden the headings 'Well Done' and 'Warnings' appeared on the chalk board in the classroom, and Jamie (white HAP pupil) had his name written underneath the 'well done' column. In that same lesson, the teacher later went on to congratulate Jamie for having done his homework when 'not so many people have been so conscientious'. This was just one instance of several recorded across all the schools where HAP pupils' names appeared on classroom 'merit' lists.

It is evident then from findings such as these that to assume that all secondary school pupils – and especially boys – are unwilling to stand out from their peers by showing that they can and do work hard and are able to achieve is a sweeping and inaccurate claim. Of course, this is not to say that these HAP pupils did not have some qualms about this: similar to the less popular achievers (see Chapter 3), the HAP pupils talked about the pressures of being both high achieving and popular and the anxieties of being seen as a 'boff' (boffin). Some of the HAP students even referred in their interviews to being rebuked by their friends as 'boffs', but tended to explain this as friends were 'only joking'. Indeed, it was clear that several of the HAP pupils invested time and effort in ensuring the 'balance' between popularity and high achievement was maintained (see Jackson, 2006a and Chapter 3). As we have already noted, this could be achieved via humour and 'clowning': as 'alpha' HAP white middle-class Laurence (Kingswood School) explains, 'Well, you try to make yourself be funny as well as do the right answers'. However, a further, and perhaps more complex factor in this 'balance' is the role of 'effortless achievement'.

The high status that achievement apparently attained without diligent application commands from both teachers and pupils has been well documented in the literature – as has the way in which notions of 'effortless achievement' have profoundly masculine associations (Clarricoates, 1980; Mac an Ghaill, 1994; Epstein and Johnson, 1998). Being seen to spend the time and effort to work towards formal educational attainment, regardless of the end result, is the behaviour most often negatively sanctioned according to this discourse. 'Effortless' attainment without seemingly putting in the time and commitment is more acceptably appropriately 'masculine'. Pupils who are constructed as hard workers in terms of school work risk being negatively sanctioned as 'nerds' or 'geeks', labels that are (derogatively) constructed as feminized and as 'gay' in opposition to 'appropriate' heterosexual masculine positions (Epstein, 1998).

'Effortless achievement' was a notable feature of the classroom constructions of many of the HAP young people in our study. The notion of 'natural brilliance' – or at least (in the case of girls) 'natural cleverness' – is central to this discursive production. However, this could manifest in a range of (gendered) ways, some of them highly complex. For example, we discussed in the previous chapter the need for young people to be seen as 'authentic' in order to be judged as popular (a perception commonly perpetuated by those young people seen as popular themselves). In contrast, however, another thread can be picked out whereby it was seen as acceptable to be clever if you wanted to be popular, so long as you didn't 'act' clever. Here a contradiction emerges – it seems that acting like someone 'you are not' is tacitly accepted so long as it is acting the role of someone 'less clever' than you 'actually are'. This may be more acceptable due to the actor presenting themselves in a way that minimizes or downplays an aspect that actually gives them greater capital and academic status in the eyes of teachers – i.e. they are acting 'modestly'. Although the number of students drawing on such discourses within our sample is very small, it is potentially significant in that it related to girls (see also Renold and Allan, 2006). This performance of modesty can be presented as springing internally from the supposedly *natural* (feminine) self, and thus paradoxically *not* an act of fakery, as described by Salima below:

> *Interviewer:* Some people have said that if a pupil does well at school, it's sometimes harder for them to be popular. Do you agree with this?
>
> *Salima:* Sometimes – if you rub it in people's faces that you're smarter. But if you're modest and say you have more imagination [instead?] It depends. I don't [put on an act?] It's just genuinely modest.
>
> (Salima, South Asian working-class, Winterfell School)

This notion of 'natural modesty' resonates with the 'niceness' identified by Renold and Alan (2006) as so crucial in girls' balanced constructions of acceptable femininity that incorporates high attainment. Crucial to this performance of downplaying yourself is that other people must be aware of your actual high performance in order to perceive that you are acting modestly (and due to the testing regimes pervasive in the UK education system pupils are often aware of who are the highest achieving among them). This is seemingly the only sanctioned form of inauthentic presentation of self, allowable due to its 'double bluff' – an inauthentic performance seemingly revealing an inner modest self conforming to dominant constructions of femininity especially. In this sense, although our findings are tentative, we are suggesting that while the dominant discourse of effortless achievement is a masculinized one, there may be feminine modes of 'balancing' that also articulate 'natural cleverness' in a different way (see also Renold and Allan, 2006; Jackson, 2006a).

Jackson (2006a) maintains that some high achieving pupils who succeed in performing their achievement as effortless are actually 'covert' or 'private' achievers – for example, working hard at home when beyond the surveillance of classmates. Such practices are likely (and occasionally were recorded) to be adopted by young people in our study. However, it was also notable how HAP young people in our study were maintaining achievement – often apparently effortlessly – within the classroom itself.

Such 'effortlessness' of HAP pupils was not only in relation to their engagement with and completion of the tasks set by the teacher but was also evident in the time they gave to the 'sociable' aspects of classroom interactions. It was said earlier that the sociability and confidence of the HAP pupils was plainly apparent (especially amongst the 'alpha' pupils) as they were frequently observed to be at the heart of classroom events, and often directing them. Indeed, all of the 'alpha' pupils, and many of the HAP pupils, might be regarded as 'attention seeking' in their gregarious performances. Having said that, it should be noted that the poststructuralist approach we adopted would inhibit such judgemental explanations by interrogating the discursive environmental conditions which produce/interpolate these performances. However, to illustrate what we are saying here, the following vignettes are just some of many that we observed:

> Someone says 'hallucination' and the teacher asks if anyone knows what that means. Lots of them shout 'yeah!' including Gail [British Chinese, working-class, HAP, alpha] really loudly. Gail carries on, 'it's like when you see a pink alien. . .'
>
> . . .
>
> Gail says loudly 'I've got two things to say!' One thing is that her and her family saw some cocaine in a car once. And the second thing is 'People often ask me if I'm on drugs cos I'm so hyper!'
>
> . . .
>
> Now the teacher is going to make statements and they have to stand up if they agree with them. The first one is 'are some drugs acceptable?' Most people stand up. Gail's still sitting down – she says 'hang on, I'm doing my hair'. The next statement is 'I look forward to being old enough to use some drugs – for example smoking, drinking'. . . Seth [African Caribbean, working-class, HAP, alpha] stands up straight away, smiling, and then sits down again (Ironoaks, PHSE, Q&A on drugs)
>
> Marie [white, working-class, HAP, alpha] says out loud 'I'm bored'. Roxanne says, 'What do you expect?'
>
> The teacher comes over to Marie and Ned, talks to them about something and then goes off again. Marie calls out to the whole class 'Ned just called Miss "Mum"!!' Ned's blushing profusely and smiling (Winterfell, Geography)

Although we would describe all of the HAP pupils as 'outgoing', some were more extrovert than others. At the same time, this did not mean that we evidenced any stereotypes of gregariousness with boys being more assertive than girls: 'alpha' girls would happily and confidently draw attention to themselves in the classroom. However, unlike the implications attributed to 'laddish boys' where their 'classroom frolics' result in underachievement (Francis, 2000; Francis and Skelton, 2005; Younger et al., 2005; Jackson, 2002, 2006a), the constant bantering and cavorting of the HAP students apparently made no impact on their abilities to academically succeed. This is not to say that, over time, these pupils' achievements might begin to decline as a consequence of their classroom 'high jinx', and that this might be particularly the case in some of the schools in the study. But, the HAP pupils were seen to take up certain practices in the class itself that would lessen the likelihood of their academic work being affected. They did this by, as we said earlier, managing to 'balance' the demands of both working on tasks set by the teacher in the lesson and ensuring they were central to the social interactions that were taking place in the classroom at the same time. Also, we were intrigued to discover that there was a tendency, especially amongst the 'alpha' HAP pupils, to have a close friend who was less achieving and more disruptive. This 'friend' detracted attention away from the alpha HAP pupil because they were more disruptive, thus claiming the main attention of the teacher. Of course, this allowed the 'alpha' HAP pupil to take part in any challenging events in the classroom but without attracting the ire of the teacher, thus avoiding any possibility of being seen as a 'troublemaker'.

Jamie's friendship with Joel (an alpha not included in the study) provides an example of such a friendship pairing. Jamie was a white, middle-class, high achieving and popular boy whilst Joel, also white, was far less engaged and generally known for being more disruptive. During one mathematics session at Highgarden School the researcher noted down that Jamie was taking an active part in the lesson and answering all the teacher's questions. In contrast, Joel was constantly sighing and demanding in a loud voice "who cares?". There were numerous times in various lessons where the teachers would frequently warn Joel about his behaviour, write his name on the board and, in one lesson, the teacher told him to leave the class. Although Jamie was also taking part in the events that were invoking the teachers' reprimands, he was never told off. For example, in one incident from our observations some of Jamie's friends were throwing scrunched up paper balls at each other and others. The teacher sees and sends Joel (who was involved), outside:

> Cory chants [to Joel] 'you got caught! You got caught!' Joel then also gets sent outside.

Joel comes back in, all indignant. 'Was I throwing something, Jamie?' Jamie shakes his head and says in an amiable voice 'He wasn't throwing something to be honest'. The teacher says to Joel 'okay, but you could say it less rudely'.

The patrol teacher then arrives outside and the teacher goes out to talk to them. While she's doing so, Jamie, Paul and Hamid get a lot of fun out of throwing lots of pens into the teacher's bin.

Looking at Jamie specifically, this data extract is interesting on a number of levels. His peers see Jamie here as a friend who is backing them up by lying to the teacher about who was throwing the paper balls, and who himself is acting in an appropriately 'laddish', mildly anti-authority way by flicking pens into the teacher's waste bin along with his friends. However to his teacher, Jamie is careful to not get caught throwing anything (only taking part in his friend's behaviour when the teacher is talking to people outside), so she doesn't see any bad behaviour. She hears him talk in a calm, rational tone that is arguably very much part of middle-class cultural habitus: 'He wasn't throwing something to be honest'. The teacher seems to accept Jamie's answer, and there is a contrast between her acceptance of Jamie's style and tone of speech with her censuring of the working-class Joel – emphasized by her saying to Paul 'okay, but you could say it less rudely'. So for the teacher Jamie presents a self that is the epitome of the 'ideal pupil' – calm, rational, assertive but respectful of the teacher's authority, whilst simultaneously Jamie is presenting a totally different self to his peers – this time in a laddish, anti-authority way.

It was common to find that the HAP pupils were on good terms with the teachers. Performances of 'attitude' tended not to be confrontational, rather they could be seen as 'cheeky'; that is, playing on the idea of mischievousness. But, here again, a 'balance' was being struck in that 'mischievousness' and 'confrontational' can be interpreted as similar forms of behaviour. As such, 'balance' is constructed and maintained by HAP pupils between resistance to schooling and engagement of the teacher, and this is crucial, both in terms of the production of behaviour and how that behaviour is read by teacher and classmates.[8]

Another example of this production of these friendship pairings, this time amongst the girls, could be found in that of Kennedy, an alpha white middle-class HAP girl and her friend Karen. Both girls were seen to be 'quite assertive and stroppy with the teachers' (observation notes). As with Joel, it was Karen, the less achieving pupil, that was observed being at the receiving end of teachers' annoyance for her disruptive behaviour. Again, she is recorded being sent out of class and disciplined by different teachers.

Karen kicks up a huge fuss at being told to move away from Kennedy. [Said loudly and stroppily but with underlying humour] 'Me and Kennedy protest, we're not going to work! Okay, maybe Kelly *will* work, but she doesn't want to *deep down*!' (Highgarden, RE)

Inevitably, it was Karen, rather than Kennedy, who was told off. Although Kennedy was frequently observed as being at the centre of any disruptive actions, she was never either aggressive or even strongly confrontational in her dealings with the teachers. Rather, it was Karen who adopted such attitudes.

To provide a few more examples of these kinds of friendship pairings: Albert, an alpha, HAP white middle-class boy was friends with Aron. On one occasion at Winterfell School, the teacher put Albert's name on the board for 'merits' (doing good work) whilst Aron's also appeared on the board but on the 'naughty list'. Another alpha HAP white working-class boy, Billy, was best friends with Larry, who was noted for defying the teachers and acting in confrontational ways. These kinds of friendships could be described as a 'fall guy' phenomenon (at the risk of using a gendered term[9]). That is, the HAP pupils were able to draw kudos from their friends' disruptive and insubordinate actions amongst their peers but, at the same time, were not subject to the teachers' punishments nor were they regarded in any negative ways by them. As such, the HAP pupil part of the friendship did not suffer any consequences of these actions in terms of either failure to do their school work, or in being castigated by teachers. Also, the 'fall guy' phenomenon extended further than close friendship pairings but could also be found more generally in the classroom, as we show here from a science lesson observed at Summerhall school:

At the end of the session, I could see some boys in the corner flicking pencils across the (very large) science suite – Finlay [white middle-class HAP, alpha] and Patrick [white, middle-class, HAP] were there but neither joined in.

On only one occasion did we witness an episode where an HAP pupil, Billy, was defiant. This incident took place in a class taught by a teacher whose management style was such that punishments were rarely enacted, and, as was the case on this occasion, Billy was not chastised for his behaviour.

Apart from illuminating one means by which HAP pupils are able to enact 'intelligible' (see Butler, 2004) gender subjectivities and academic attainment through their friendships with more confrontational classmates, these findings also raise questions about 'success' and 'failure' in neoliberal educational policies and practices. We have suggested in Chapter 1 that discussions of high achievement and academic success also invoke reference to its 'Other'; that is, failure (see Reay and Lucey, 2002 for a discussion). Just as some children are identified as 'failures' in order to shine a light on those who are 'gifted and talented', the 'fall guy' phenomenon highlights a similar symbiotic relationship. Furthermore, in an atmosphere where qualifications are reified and there is an emphasis on competition as a means of facilitating 'excellence' – allowing the best to filter up to the top – those with social and financial capital are able to use this to build up further capitals (Reay and Lucey, 2002; Ball, 2003). Of course, not all of the HAP pupils were middle class but, regrettably, the possibility of undertaking a social class analysis of the 'fall guy' phenomenon was restricted as we did not have information about the social class background of all the pupils in all of the schools (only for those that were identified in our sample). It is worth noting, however, and would be an important aspect to consider in the future; that is, to ascertain whether this 'fall guy' phenomenon is indeed a socially classed occurrence. What we do not want to imply here is that we are accusing the HAP pupils of being devious and deliberately identifying a classmate as a 'fall guy' whom they can use to mask their own rebellious actions. Also, the benefits of a 'fall guy' friendship are not just in one direction – from the 'friend' to the HAP partner. There is conceivably much to be gained by relationships with HAP pupils. Nonetheless, whether, or to what extent, these friendship pairings are characterized by gender, social class or 'race' hierarchies are one that need to be considered.

In summarizing this section, it has been shown how HAP pupils' production of 'effortless achievement' was secured through a simultaneous engagement with their school work alongside maintaining a central position vis-a-vis the social interaction in the classroom. More so, this was carried out through the HAP pupils' common production of 'attitude' within both work and social activities, and this was especially so in the case of the 'alpha' HAP pupils. Having said that, and as we have shown, this construction of rebellious confidence constituting 'attitude' was placed within 'safe limits' in that the HAP pupils presented their responses as mischievous, 'cheeky' and as 'clowning around' as opposed to the more confrontational and disruptive behaviours of their, lower achieving, friends.

Discussion

What we have shown here in this chapter is how some pupils are able to be both open and indeed draw attention to their high achievement and yet still be seen as popular by their peers. Whilst the underachievement and 'laddish' behaviours of boys is perceived as highly gendered, the simultaneous social and academic achievement of the HAP pupils was secured by both genders, of different social class groups, and of different ethnicities.[10] Also, as 14 of the 71 pupils were 'alpha' pupils – that is they were the very highest achievers – we should recognize that high achievement is not necessarily equated with 'boffinness', nor are all boys turning their back on academic work in order to preserve their social status amongst their peers. One aspect that proved uncomfortable was that our analysis of the shared characteristics of these HAP pupils showed that an enabling factor for maintaining balance between academic work and sociability was their 'good looks'. For boys, it was also their (adept) ability at sport that added another positive contribution.

This relationship between the 'body' and discourse has been identified in the writing of Judith Butler whose view is that 'discourse cannot fully "capture" the body, and the body cannot fully elude discourse. This formulation was meant to open up a space of slippage in which neither theories of natural determinism, nor accounts of cultural constitution could claim a unilateral or prior place to one another' (Butler and Kirby, 2006:145).

In keeping with Butler then, our findings illustrate the ways in which bodies are both produced through discourse but also impact and influence discursive productions. Whilst recognizing that ideas of 'attractiveness' are socially constructed, it is still the case that some pupils are fortunate to possess physical features that conform to such constructions, whilst others are not so lucky. The same can be said of the abilities of some boys to be able to demonstrate sporting prowess. Social constructions continue to take a part – for instance it may be that 'athletic' looking boys are more likely to be regarded as adept sportsmen by their peers. The point being made here is that 'the body' is of central importance in pupils' performance of gendered subjectivity, and in facilitating 'balance' between popularity and academic achievement. In other words, we want to reiterate the role of embodiment in the formation of subjectivities – in informing and constraining young people's 'modes of being', as we have put it.

Of course, the chapter has highlighted that appearance is by no means the only factor at stake. We have used our study data to illustrate how young people are having to continuously pay attention to ways of managing their performances in the classroom. Tremendous effort is put in to these productions of 'effortlessness'! The HAP pupils discussed in this chapter act in ways that are rarely excessive and maintain a 'balance' between social interactions with classmates and completing (well) the tasks set by the teacher. In this latter sense they are no different from the pupils in the sample who were high achieving but not popular, specifically those regarded as 'geeks' or 'boffins' discussed in Chapter 4. However, whilst the HAP pupils paid equal attention to the sustenance of social relationships in the class, the 'boffins' tended to be far more exclusively focused on the pedagogic demands. In a related way, the behaviours of the HAP girls and boys were neither overly disruptive nor 'good', instead presenting themselves as having good humoured 'attitude' and 'cheek'. Rather, the HAP pupils were often friends with someone who deflected attention away from any misdemeanours they may be involved with, acting as a 'fall guy'. Here 'alpha' HAP pupils gained kudos because of their association with more disruptive friends but without incurring the kinds of teacher attention and disciplining that their more troublesome friends received. In so doing, the HAP pupils succeeded in managing the 'balance' between sociability and achievement that Caroline Jackson (2006a) has argued to be so difficult for school pupils to accomplish.

We want to reiterate that performances involved in the production of such 'effortless' achievement are themselves far from effortless: rather, onerous and consistent identity work underpins these productions. What we have shown is how highly gendered this identity work is and how the pupils who were high achieving and popular, especially the 'alpha' students, produced gender in ways which reflected normative, monological productions of 'girling' and 'boying'. These performances, together with the good fortune to be regarded as 'physically attractive', enabled intelligible gender performances – which facilitated popularity – simultaneous to academic achievement. The practices of HAP pupils' also helped to highlight the (oppositional) tensions that can be seen in neoliberal education contexts: between 'success' and 'failure'; between achievement and underachievement; between good and bad behaviour, amongst others. It is, as we have shown, a variety range of different capitals (including the physical) that smooth the progress of HAP pupils' productions, although we recognize the importance of carrying out further research in order to ascertain the veracity of the claims made here.

Despite gender, 'race' and social class differences, there was a marked consistency in the way HAP pupils managed to be both academically successful and sociable in the classroom. Having said that, we have also shown how the *content* of these performances differed considerably according to (especially) gender, 'race' and social class differences. Illustrations of how HAP pupils produced comparatively monological, normative performances of gender (mainly with respect to embodiment and constructions of heterosexuality) have been provided. At the same time, we have shown how, simultaneously, these performances were dialogic and marked throughout with contradiction, and often containing aspects which might be associated with the opposite gender. Questions arising from this are: whether popularity allows pupils to be more or less able to produce non-traditional performances of gender; and whether embodiment of 'authentic' gendered attributes limits or assists non-traditional performance (Francis, 2000)?

Of particular significance is that our findings suggest that all the HAP, but especially the 'alpha' students, in many ways stand in opposition to Butler's (2004) 'impossible subjects' – they are the epitome of the authentic subject, those privileged subjects against which other pupils are Othered. Furthermore, they appear to be the 'ideal' neoliberal subjects in that they are both popular *and* academically successful. What needs to be kept in mind though is how the 'success' of these pupils positions those pupils who are less academically and socially able and what impact this has on their gender subjectivities. To refer to Schippers (2007, p. 100):

> Gender inequality is not simply the unequal distribution of resources, power, and value between men and women, but also between those who embody intelligible gender and those who do not. And gender hegemony . . . explains how masculinity and femininity ensure and legitimate those relations of domination as well.

Despite this, and as we have shown here, 'authentic' subjectivity must be worked at and maintained by pupils who are both high achieving and popular. And, it could well be that the heteroglossic tensions arising within HAP pupils' productions of gender and achievement becomes 'impossible' (see Butler, 2004; Youdell, 2006). In so doing, the consequence would be either a fading away of popularity or a decline in the high levels of achievement.

Notes

1   We are aware that this term can be underpinned by psychological and essentialist narratives, and its application in other ways from which we would wish to disassociate ourselves (e.g. the recent

coining of the term 'alpha girls' [Kindlon, 2006] to evoke the post-feminist discourse of the 'Top Girl' [see McRobbie, 2007] as powerful, autonomous and successful – 'having it all' [see McRobbie, 2004; Renold and Ringrose, forthcoming, for critique]). We have adopted the term because it so neatly evokes the concept of being at the pinnacle of popularity and influence in hierarchized class-room social relations. However, we intend our application of 'alpha' in an ironic sense that recog-nizes the tenuous and shifting positioning of these young people in classroom interaction.

2   We also noted 6 AP students who could be classified as 'alphas' (one white working-class girl, 4 white girls whose social class were not recorded, and one white boy whose social class was not recorded. Finally, we also noted from the observations 6 students who were popular enough to be considered 'alphas' but who were not achieving highly enough to be part of the sample for our study – one black minority ethnic girl, plus three white boys and two white girls.

3   Following findings concerning the importance of 'embodied' aspects such as fashionability and physical attractiveness in classroom relations (see e.g. Francis, 2000; Swain, 2002; Jackson, 2006), we had made efforts to record physical descriptions of pupils as part of our observational data, albeit experiencing tensions and ethical questions about our own constructions in doing so.

4   It was notable that 'alpha' boys were often considered by peers/researchers as 'cute', rather than hav-ing an overtly 'macho' appearance, but this 'cuteness' still signified within a masculine 'cheeky chap' production.

5   We are attuned to both the notions of 'cleverness', and 'early development' or 'blossoming' evident in definitions of this adjective, and indeed our data reported here exemplifies the (hetero)sexualized element of such performances.

6   Such carefully balanced and occasionally transgressive productions of sexuality, including examples of what we are referring to as 'precocious femininity', have also been analysed in cultural studies, which have, for example, identified how representations of women in advertising demand young women to produce themselves as simultaneously as sexual objects, sexually innocent and sexual subjects (Gill, 2006). Hence girls are expected to produce themselves as sexual and available, but as sexually passive and even innocent, an extremely complex and contradictory positioning (Gill, 2006; Ringrose, 2008; Renold, 2008).

7   Albeit as we have shown, the nature and content of such discussion tended to differ according to gender. As we observe elsewhere, the 'alpha' pupils' performances of heterosexuality tend to per-petuate traditional constructions of females as sexually passive, and invested in the emotional rather than physical aspects of relationships; and males as actively sexual and prioritizing this element (Lees, 1992; Fine, 2003; Renold, 2006). On the other hand, it is also important to consider that the performance of 'precocious' femininity sometimes incorporated active constructions of sexuality on the part of girls.

8   Our data supports previous findings that teachers tend to find popular, high-status pupils – par-ticularly boys – appealing and entertaining (Francis, 2000). Teachers may seek to draw capital in the classroom from being seen to 'bond' with such pupils (Connolly, 1998; Skelton, 2001) and research has pointed to the excluding consequences of such practices for other pupils.

9 We envisage this metaphor not simply applying to boys, as girls too may behave in such ways, and we do not through the metaphor seek to posit any intentionality on the part of players. However, the metaphor retains a masculinist resonance in our application here in reference to the ways in which 'others' are used as capital for sustaining popularity.

10 Albeit the under-representation of minority ethnic pupils in our sample of high-achieving pupils remains notable given the diverse nature of some of the school populations, see discussion in Chapter 2.

7 Implications for Schools

Recent explorations of gendered identities in relation to achievement have tended to focus on underachieving pupils[1] but what we have shown in this book is how academic excellence is also something that demands attention. High achievement is not just about being adept at obtaining good grades and qualifications but involves students in skilful negotiation of social relationships. We have demonstrated how some high achieving students are able to remain popular with classmates whilst others struggle to negotiate friendships amongst their peers. Educationalists need to attend carefully to the idea that academic success is, for many secondary school students, constructed as incompatible with social popularity; and the consequences of such constructions both for those working to produce themselves as 'popular' (see Chapter 5) and for those derided as 'boffins' (see Chapter 4).

In summarizing the key points of the preceding chapters, we would start by reiterating our argument that the way in which educators are encouraged to understand 'achievement' and 'gender' presents a major challenge to educationalists and activists concerned to tackle inequities in school. Today, the moral panics around 'boys' underachievement' promote a perception of girls having taken up the kinds of gender performances in the classroom previously associated with boys. Yet, as we have shown, even the highest achieving girls continue to be anxious about doing well, seek their teachers' approval

and are uneasy about what their academic success means for their relationships with other pupils. The challenge for policymakers and practitioners
resides in shifting educational policy thinking away from defining gendered
achievement in a way that relies on oppositional gender binaries (where being
a 'proper girl' means shunning any associations with masculinity and vice
versa). Whilst in academic circles the use of gender binaries as a means of
understanding gender performance has been widely critiqued for some considerable time (Davies, 1989; Francis, 1998), these have remained resilient
in the equal opportunities policies and practices of schools. If schools were
enabled to dismantle their view of gender as directly related to sex (i.e. bodies) this would generate more holistic approaches to tackling achievement.
We shall elaborate this further below. However, herein lies a challenge for
academic researchers as well as educational practitioners, as clearly trends
and patterns of inequality according to gender remain, and the challenge is
to recognize and address such inequalities while simultaneously avoiding the
reification of gender difference.

As we have suggested, pupils recognized as achieving within school contexts are placed in a privileged situation and are in a position to realize the
opportunities presented through the interplay of gender, achievement and
neoliberalism . The emphasis of these policies on 'success', 'achievement' and
'effectiveness' inevitably invokes their opposite, 'failure', 'underachievement'
and 'ineffectiveness'. As such, in an education system whereby the securing of
more and 'better' credentials is the major concern, those who already possess
social, cultural and financial capital are better able to enhance their credentials; and those who lack such capitals are further disadvantaged.

We now turn our attention to considering how some schools succeed in
raising the achievement of all pupils (including groups previously regarded
as 'failing') by taking an approach that tackles inequities through challenging misdirected strategies such as 'boy friendly' reading materials, single-sex
classes and so on.[2] It is to these that we now turn our attention.

Schools and Achievement

Articulations of how high achieving pupils approached school and school
work demonstrated certain commonalities that were not gender-related. Also,
as we have shown in Chapter 3, for all young people the school context was
crucial, particularly their relationships with teachers. There were different

cultural expectations of pupil behaviour within schools which inevitably had consequences for the ease in which pupils were enabled to manage their high achievement. For example, those schools which enjoyed sound academic reputations and were well known in their local areas to be 'good' schools shared certain common features including high expectations of pupils, relatively low teacher turnover and the enforcement of strict uniform and behavioural policies. Those students who attended schools whose policies relating to punctuality, school uniform and so on were more likely to be circumvented by the pupils were also more likely to articulate problems encountered in trying to maintain academic achievement.

In *Breaking Down The Stereotypes* (EOC, 2007) two of us set out the key factors that research literature had shown were evident in schools which were successful in raising achievement for all pupils, irrespective of gender, social class and ethnicity. These strategies would help to address the tensions experienced by those students in our study who were high achieving in terms of their academic skills but who, nevertheless, found themselves alienated and marginalized in classroom interactions.

A Whole-School Approach

In order to raise achievement for all pupils, schools need to adopt a whole-school approach which, according to Molly Warrington and colleagues (2006), involves three key aspects: the leadership provided by the headteacher; partnership; and teaching practices. Excellent leadership has of course been shown to be a vital component of school improvement more generally, however here we mean a visionary and deep commitment to gender equality and high achievement on the part of the headteacher and senior leadership team, which permeates the school and its policies, and is determinedly driven forward, implemented, monitored and reflected upon across the school with the senior team's support. Partnership refers to the drawing in of all concerned stakeholders within this vision and the mode of its practical implementation – young people, teachers, support staff and parents. Teaching practice has been shown to be central, both in raising achievement more generally, but especially in the avoidance of reproducing gender inequalities and meeting the needs of particular groups of pupils at the expense of others. When all three key aspects are evident then these create a culture in which pupils and teachers are supported and provide the elements through which achievement can be realized. Certainly our findings showed that students had different resources at their disposal for facilitating or constraining their performance of the 'good pupil'. It is important then for schools to be aware of such inequalities, in relation to classroom interaction and management. In particular, attention need to be given as to how school management and organizational practices might be facilitating constructions of distinction between pupils leading to marginalization, exclusion and bullying.

Warrington et al. (2006, pp. 192–193) set out the components of school cultures that provide a supportive environment for achievement:

- *Behaviour*: This involves the school establishing an expectation of high levels of self-discipline, supporting this by prompt attention to misdemeanours and responding in a constant and ongoing manner to issues of behaviour. Staff should show courtesy to pupils.
- *Equal opportunities*: This involves a commitment to valuing diversity through curriculum content, classroom grouping arrangements, school activities and worship.
- *Fostering pride and achievement*: This involves a school placing emphasis on pride in work and behaviour, as well as having high expectations of responsibility and independence. Pupils are aware that staff care for their progress and happiness.
- *Imaginative thinking*: This concerns the ways in which pupils can become engaged in the life of the school, and the willingness of the school to ensure that individual pupils become involved in its activities.
- *Values and aims*: These need to be transparent, consistent, shared by colleagues, and permeate all the work of the school.

For the above to be realized then Younger et al. (2005) and Warrington et al. (2006) identified leadership, partnership and teaching practices as the factors that need to be in place. Each of these as manifested in their study will be elaborated briefly.

The Headteacher: Effective Leadership

Effective leadership among headteachers is characterized by an emphasis on teamwork and this was evidenced by the headteacher's involvement with their staff and pupils. Also, school policy was developed around people and relationships rather than being initiatives in isolation from those they would effect. Furthermore there was evidence that there was a willingness to take risks. Headteachers encouraged their staff by allocating time, training and resources to concentrate on all aspects of achievement. Effective leaders ensured that their policies developed in the school were given a high profile, for example, a policy that set out expectations relating to attendance and behaviour were seen to be implemented and monitored (Younger et al., 2005).

Partnership

The term 'partnership' illustrates the democratic, inclusive and mutually supportive aspects of this approach. In order to implement successful strategies which address gender, ethnicity, social class and raise achievement requires democratic partnerships between all those in the school from teachers, pupils, school governors, parents, administrative and support staff etc.[3] As has been shown, schools which develop a sense of belonging in pupils, which generate feelings of responsibility and in which students perceive they are listened to and that their voices occupy a place in school policy and practice have been the most successful in raising pupils' achievements (Younger et al., 2005; Warrington et al., 2006).

Teaching Practice

In explaining what is meant by 'good teaching practice' Younger et al. (2005) include: well-planned, structured lessons with clear learning aims and outcomes; approaches to encourage children to reflect on their learning practices; pupils' involvement in self and peer assessment. At the same time, because such approaches benefit boys and girls alike, they will not of themselves address gender performances in (under)achievement. To address gender cultures underpinning gendered patterns in behaviour requires approaches that have been found to produce 'improved and more equitable student outcomes' (Martino et al., 2005, pp. 251–252) such as that found in Productive Pedagogies. Martino et al. go on to explain that effective pedagogies are characterized by

> a high degree of intellectual quality, high levels of connectedness in terms of curriculum content and its application to the students' lives outside school, supportive classroom environments where students feel valued and are encouraged to take risks in their learning, along with a strong recognition and celebration of difference. (Martino et al., 2005, p. 252)

Productive Pedagogies comprise a progressive approach to teaching and learning that foregrounds socially-just principles along with an emphasis on intellectual quality. As such it may be seen to especially facilitate best practice around addressing gender and other inequality issues. For more discussion of how Productive Pedagogies might be used in schools than space allows here, see Lingard et al. (2003).

From what we have said so far, it is evident that a 'whole school approach' requires schools, from the outset, to ascertain their current position in relation to achievement in order to identify what steps need to be taken. A starting point is for school staff to establish the following:

- What are our understandings of 'achievement' as a school? Do we want to change this? Do students, staff and other members of the school share the same understandings of 'achievement'?
- How is our school organized? What expectations are there about behaviour and how are these fulfilled? Who makes the decisions? How are these decisions communicated? What strategies can we adopt to ensure everyone shares responsibility for what the school expects and also takes part in decision making?
- What information do we have about the patterns of success and failure amongst different groups in the school?
- What information do we have about the ways in which teachers and pupils see themselves and each other (what part does gender, social class, ethnicity, sexuality and so forth feature in these perspectives?)

Inevitably, all schools will have a different set of responses to these questions. As has been recommended by such educationalists as Younger et al. (2005), Warrington et al. (2006) and Keddie and Mills (2007), what is of key importance is the context in developing strategies to address issues of gender/ethnicity/social class and achievement. To ascertain what patterns of achievement exist in a school, information could be collected that includes statistical data on pupil performance (such as RaiseOnline and so on) and also qualitative data on the views of both pupils and staff around gender/ethnic/social class stereotyping.

However, what readers may have noticed about these 'whole school' accounts is that they are relatively generalist. They reflect best practice which we might in any case expect in outstanding schools. What do we need to do in addition to addressing gender issues in the classroom and playground – and indeed in the assumptions and values permeating schooling? We will address this point once we have considered a further factor in addressing social justice barriers in achievement: teachers' expectations of students.

Teachers' Expectations of Pupils and Achievement

When looking at the characteristics of schools which are successful in reducing gaps in achievement, Christine and Becky found that it was schools that had *rejected* the kinds of strategies which emphasize gender, such as 'books for boys', 'boys' learning styles' etc. that had been successful in narrowing the gap. As Warrington et al. (2006) observed, it was in schools where differential gender cultures were less overt, and/or had been challenged, that the gap for achievement tended to be narrower. This also resonates with Pickering's (1997) finding that it is in schools where children did not see reading as a gendered activity (i.e. 'for girls') and that boys tended to read more. Instead, successful schools were those that placed *less* attention on differences between boys and girls. To achieve this required teachers to become aware of how children's gendered identities are constructed as binary opposites, whereby being 'a boy' means not being 'a girl' and vice versa. As such, teachers start by considering their own assumptions and examine the implications of these for gender and learning.

This is fundamental. Society is so saturated in gender stereotypes and distinctions, and assumptions about what is 'naturally different' between girls and boys, that it is often difficult to avoid applying different expectations and understandings of girls' and boys' behaviour. Our own research has shown that beliefs about the 'natural differences' and 'different learning styles' between boys and girls are rife among teachers, and we have illustrated the many instances when we found teachers using such assumptions to inform their teaching and classroom management practices. For example, we have come across instances where teachers provide primary age boys with football-shaped cushions to sit on during storytime to keep them seated, or focus lessons about food and nutrition on girls' concerns about their weight in the belief that children will respond best to such approaches (see e.g. Skelton et al., 2009). Primary teachers frequently cited pupils' gendered learning styles as something they attempt to play to (usually focusing on the perceived kinaesthetic needs of boys). However, even exponents of gendered learning styles – whereby girls are said to prefer group work and boys individual learning exercises – acknowledge that there is often diversity (Gurian, 2002). That is, there are boys who prefer group work and girls who favour individual learning so any gender stereotypical assumptions on the part of the teacher might well alienate many children in the class who do not conform to such categorization. Our analysis of young people's monoglossic and heteroglossic gender productions – whereby we would argue that all of us (including pupils) are constantly performing both masculine and feminine aspects – takes such recognition of diversity far further. In this case, to expect and teach *to* differences according to gender (or ethnicity/social class) is to perpetuate and exacerbate stereotypical distinctions, rather than doing the responsible pedagogical job of extending horizons and broadening pupils' repertoires.

Of course it is not just gendered expectations of pupils' potential that affect their schooling experiences as ethnicity and social class positions have also been shown to influence teachers' practices and expectations of achievement (Archer and Francis, 2005; Gillborn, 2008; Mirza, 2009). Importantly, as we have found in our research of high achievers, the school environment, uniform policy, setting of pupils, use of 'gifted and talented' registers, all have the potential to play down or play up differences according to gender and other aspects of social identity. This is not simply, or solely, a consequence of individual teacher 'bias' but rather as a result of policy that draws attention to and demands results around raising the achievement of particular groups. When policymakers suggest that schools have failed to recognize 'boys' learning needs' and that 'girls outstrip boys', for example, then teachers are encouraged to believe there are gender differences in children's approaches to learning and play to these differences (Skelton and Read, 2006).

An example of the kinds of activities that school staff could undertake is to identify an event where gendered (or 'race'/social class) implications might arise. It may be an English lesson where pupils are asked to write a news item for a radio broadcast and boys are allowed or encouraged to provide a sports-related event whilst girls draw on a 'human interest' story (see Ivinson and Murphy, 2007). The questions the staff might ask are:

- What is the aim or incentive for adopting this kind of classroom practice?
- What opportunities were being foreclosed or opened up for students in adopting this approach?
- What is the message being promoted by this kind of practice?

In their book *Raising Boys' Achievement in the Secondary Schools*, Mike Younger, Molly Warrington and Ros McLellan (2005) describe how staff found it useful to work with teachers in other schools on this kind of exercise as it helped to have alternative views of their own and other school cultures.

There are also issues that teachers can explore as individuals; for example, Francis (2007b) set out four questions that teachers might ask in order to ascertain how they might challenge their own gender attitudes and expectations. These are:

- Do I spend more time and attention on certain groups of pupils? If so, why?
- Do I apply the same expectations to all pupils, and respond to their behaviours in a consistent way in spite of factors such as gender, social class and so on? Which

pupils do I like/dislike, and why? Am I complicit with gendered expectations, for example that boys behave in 'laddish' ways, or that girls be 'ladylike'?

- Do I ever find myself giving more time and mental energy to boys, due to a pragmatic need to hold their attention in order to complete tasks?
- Do I adopt particular approaches with boys, and/or girls (e.g. 'roustabout'/gentle), which may aid classroom constructions of gender as oppositional?

There are too the ways in which the intersectionality of gender, social class and ethnicity influence teacher expectations and relationships with students. Here staff might ask themselves:

- Do I expect students to act differently in class depending on their gender/'race'/social class?
- Do I question what might be stereotypical career choices of students?
- What are the messages that students are presented with in the books used in the classroom around gender/'race'/social class and do I work with them in confronting the ways in which pupils are expected to think, act and behave in order to be a 'proper boy' or a 'proper girl'?
- Am I aware of how my own theories of teaching my subject might contribute towards the gendered learning expectations of my students?

In the current climate of constant accountability, targets, monitoring, Ofsted inspections and the like, and the constant scrutiny of what goes on in classrooms, we are hesitant in suggesting that teachers should conduct yet more self-assessments. However, the following pointers could be carried out as part of these official self-assessments, or separately as action research or collaborative peer review, to enable teachers to become aware of how certain groups of pupils within the classroom are treated differently. As Becky Francis (2007) has set out, this might include asking:

- How much time is spent communicating with boys and girls? This involves recording which girls and boys will supply a more nuanced reflection of interaction that recognizes factors such as ethnicity and social class.
- What sort of attention is given to pupils in the class? Do boys (or girls) tend to require more discipline? Is praise given proportionately to different groups in the class?
- Do boys and girls have equal access to different classroom resources, and are they encouraged to utilize these?
- What sort of language is the teacher using? Does it differ depending on the gender (or other social factors) of the child?

- What sort of language are the children using? Does gender or sexuality take a prominent role, e.g. making references to 'pretty girls, tough boys'; or accusations such as 'acting like a mummy's boy'.
- What is the social status/power dynamics among pupils in the class? Are some pupils 'silenced' by others? How does gender inform these patterns?
- How are pupils conceptualizing achievement amongst themselves? For example is there evidence of name-calling in relation to achievement, or demonstrations of achievement? Again, how does gender (or other facets of identity) inform these patterns[4]?

None of the schools in our study of high achieving pupils indicated that the kinds of 'whole-school approaches' discussed in the above sections were in place. Clearly, the high achieving students in our study experienced an array of forms of classroom management and organization but none of these might be considered to be 'good practice' of the kind described above. Indeed our observations suggested that few of the teachers were aware of how gender was shaping the experiences of the students. There are implications then for teacher education programmes. Our findings support arguments in our previous research that student teachers need to be facilitated to engage in critical reflection on issues such as gender, 'race' and social class in the classroom, and their relation to achievement (Francis, 2000; Skelton and Read, 2006; Francis, 2007; Skelton, et al., 2009). This may help teachers not only to be reflexive about their own practice, but also may help them feel confident in facilitating chances for explicit discussion/debate on these issues amongst pupils themselves (see below).

In other words, the social and cultural contexts of teaching and learning need firmly reinstating in the initial teacher education curriculum. Also, staff training in behaviour management – including within this a focus on high expectations and on expression of care for/interest in pupils – is of critical importance. The evidence reported in this book supports a raft of previous research showing how young people appreciate and respond to teachers who seem interested in them and their needs, and who hold high expectations of them (Woods, 1990; Flutter and Rudduck, 2004; Thornberg, 2008).

Our findings demand further reflections and conversations on all our parts – academics and teachers alike – to acknowledge our implications in these complex and nuanced classroom constructions of popularity and achievement. A few researchers have noted the ways in which teachers are often attracted to the most popular pupils. Association with such 'alpha' young people brings the teacher status with the rest of the class (Connolly,

1998; Skelton, 2001); but more than this, they are often simply highly appealing and amusing – we as adults are also imbued with the general values of wider society. We earlier discussed feminist accusations that male researchers are drawn to study the disruptive, rebel boys. But beyond this Francis (2000) and Renold (2007) have discussed researchers' lack of immunity to such popularity dynamics – how researchers likewise tend to be drawn to popular, confident, appealing young people, and to find needy, unfashionable and attractive respondents less appealing (and even distasteful). Yet how are our behaviours, however subtle, acting to strengthen existing dynamics – including hierarchies, inclusions and exclusions, which are gendered, 'raced' and classed – in the classroom? How might we act instead to relax such dynamics?

Deconstructing Gender Cultures through Pedagogy

As we have said, in addition to practices that have a strong inclusive ethos and work against gender differentiation and stereotyping, there is additionally a need to go beyond what we would see as prerequisite approaches, in order to encourage students to reflect upon and challenge dominant gender distinctions.

We do not intend to repeat prior works, as there are a raft of existing resources that suggest practical ways to facilitate such work with pupils (although arguably there could be more, especially contemporary examples). However, what is important to highlight is that all the work in this area, including our own, has found that young people – both primary and secondary pupils – relish the opportunity to discuss gender and the gender stereotypes to which we are all subject. Hence this is an often enjoyable, stimulating activity in which young people may be enabled to consider the ways in which gender operates to constrain the behaviours and practices of young people within the school (and indeed the operations of the school itself). Francis (2000) presents different ideas for facilitating group discussion and analysis of gender among pupils, and has suggested that such discussion can be extended to reflection on the impact of gender on pupils' school achievement. Various works offer teaching materials that can be applied in such endeavours – examples include Salisbury and Jackson (1996), Wing (1997), Francis (2007b), DCSF (2009a, b) and Keddie and Mills (2007).

In relation to the specific focus of this book, there might be opportunities for teachers to discuss in class pupils' conceptions of gender, class and 'race' in relation to popularity and achievement. Again, the vast majority of our participants seemed to greatly enjoy the chance to reflect and discuss issues around friendship and popularity, and the need to 'balance' being seen to work hard and spending time with friends. Although care would need to be taken to ensure a 'safe' environment in which to discuss such sensitive issues, it is possible that debating aloud the pressures around popularity and achievement may help students feel more comfortable in asserting presentations of self that run counter to dominant pressures.

But herein a question is raised. Do we wish to say that young people should be 'freed up' from the pressure to balance? If so, what would this look like? Clearly, in the current policy environment where educational benchmarking, assessment and credentialism is becoming an increasingly global phenomenon, and educational offers increasingly globally standardized as a result, suggesting that young people should be freed up from the pressure to achieve (interpreted in the current climate as obtaining academic credentials) is untenable. There are movements against the obsessive and exclusive focus on credentials (see e.g. the 'Whole Education' campaign in England). And it may be that this is where the truly radical agenda lies in returning to questions about the real purpose of education. However, in the current, increasingly marketized education environment, wherein competition for places at 'the best' schools and universities and the highest credentials is mirrored on a global scale by inter-country competition in assessments such as OECD PISA and international higher education league tables, it is unlikely that attainment will be seen to be less important any time soon. In this context, ensuring that all students have equal access to securing such credentials – which, following the Rawlsian 'difference principle', means that some disadvantaged groups will need to be given further support/advantage in order to ensure an even playing field – becomes a key issue for social justice.

So if students are not to cease attempts to balance achievement, should they be freed up to cease balancing sociability? This would of course be the extreme logic of competitive, middle-class endeavours to secure the highest possible attainment. It is encapsulated by Amy Chau's (2011) highly mythic book on her perception of 'good' Chinese mothering, where it is claimed that offspring should be banned from recreational pursuits barring playing the piano and violin, to facilitate an unrelenting focus on their studies, and wherein anything below a top mark is perceived a failure. Chau's book created much excitement in the British press, arguably because it played so strongly to the concerns (and perhaps barely hidden empathies) of the middle classes and their journalist commentators.

We would argue that a view that 'education' is only about excelling at academic study, or indeed that this is the only meaningful method and content of 'learning', is a nonsense. Clearly, young people are learning far more than the content of the official curriculum while they are at school (gender reproduction being just one example!) But the social and creative elements of school life are absolutely fundamental for learning the skills needed for adult life. Excelling at maths and geography, important as this may be, does not prepare one for active citizenship. Moreover, academic application does not necessarily indicate the competences needed for the contemporary world of work.

In this sense, our findings concerning the intricate balancing performance, involving aesthetic and behavioural elements (both aspects gendered), for high achieving popular pupils, demand reflection on the context for these productions – the nature of education – and what it *should* look like. We believe that while subject knowledge is important, education should be focused on engaging young people, recognizing and speaking to their own expertise, and also providing the skills they need for life as reflective, competent citizens, workers and creative agents. This raises many questions for the existing curriculum, and its relevance for young people[5]; however these are somewhat beyond the bounds of this book. What is of direct import to assert is: (a) the need to acknowledge the other functions of schooling aside from the official curriculum and (b) the need for space *within* the official curriculum for students to undertake the study of society and relationships that enable the development of the aforementioned skills, and also which crucially develop criticality on schooling (both official and unofficial curriculum) and other aspects of public and private life, including the various axes of social inequality. We would argue that such criticality is vital for civic competence, and certainly to enable the development of a socially just society. More specifically, in relation to the content of this book, such space enables discussion and reflection on gender (and 'race' and class), and for students themselves to reflect on the often harsh normative regimes, distinctions and hierarchies they (and we) are involved in perpetuating according to gendered aesthetics, behaviours, friendship groupings, subject preferences and so on.

In conclusion, we would urge that matters of (under)achievement should be shifted away from a preoccupation with gender gaps, and particularly boys' underachievement, towards one that adopts more holistic considerations.

Rather than taking various elements of school and school populations in isolation and responding to these through separate initiatives (e.g. 'school effectiveness' or 'gender' or 'ethnicity' or 'pedagogy and achievement') attention might be more usefully given to the interplay of these within specific school sites. There are boys, as well as girls, who are high achievers and, indeed, differential educational experiences based on gender/social class/minority ethnic positionings appear to be less evidently influential in the perceptions and experiences of these pupils. As such, the findings of our study lend weight to those that have identified a whole school approach as a means of raising expectations and attainments for all groups.

Of importance is how the constructions of high achieving pupils draw attention to the construction and relationship between 'success' and 'failure' in neoliberal educational policies and practices. The policy preoccupation with educational 'excellence' as indicated throughout the book exclusively via educational credentials has resulted in an acute awareness among pupils of attainment hierarchies within classrooms. As Lucey and Reay (2003) observe, the notion of academic excellence and success cannot exist without reference to its Other, failure. Hence some children must be marked out as failures in order that others can be identified as successes, and our identification of the 'fall guy' phenomenon between HAP and less academically achieving pupils illustrates the symbiotic relationship here. It also illuminates the ways in which, in an environment obsessed with credentials and the 'channelling' of excellence through competition, and wherein those with social and financial capital are able to accrue further capitals (Lucey and Reay, 2002; Ball, 2003), capitals may be drawn by particular pupils in classroom interaction to facilitate 'balance' and attainment. Policymakers ought to reflect on the stigmatization of certain pupils (and pupil groups) as under- or over-achieving within such practices, and the impact of such stigmatization on the patterning of educational achievement by gender, social class, and ethnicity. We would argue for policies which reduce, rather than exacerbate educational selection and distinction (which as the OECD PISA Study shows, tend to promote social inequalities in educational achievement).

We hope that this book has illuminated the 'balancing act' that high achieving young people are demanded to perform in order to avoid stigmatization. The consequences for those that fail to balance, labelled boffins and geeks, have been explored, and we drew attention to the gendered nature of this 'Othering'. The complex, hierarchized world of adolescent peer relations, the delicate projections of 'acceptable selfhood' within these, and the ways in which these projections/readings are gendered, raced and classed, have been explored. We have shown how high achieving popular pupils maintain both their popularity and their high achievement – and how this successful balance was achieved via onerous identity work, in combination with (gendered) aesthetic productions including good looks/'prettiness' and fashionability. We have elaborated the complexity at play in this regard, and the contradictions and masquerades underpinning the gender performances. Primarily, we have demonstrated the ongoing importance of gender distinction in maintaining socially acceptable selves especially in relation to academic achievement. We hope that in addition to highlighting this point, we have also begun to suggest some theoretical and practice-based ways of decreasing the significance of gender in school life.

Notes

1   There are some exceptions: for example, Martino (1999); Mac an Ghaill (1994); Redman and Mac an Ghaill (1997); and Swain (2000) include groups of achieving boys in their typologies of schoolboy masculinity. The studies by Power et al. (1998) and Reay (2002, 2006) pay attention to schoolboy masculinity, social class and high achievement. And Renold and Allan (2006) have undertaken analyses of the gender subjectivities of a small sample of high achieving girls.

2   Of course, these various suggested strategies for addressing 'boys' underachievement' have been extensively researched and critiqued, demonstrating their general lack of impact (or at least lack of impact in producing the outcomes intended!) See, e.g. Francis and Skelton (2005), Ivinson and Murphy (2007); Lingard et al., (2009); Martino et al. (2009).

3   Of course, a range of research has established how and why it is far easier for some social groups – of parents, for example – to work with schools than others. There are a range of reasons why working class and black and minority ethnic parents (and staff) may feel excluded from school, and unequal partners in communications. Schools need to be aware of and reflexive about such inequalities, and to take measure to ensure partnership is meaningfully extended to diverse groups.

4   In the context of our study, we have added this last bullet point to the original list offered by Francis (2007).

5   Currently being explored in England with the government's curriculum review, and the introduction of the controversial English Baccalaureate (E-Bac) which prioritizes particular 'traditional' curriculum subjects.

References

Aapola, S., Gonick, M. and Harris, A. (2005) *Young Femininity*. Basingstoke: Palgrave Macmillan.

Abraham, J. (1995) *Divide and School*. London: Falmer.

Adler, P., Kless, S., and Adler, P. (1992) Socialization to gender roles: Popularity among elementary school boys and girls, *Sociology of Education*, 65, 169–187.

Ali, S. (2003a) 'To be a girl': Culture and class in schools, *Gender and Education*, 15:3, 269–283.

Ali, S. (2003b). *Mixed Race, Post Race?* Oxford: Berg.

Allan, A. (2010) 'Rebels', 'bad girls' and 'misbehavers': Exploring 'underachievement' in single-sex, selective schooling, in: C. Jackson, C. Paechter and E. Renold (eds), *Girls and Education 3–16*. Maidenhead: Open University Press, 50–61.

Anyon, J. (1983) Intersections of gender and class: Accommodation and resistance by working-class and affluent females to contradictory sex-role, in: S. Walker and L. Barton (eds), *Gender, Class and Education*. Lewes: Falmer.

Apple, M. (2004) *Ideology and Curriculum* (3rd edition). New York: Routledge.

Apple, M. (2006) *Educating the 'Right' Way: Markets, Standards, God, and Inequality* (2nd edition). New York: Routledge.

Archer, L. (2005) The impossibility of girls' educational 'success', paper for ESRC Seminar Series *Girls in Education 3–16*, Cardiff University, 24/11/05.

Archer, L. (2003) 'Knowing their limits'? Identities, inequalities and inner city school leavers' post-16 aspirations, *Journal of Education Policy*, 18:1, 53–69.

Archer, L. and Francis, B., (2005) 'They never go off the rails like other ethnic groups': Teachers' constructions of British Chinese pupils' gender identities and approaches to learning, *British Journal of Sociology of Education*, 26:2, 165–182.

Archer, L. and Francis, B. (2007) *Understanding Minority Ethnic Achievement*. London: Routledge.

Archer, L. and Yamashita, H. (2003) Theorising inner-city masculinities: 'race', class, gender and education, *Gender and Education*, 15:2, 115–132.

Archer, L., Halsall, A. and Hollingworth, S. (2007) Inner-city femininities and education: 'race', class, gender and schooling in young women's lives, *Gender and Education*, 19:5, 549–567.

Archer, L., Hutchings, M. and Ross, A. with Leathwood, C., Gilchrist, R. and Phillips, D. (2003) *Higher Education and Social Class: Issues of Exclusion and Inclusion*. London: Routledge.

Arendt, H., (1978) *The Jew as Pariah: Jewish Identity and Politics in the Modern Age*. New York: Grove Press.

Arnot, M. (1991) Equality and democracy: a decade of struggle over education, *British Journal of Sociology of Education*, 12:4, 447–466.

Arnot, M. (2009) *Educating the Gendered Citizen*. London: Routledge.

Arnot, M. and Reay, D. (2006) The framing of performance pedagogies: Pupil perspectives on the control of school knowledge and its acquisition, in: H. Lauder, P. Brown, J-A. Dillabough and A.H. Halsey (eds), *Education, Globalization and Social Change*. Oxford: Oxford University Press, pp. 766–778.

Arnot, M. and Reay, D. (2007) A sociology of pedagogic voice: Power, inequality and pupil voice, *Discourse*, 28:3, 311–325.

Arnot, M., David, M. and Weiner, G. (1999) *Closing the Gender Gap*. Cambridge: Polity Press.

Assiter, A. (1996) *Enlightened Women: Modernist Feminism in a Postmodern Age*. London: Routledge.

ATL (Association of Teachers and Lecturers) (2010) ATL president tells politicians to stop using education as a political football and leave learning to the professionals, 29 March 2010 (http://www.atl.org.uk/media-office/media-archive/lesley-ward-conference-2010-release.asp) (Accessed 16 August 2010)

Australian Government: Department of Education, Science and Training (2004) *Learning Together: Achievement through Choice and Opportunity* (http://www.dest.gov.au/sectors/school_education/publications_resources/profiles/government_funding_schools_2005_2008.htm) (Accessed 24 March 2011).

Baker, S. (2001) 'Rock on, baby!': Pre-teen girls and popular music, *Journal of Media and Cultural Studies*, 15:3, 359–371.

Bakhtin, M. (1981) *The Dialogic Imagination: Four Essays*. M. Holquist (ed) C. Emerson and Michael Holquist (trans.) Austin and London, University of Texas Press.

Balbus, I. (1987) Disciplining women: Michel Foucault and the power of feminist discourse, in: S. Benhabib and D. Cornhill (eds), *Feminism as Critique*. Cambridge: Polity Press.

Ball, S. (1981) *Beachside Comprehensive*. Cambridge: Cambridge University Press.

Ball, S. (2003) *Class Strategies and the Education Market: The Middle Classes and Social Advantage*. London: Routledge Falmer.

Ball, S. (2007) *Education PLC*. London: Routledge.

Ball, S.J., Maguire, M. and Macrae, S. (2000) *Choices, Transitions and Pathways: New Youth, New Economies in the Global City*. London: Falmer Press.

Bauman, Z. (2005) *Work, Consumerism and the New Poor* (2nd edition). Buckingham: Open University Press.

Beck, U. (1992) *Risk Society*. London: Sage.

Benjamin, S., Nind, M., Hall, K., Collins, J., and Sheehy, K. (2003) Moments of inclusion and exclusion: Pupils negotiating classroom contexts, *British Journal of Sociology of Education*, 24:5, 547–558.

Berger, P. and Luckman, T. (1966) *The Social Construction of Reality*. Harmondsworth, Penguin.

Best, R. (1989, orig. 1983) *We've All Got Scars: What Boys and Girls Learn in Elementary School*. Bloomington: Indiana University Press.

Bettie, J. (2002) Exceptions to the rule: Upwardly mobile white and Mexican American high school girls, *Gender and Society*, 16:3, 403–422.

Bettis, P. and Adams, N. (2003) The power of the preps and a cheerleading equity policy, *Sociology of Education*, 76, 128–142.

Bhavnani, R. (2006) *Ahead of the Game: the Changing Aspirations of Young Ethnic Minority Women. Moving on up?* Series. Manchester: Equal Opportunities Commission.

Bleach, K. with Blagden, T., Ebbutt, D. et al. (1996) *What Difference Does it Make? An Investigation of Factors Influencing the Motivation and Performance of Year 8 boys in a West Midlands Comprehensive School.* Wolverhampton, Educational Research Unit, University of Wolverhampton.

Bloustein, G. (1999) On not dancing like a 'try hard', in G. Bloustien (ed), *Musical Visions: Selected Conference Proceedings* from the 6th National Australian/ New Zealand IASPM and Inaugural Arnhem Land Performance Conference. Kent Town: Wakefield Press, pp. 8–20.

Bourdieu, P. (1986a) The forms of social capital, in: J.G. Richardson (ed), *Handbook for Theory and Research for the Sociology of Education.* New York: Greenwood, pp. 241–258.

Bourdieu, P. (1986b) *Distinction: A Social Critique on the Judgement of Taste.* London: Routledge.

Brah, A. and Minhas, R. (1985) Structural racism or cultural difference: Schooling for Asian girls, in G. Weiner (ed), *Just a Bunch of Girls.* Milton Keynes: Open University Press.

Brown, P., Halsey, A.H., Lauder, H. and Stuart Wells, A. (1997) The transformation of education and society: An introduction, in: A.H. Halsey, H. Lauder, P. Brown and A. Stuart Wells (eds), *Education: Culture, Economy and Society.* Oxford: Oxford University Press.

Bujak, P. (2010) 'Election winner must not treat education as a political football'. *Telegraph* (5 October.2010) (http://www.telegraph.co.uk/education/educationnews/7681648/Election-winner-must-not-treat-education-as-a-political-football.html) (Accessed 16 August 2010).

Burgess, S., Briggs, A., McConnell, B. and Slater, H. (2006) *School Choice in England: Background Facts,* CMPO Working Paper No. 06/159. Bristol: Centre for Market and Public Organisation, University of Bristol.

Butler, J. (1990) *Gender Trouble.* London: Routledge.

Butler, J. (1993) *Bodies That Matter: On the Discursive Limits of 'Sex'.* London: Routledge.

Butler, J. (2004) *Undoing Gender.* London: Routledge.

Butler, J. and Kirby, V. (2006) Butler live, in V. Kirby (ed), *Judith Butler: Live Theory.* London: Continuum, pp. 144–158.

Byrne, E. (1978) *Women and Education.* London: Tavistock.

Carrington, B., Francis, B., Hutchings, M., Skelton, C., Read, B. and Hall, I. (2008) Does the gender of the teacher really matter? Seven to eight year olds' accounts of interactions with their teachers, *Educational Studies*, 33:4, 397–413.

Cassen, R. and Kingdon, G. (2007) *Tackling Low Educational Achievement.* Report for Joseph Rowntree Foundation. (http://www.jrf.org.uk/publications/tackling-low-educational-achievement) (Accessed 9 February 2011).

Chambers, D., Tincknell, E., and Van Loon, J. (2004) Peer regulation of teenage sexual identities, *Gender and Education*, 16:3, 397–415.

Charlton, E., Mills, M., Martino, W. and Beckett, L. (2007) Sacrificial girls: A case study of the impact of streaming and setting on gender reform *British Educational Research Journal*, 33:4, 457–478.

Chau, A. (2011) *Battle Hymn of the Tiger Mother*. London: Bloomsbury.

Chodorow, N. (1978) *The Reproduction of Mothering: Psychoanalysis and the Sociology of Gender*. Berkeley, CA: University of California Press.

Chubb, J.E. and Loveless, T. (eds) (2002) *Bridging the Achievement Gap*. Washingtron, DC: Brookings Institution Press.

Chubb, J.E. and Moe, T. (1997) Politics, markets and the organisation of schools, in: A.H. Halsey, H. Lauder, P. Brown and A.S. Wells (eds), *Education, Culture, Economy and Society*. Oxford: Oxford University Press, pp. 363–381.

Clarricoates, K. (1980) The importance of being Ernest . . . Emma . . . Tom . . . Jane. The perception and categroization of gender conformity and gender deviation in primary schools, in R. Deem (ed.) *Schooling for Women's Work*. London: Routledge & Kegan Paul.

Cohen-Shabot, S.C. (2007) Grotesque bodies: A response to disembodied cyborgs, *Journal of Gender Studies*, 15:3, 223–235.

Colley, H. (2007) Understanding time in learning transitions through the lifecourse: A feminist materialist perspective, paper presented in the Keynote Symposium The Return of the Thing: Feminism and the Material in Educational Research (convened by Helen Colley), *British Educational Research Association Annual Conference*, London, 6 September 2007.

Connell, R. W. (1987) *Gender and Power*. London: Routledge.

Connell, R.W. (1989) Cool guys, swots and wimps: the interplay of masculinity and education, *Oxford Review of Education*, 15:3, 291–303.

Connell, R.W. (1995) *Masculinities*. London: Polity Press.

Connell, R.W. (2000) *The Men and the Boys*. Oxford: Polity Press.

Connell , R. W. and Messerschmidt, J. (2008) Hegemonic masculinity: rethinking the concept, *Gender and Society*, 19:6, 829–859.

Connell, R.W., Ashenden, D.J., Kessler, S. and Dowsett, G.W. (1982) *Making the Difference*. Sydney: Allen and Unwin.

Connolly, P. (1998) Racism, Gender Identities and Young Children. London: Routledge.

Cook, T., Deng, Y. and Morgano, E. (2007) Friendship influences during early adolescence: The special role of friends' grade point average, *Journal of Research on Adolescence*, 17:2, 325–356.

Cooper, H. and Hyland, R. (eds) (2000) *Children's Perceptions of Learning with Trainee Teachers*. London: Taylor and Francis.

Corrigan, P. (1979) *Schooling the Smash Street Kids*. London: Macmillan.

Crozier, G. Reay, D. James, D. Jamieson, F. Hollingworth, S. Williams, K. Beedell, P., (2008) White middle class parents, identities, educational choice and the urban comprehensive school: Dilemmas, ambivalence and moral ambiguity, *British Journal of Sociology of Education*, 29:3, 261–272.

Currie, D., Kelly, D. and Pomerantz, S. (2007) 'The power to squash people': Understanding girls' relational aggression, *British Journal of Sociology of Education*, 28:1, 23–37.

Dalley-Trim, L (2007) 'The boys' present . . .' Hegemonic masculinity: A performance of multiple acts, *Gender and Education*, 19:2, 199–217.

Davies, B. (1989) *Frogs and Snails and Feminist Tales*. Sydney: Allen and Unwin.

Day, C., Sammons, P., Stobart, G., Kington, A. and Gu, Q. (2007) *Teachers Matter*. Maidenhead: Open University Press.

de Beauvoir, S. (1973) *The Second Sex*. London: Vintage Book.

Deem, R. (1981) State policy and ideology in the education of women, 1944–80, *British Journal of Sociology of Education*, 2: 2, 131–143.

Delamont, S. (1980) *Sex Roles and the School*. London: Methuen.

Delamont, S. and Galton, M. (1986) *Inside the Secondary Classroom*. London: Routledge and Kegan Paul.

Department for Education and Skills (2003) *Using the National Healthy School Standard to Raise Boys' Achievement*. Wetherby: Health Development Agency.

Department for Children, Schools and Families (2007a) *Engaging Parents in Raising Achievement: Do Parents Know They Matter?* (http://publications.education.gov.uk/default.aspx?PageFunction=downloadoptions&PageMode=publications&ProductId=DCSF-RW004&)

Department for Children, Schools and Families (2007b) *Confident, Capable and Creative: Supporting Boys' Achievements*. London: DSCF.

Department for Children, Schools and Families (2009a) *Gender and Education – Mythbusters*. Nottingham: DCSF Publications.

Department for Children, Schools and Families (2009b) *Gender Issues in School – What Works to Improve Achievement for Boys and Girls*. Nottingham: DCSF Publications.

Department of Education (United States) (2010) *Accelerating Achievement and Ensuring Equity*. (http://www2.ed.gov/about/overview/budget/budget11/justifications/b-aaee.pdf) (Accessed 9 February 2011).

Department of Education, Science and Training (Australia) (2004) *Learning Together – Achievement through Choice and Opportunity*. (http://www.dest.gov.au/sectors/school_education/publications_resources/profiles/government_funding_schools_2005_2008.htm) (Accessed 9 February 2011).

Directgov (2010) *Supporting Gifted and Talented Children*. (http://www.direct.gov.uk/en/Parents/Schoolslearninganddevelopment/ExamsTestsAndTheCurriculum/DG_10037625) (Accessed 18 August 2010).

Dobson, J. (2005) *Bringing up Boys*. Wheaton, IL: Tyndale House Publishers.

Dorman, J. and Adams, J.(2004) Associations between students' perceptions of classroom environment and academic efficacy in Australian and British secondary schools, *Westminster Studies in Education*, 27:1, 69–85.

Dubberley, W.S. (1993) Humour as resistance, in: P. Woods and M. Hammersley (eds), *Gender and Ethnicity*. London: Routledge.

Dunne, M. and Gazeley, L. (2008) Teachers, social class and underachievement, *British Journal of Sociology of Education*, 29:5, 451–463.

Emmerich, W., Goldman, S., Kirsh, B. and Sharabany, R. (1977) Evidence for a transitional phase in the development of 'gender constancy', *Child Development*, 48, 930–936.

Equal Opportunities Commission (1984) *Do You Provide Equal Educational Opportunities*? Equal Opportunities Commission, Manchester.

Epstein, D. (1997) Boyz Own Stories: masculinities and sexualities in schools, *Gender and Education*, 9:1, 105–116.

Epstein, D. and Johnson, R. (1998) *Schooling Sexualities*. Buckingham: Open University Press.

Epstein, D., Elwood, J., Hey, V. and Maw, J. (eds) (1998) *Failing Boys?* Buckingham: Open University Press.

Evans, J., Rich, E. and Holroyd, R. (2004) Disordered eating and disordered schooling: What schools do to middle-class girls, *British Journal of Sociology of Education*, 25:2, 123–142.

Fairclough, K. (2008) Fame is a losing game: Celebrity gossip blogging, bitch culture and postfeminism, *Genders: Presenting Innovative Work in the Arts, Humanities and Social Theories* 48 (http://www.genders.org/g48/g48_fairclough.html) (accessed 13 September 2009).

Fairclough, N. (2000) *New Labour, New Language?* London: Routledge.

Farrow, S., Tymms, P. and Henderson, B. (1999) Homework and attainment in primary schools, *British Educational Research Journal*, 25:3, 323–341.

Fine, M. (2003) Sexuality, schooling and adolescent females: The missing discourse of desire, in: M. Fine and L. Weis (eds), *Silenced Voices and Extraordinary Conversations*. Amsterdam: Teachers College Press.

Fine, M., Burns, A., Torre, M. and Payne, Y. (2008) How class matters, in Weis, L. (ed), *The Way Class Works*. New York: Routledge.

Flutter, J. and Rudduck, J. (2004) *Consulting Pupils: What's in it for Schools?* London: Routledge Falmer.

Fordham, S. (1996). *Blacked Out: Dilemmas of Race, Identity, and Success at Capital High*. Chicago, IL: University of Chicago Press.

Forsey, C. (1990) *The Making of Men: Guidelines for Working with Boys to Counter the Male Sex-Role*. Footscray, Vic: West Education Centre.

Foucault, M. (1980) *Power/Knowledge: Selected Interviews and Other Writings, 1972–77*. New York: Pantheon.

Francis, B. (1998) *Power Plays: Primary School Children's Constructions of Gender, Power and Adult Work*. Stoke-on-Trent: Trentham.

Francis, B. (1999) Modernist reductionism or post-modernist relativism: Can we move on?, *Gender and Education*, 11: 4, 381–394.

Francis, B. (2000) *Boys, Girls and Achievement*. London: Routledge Falmer.

Francis, B. (2001) Beyond Postmodernism: feminist agency in educational research, in: Francis, B. and Skelton, C. (eds), *Investigating Gender: Contemporary Perspectives in Education*. Buckingham: Open University Press.

Francis, B. (2007a) Postmodern and poststructural theories, in: B. Banks (ed), *Gender and Education: An Encyclopedia*. Westport CT: Praeger.

Francis, B. (2007b) Classroom interaction, in: K. Myers (ed), *Gender Watch: Still Watching*. Stoke-on-Trent: Trentham Books.

Francis, B. (2008a) Engendering debate: how to formulate a political analysis of the divide between genetic bodies and discursive gender, *Journal of Gender Studies*, 17:3, 211–223.

Francis, B. (2008b) Teaching manfully? Exploring gendered subjectivities and power via analysis of men teachers' gender performance, *Gender and Education*, 20:2, 109–122.

Francis, B. (2009) The role of the boffin as abject Other in gendered performances of school achievement, *Sociological Review*, 57:4, 645–659.

Francis, B. (2010) Re/theorising gender: Female masculinity and male femininity in the classroom? *Gender and Education*, 22:6, 477–490.

Francis, B. (forthcoming) Gender monoglossia, gender heteroglossia: The potential of Bakhtin's work for re-conceptualising gender, accepted for publication in *Journal of Gender Studies*, 21(1).

Francis, B. and Archer, L., (2005) Negotiating the dichotomy between boffin and triad: British-Chinese constructions of 'laddism', *Sociological Review*, 53:3, 495–522.

Francis, B. and Skelton, C. (2005) *Reassessing Gender and Achievement*. London: Routledge.

Francis, B. and Skelton, C. (2008) The self-made self: Analysing the potential contribution of theories to the field of gender and education that disembed selfhood, *Discourse*, Special Issue: 'Troubling Gender in Education', 29:3, 311–323.

Francis, B., Skelton, C. and Read, B. (2010) The simultaneous production of educational achievement and popularity: how do some pupils accomplish it? *British Educational Research Journal*, 36:2, 317–340.

Frazier, N. And Sadker, M. (1973) *Sexism in School and Society*. New York: Harper and Row.

Frosh, S., Phoenix, A. and Pattman, R. (2002) *Young Masculinities: Understanding Boys in Contemporary Society*. London: Palgrave.

Fry, S. (2010) *The Fry Chronicles*. London: Michael Joseph.

Garfinkel, H. (1967) *Studies in Ethnomethodology*. Englewood Cliffs, NJ: Prentice-Hall.

Gaskell, J. (1992) *Gender Matters From School to Work*. Buckingham: Open University Press.

George, R. (2007) *Girls in a Goldfish Bowl: Moral Regulation, Ritual and the Use of Power Amongst Inner City Girls*. Rotterdam, Netherlands: Sense Publishers.

Gewirtz, S., Ball, S.J. and Bowe, R. (1995) *Markets, Choice and Equity in Education*. Buckingham: Open University Press.

Giddens, A. (1998) *The Third Way*. Cambridge: Polity.

Gill, R. (2006) *Gender and the Media*. Cambridge, Polity.

Gillborn, D. (2008) *Racism and Education: Coincidence or Conspiracy*? London: Routledge.

Goffman, E. (1959) *The Presentation of Self in Everyday Life*. Anchor: New York.

Gorard, S. and Taylor, C. (2002) A comparison of segregation indices in terms of strong and weak compositional invariance, *Sociology*, 36, 4, 875–895.

Gregory, R. (1969) *A Shorter Textbook of Human Development*. Maidenhead: McGraw-Hill.

Griffin, C. (1985) *Typical Girls*? London: Routledge and Kegan Paul.

Griffin, C. (2004) Anglocentrism and diversity in the constitution of contemporary girlhood, in A. Harris (ed), *All About the Girl: Culture, Power and Identity*. London: Routledge.

Gurian, M. (2002) *Boys and Girls Learn Differently*! Jossey Bass: San Francisco, CA.

Halberstam, J. (1998) *Female Masculinity*. Durham and London: Duke University Press.

Hallam, S. (2004) *Homework: The Evidence*. London: Institute of Education, Bedford Way Papers.

Hargreaves, D.H. (1967) *Social Relations in a Secondary School*. London: Routledge and Kegan Paul.

Hargreaves, L. and Galton, M. (2002) *Moving From the Primary Classroom: 20 Years On*. London: Routledge.

Harness, J. (2009) *Are you a Nerd, Geek or Dweeb?* (www.neatorama.com/2009/09/16/are-you-a-nerd-dork-geek-or-dweeb/) (last accessed 14 August 2011)

Hartsock, N. (1990) Foucault on power: a theory for women, in L. Nicholson (ed), *Feminism/Postmodernism*. London: Routledge.

Hey, V. (1997) *The Company She Keeps: An Ethnography of Girls' Friendships*. Buckingham: Open University Press.

Hey, V. (2010) Framing girls in girlhood studies, in: C. Jackson, C. Paechter and E. Renold (eds), *Girls and Education 3–16*. Maidenhead: Open University Press.

Hill, D. (2001) State theory and the neo-liberal reconstruction of schooling and teacher education: a structuralist neo-marxist critique of postmodernist, quasi-postmodernist, and culturalist neo-marxist theory, *British Journal of Sociology of Education*, 22:1, 137–157.

Hill, A. (2004) Watching Big Brother UK, in: E. Mathijs and J. Jones (eds), *Big Brother International: Format, Critics and Publics*. London: Wallflower Press, pp. 25–39.

Hobbs, G. and Vignoles, A. (2007) *Is Free School Meal Status a Valid Proxy for Socio-Economic Status (in Schools Research)?* London: Centre for the Economics of Education, London School of Economics.

Hoffer, C.P. (1974) Madam Yoko: ruler of the Kpa Mende Confederacy, in: M. Z. Rosaldo and L. Lamphere (eds), *Women, Culture and Society*. Stanford, CA: Stanford University Press.

Holland, J., Ramazanoglu, C., Sharpe, S. and Thomson, R. (1998) *The Male in the Head: Young People, Heterosexuality and Power*. London: Routledge.

Holm, A-S. (2007) Crossing boundaries? Complexities and drawbacks to gendered success stories, in: M. Carlson, F. Gök and A. Rabo (eds), *Education in 'Multicultural' Societies: Turkish and Swedish Perspectives*. Istanbul: Swedish Research Institute in Istanbul, Tauris Publishers, pp. 181–195.

Hood-Williams, J. (1998) Stories for sexual difference, *British Journal of Sociology of Education*, 18, 81–99.

Hufton, N.R., Elliott, J.G. and Illushin, L. (2002) Educational motivation and engagement: Qualitative accounts from three countries, *British Educational Research Journal*, 28:2, 265–289.

Hutchings, M., Carrington, B., Francis, B., Skelton, C, Read, B. and Hall, I. (2008) Nice and kind, smart and funny: What children like and want to emulate in their teachers, *Oxford Review of Education*, 34:2, 135–147.

Ivinson, G. and Murphy, P. (2007) *Rethinking Single Sex Teaching*. Maidenhead: Open University Press and McGraw-Hill Education.

Jackson, C. (2002) 'Laddishness' as a self-worth protection strategy, *Gender and Education*, 14:1, 37–51.

Jackson, C. (2006a) *Lads and Ladettes in School*. Maidenhead: Open University Press.

Jackson, C. (2006b) 'Wild' girls? An exploration of 'ladette' cultures in secondary schools, *Gender and Education*, 18: 4, 339–360.

Jackson, C. and Dempster, S. (2009) 'I Sat Back On My Computer . . . With a Bottle of Whisky Next to Me': Constructing 'cool' masculinity through 'effortless' achievement in secondary and higher education, *Journal of Gender Studies*, 18:4, 341–356.

Jackson, C. (2010) Demanding time: Balancing school and out-of-school demands, in: C. Jackson, C. Paechter and E. Renold (eds), *Girls and Education 3–16*. Maidenhead: Open University Press.

Jones, L.G. and Jones, L.P. (1989) Context, confidence and the able girl, *Educational Research*, 31:3, 189–194.

Jones, A. (1997) Teaching poststructuralist feminist theory in education: Student resistances, *Gender and Education*, 9:3, 261–269.

Keddie, A. and Mills, M. (2007) *Teaching Boys?* Crows Nest, NSW: Allen and Unwin.

Kehily, M. J. (2002) *Sexuality, Gender and Schooling: Shifting Agendas in Social Learning*. London: Routledge Falmer.

Kehily, M.J. (2004) *Girls and sexuality: continuities and change for girls in school*, in A. Harris (ed.) *All About the Girl, Power, Culture and Identity*. New York: Routledge Falmer.

Kehily M. and Nayak, A. (1997) 'Lads and laughter': Humour and the production of heterosexual hierarchies, *Gender and Education*, 9:1, 69–87.

Kenway, J. and Fitzclarence, L. (1997) Masculinity, violence and schooling: Challenging 'poisonous pedagogies', *Gender and Education* 9:1, 117–133.

Kenway, J. and Willis, S. with Blackmore, J. and Rennie, L. (1998) *Answering Back: Girls, Boys and Feminism in Schools*. London: Routledge.

Kessler, S. and McKenna, W. (1978) *Gender, an Ethnomethodological Approach*. Chicago, IL: University of Chicago Press.

Kiesner, J., Cadinu, M., Poulin, F. and Bucci, M. (2002) Group identification in early adolescence: Its relation with peer adjustment and its moderator effect on peer influence, *Child Development* 73:1, 196–208.

Kindlon, D. (2006) *Alpha Girls: Understanding the New American Girl and How She is Changing the World*. New York: Rodale Books.

Kindlon, D. and Thompson, M. (2000) *Raising Cain: Protecting the Emotional Life of Boys*. New York: Ballantine.

Kohlberg, L. (1966) A cognitive-developmental analysis of children's sex-role concepts and attitudes, in E. Maccoby (ed), *The Development of Sex Differences*. Stanford, CA: Stanford University Press.

Lacey, C. (1970) *Hightown Grammar: School as a Social System*. Manchester: Manchester University Press.

Lake, A. (1975) Are we born into our sex roles or programmed into them? *Woman's Day*, January 1975, 24–25.

Lambart, A. (1976) The sisterhood, in: M. Hammersley and P.Woods (eds), *The Process of Schooling*. London: Routledge and Kegan Paul.

Lauder, P. Brown, J. Dillabough and A.H. Halsey (eds) (2006) *Education, Globalization and Social Change*. Oxford: Oxford University Press.

Lees, S. (1992) *Sugar and Spice*. London: Penguin.

Lingard, B., Hayes, D., Mills, M. and Christie, P. (2003) *Leading Learning: Making Hope Practical in Schools*. Buckingham: Open University Press.

Lingard, B., Martino, W. and Mills, M. (2009) *Boys and Schooling*. London: Palgrave.

Lobban, G. (1978) The influence of the school on sex-role stereotyping, in J. Chetwynd and O Hartnett (eds), *The Sex Role System*. London: Routledge and Kegan Paul.

Lucey, H. (2001) Social class, gender and schooling, in: B. Francis and C. Skelton (eds), *Investigating Gender: Contemporary Perspectives in Education*. Buckingham: Open University Press.

Lucey, H. and Reay, D. (2000) Excitement and anxiety in the move to secondary school, *Oxford Review of Education*, 26: 191–205.

Lucey, H. and Reay, D. (2002) A market in waste: Psychic and structural dimensions of school-choice policy in the UK and children's narratives on 'demonised' schools, *Discourse*, 23:1, 23–40.

Lundh, L-G., Karim, J. and Quilisch, E. (2007) Deliberate self-harm in 15-year-old adolescents: A pilot study with a modified version of the Deliberate Self-Harm Inventory, *Scandinavian Journal of Psychology*, 48:1, 33–41.

Lynch, K. (2006) Neoliberalism and marketisation: The implications for higher education, *European Education Research Journal*, 5:1, 1–12.

Mahony, P. (1985) *Schools for the Boys: Coeducation Reassessed*. London: Hutchinson.

Mahony, P. (1998) Girls will be girls and boys will be first, in: D. Epstein, J. Elwood, V. Hey and J. Maw (eds), *Failing Boys*? Buckingham: Open University Press.

Mac an Ghaill, M. (1994) *The Making of Men: Masculinities, Sexualities and Schooling*. Buckingham: Open University Press.

Mansell, W. (2010) Speech to the Society for Educational Studies Annual Seminar, London, November 2010.

Martino, W. (1999) 'Cool boys', 'party animals','squids' and 'poofters': Interrogating the dynamics and politics of adolescent masculinities in school, *British Journal of Sociology of Education*, 20:2, 239–263.

Martino, W. (2009) Beyond male role models: Interrogating the role of male teachers in boys' education, in: W. Martino, M. Kehler and M.B. Weaver-Hightower (eds), *The Problem with Boys' Education*. New York: Routledge.

Martino, W. and Pallotta-Chiarolli, M. (eds) (2003) *So What's a Boy*? Maidenhead: Open University/ McGraw Hill.

Martino, W., Mills, M. and Lingard, B. (2005) Interrogating single-sex classes as a strategy for addressing boys' educational and social needs, *Oxford Review of Education*, 31: 2, 237–254.

Martino, W., Kehler, M. and Weaver-Hightower, M. (eds) (2009) *The Problem with Boys' Education*. London: Routledge.

Maynard, T. (2002) *Boys and Literacy: Exploring the Issues*. London: Routledge.

McClure, A. (2008) *Making It Better for Boys in Schools, Families and Communities*. London: Continuum.

MacInnes, J. (1998) *The End of Masculinity*. Buckingham: Open University Press.

McIntyre, D., Pedder, D., and Rudduck, J. (2005) Pupil voice: Comfortable and uncomfortable learnings for teachers, *Research Papers in Education*, 20: 2, 149–168.

McNamara Horvat, E., Weininger, E.B. and Lareau, A. (2006) From social ties to social capital: Class differences in the relations between schools and parent networks, *American Educational Research Journal*, 40:3, 319–351.

McNay, L. (2000) *Gender and Agency*. Cambridge: Polity Press.

McRobbie, A. (2008) *The Aftermath of Feminism: Gender, Culture and Social Change*. London: Sage.

Mead, G. H. (1934) *Mind, Self and Society*. Chicago, IL: University of Chicago Press.

Measor, L. and Sikes, P. (1992) *Gender and Schooling*. London: Cassell.

Measor, L. and Woods, P. (1984) *Changing Schools: Pupil Perspectives on Transfer to a Comprehensive*, Milton Keynes and Philadelphia, PA: Open University Press.

Mendick, H. (2005) A beautiful myth? The gendering of being/ doing 'good at maths', *Gender and Education*, 17:2, 205–219.

Mendick, H. (2008) Subtracting difference: Troubling transitions from GCSE to AS-level Mathematics, *British Educational Research Journal*, 34:6, 711–732.

Mendick, H. and Francis, B. (2011) Boffin and geek identities: abject or privileged? accepted for publication in *Gender and Education*. IFirst, http://www.tandfonline.com/doi/abs/10.1080/09540 253.2011.564575

Mendick, H., Moreau, M.P. and Hollingworth S. (2008) *Mathematical Images and Gender Identities*. London: UK Resource Centre for Women in Science, Engineering and Technology.

Merten, D. (1997) The meaning of meanness: Popularity, competition, and conflict among junior high school girls, *Sociology of Education*, 70, 175–191.

Mills, M. (2001) *Challenging Violence in Schools: an Issue of Masculinities*. Buckingham: Open University Press.

Mills, M. (2003) Shaping the boys' agenda: the backlash blockbusters. *International Journal of Inclusive Education*, 7: 57–73.

Mills, M., Francis, B. and Skelton, C. (2009) Gender policies in Australia and the UK: The construction of new boys and girls, in: W. Martino, M. Kehler and M. Weaver-Hightower (eds), *The Problem With Boys' Education: Beyond the Backlash*. New York: Routledge.

Mirza, H.S. (1992) *Young, Female and Black*. London: Routledge.

Mirza, H. (2009) *Race, Gender and Educational Desire: Why Black Women Succeed and Fail*. Abingdon: Routledge.

Mitchell, J. (1974) *Psychoanalysis and Feminism*. New York: Pantheon Books.

Moir, A. and Moir, B. (1999) *Why Men Don't Iron*. London: Harper Collins.

Mojab, S. (2006) 'In the quagmires of ethnicity': A Marxist critique of liberal 'exit strategies', *Journal of Ethnicities*, 6:3, 341–361.

Mortimore, P. (2010) Fight Gove's big sell-off of education, *Guardian* (http://www.guardian.co.uk/education/2010/dec/07/fight-gove-education-reforms) (Accessed 9 February 2011).

Mouffe, C. (ed) (1996) *Deconstruction and Pragmatism*. London: Routledge.

Myers, K. (ed) (2000) *Whatever Happened to Equal Opportunities in Schools?* Buckingham: Open University Press.

Myhill, D. (2002) Bad boys and good girls? Patterns of interaction and response in whole class teaching, *British Educational Research Journal*, 28:3, 339–352.

Nash, R. (1978) *Pupils' Expectations of Their Teachers.* London: John Wiley and Sons.

Nayak, A. and Kehily, M.J. (1996) Playing it straight: Masculinities, homophobias and schooling, *Journal of Gender Studies*, 5:2, 211–230.

Nayak, A. and Kehily, M. (2006) *Gender, Youth and Culture: Young Masculinities and Femininities.* London: Palgrave MacMillan.

Norfleet James, A. (2007) *Teaching the Male Brain.* Thousand Oaks, CA: Corwin Press.

O'Brien, M. (2003) Girls and transition to secondary-level schooling in Ireland: 'moving on' and 'moving out', *Gender and Education*, 15, 249–267.

Oakley, A. (1972) *Sex, Gender and Society.* London: Temple Smith.

OECD (2007) see entry for Organisation for Economic Co-operation and Development.

Ofsted (1993) *Boys and English.* London: HMSO.

Ofsted (2002) *Achievement of Black Caribbean Pupils: Good Practice in Secondary Schools.* London: Ofsted Publications.

Ofsted (2003a) *Yes He Can – Schools Where Boys Write Well.* London: Ofsted Publications.

Ofsted (2003b) *Boys' Achievement in Secondary Schools.* London: Ofsted Publications.

Organisation for Economic Co-operation and Development (2007) *PISA 2006: Science Competencies for Tomorrow's World: Executive Summary.* (www.pisa.oecd.org.) (Accessed 29 March 2011).

Osler, A. (2006) Excluded girls: Interpersonal, institutional and structural violence in schools, *Gender and Education*, 18:6, 571–590.

Osler, A. and Vincent, K. (2003) *Girls and Exclusion: Rethinking the Agenda.* London: Routledge Falmer.

Paechter, C. (2001) *Changing School Subjects: Power, Gender and Curriculum.* Buckingham: Open University Press.

Paechter, C. (2006) Masculine femininities/feminine masculinities: Power, identities and gender, *Gender and Education*, 18:3, 253–263.

Paechter, C. (2007) *Being Boys, Being Girls: Learning Masculinities and Femininities.* Milton Keynes: Open University Press.

Paechter, C. and Clark, S. (2007) Learning gender in primary school playgrounds: Findings from the Tomboy Identities Study, *Pedagogy, Culture and Society*, 15:3, 317–331.

Paechter, C. and Head, J. (1996) Gender, identity, status and the body: life in a marginal subject, *Gender and Education*, 8:1, 21–30.

Palmer, S. (2010) *21st Century Boys: How Modern Life Can Drive Them off the Rails and How to Get Them Back on Track.* London: Orion.

Parker (1996) The construction of masculinity within boys' physical education, *Gender and Education*, 8, 141–157.

Parry, O. (1996) 'Schooling is fooling': Why do Jamaican boys underachieve in school? *Gender and Education*, 9: 2, 223–231.

Parsons, C. G., Godfrey, R., Annan, G., Cornwall, J., Dussart, M., Hepburn, S., Howlett, K. and Wennerstrom, V. (2005) *Minority Ethnic Exclusions and the Race Relations (Amendment) Act 2000*, RR 616. Nottingham: DfES.

Perry, E. and Francis, B. (2010) *The Social Class Gap for Educational Achievement: A Review of the Literature*. London: The RSA.

Pickering, J. (1997) *Raising Boys' Achievement*. Stafford: Network Educational Press.

Plummer, G. (2000) *Failing Working-Class Girls*. Stoke-on-Trent: Trentham.

Pollack, W. (1998) *Real Boys*. New York: Owl Books.

Pollard, A. (1987) *Children and their Primary Schools*. Lewes: Falmer.

Pollard, A. (2001) *The Social World of Children's Learning*. London: Continuum.

Pollitt, C. (1993) *Managerialism and the Public Service: Cuts or Cultural Change in the 1990s*, 2nd edition. Oxford: Blackwell.

Pomerantz, S. (2008) *Girls, Style and School Identities: Dressing The Part*. Basingstoke, Palgrave Macmillan.

Power, S., Edwards, T., Whitty, G. and Wigfall, V. (1998) Schoolboys and schoolwork: Gender identification and academic achievement, *International Journal of Inclusive Education*, 2:2, 135–153.

Pratt, S. and George, R. (2005) Transferring friendship: Girls' and boys' friendships in the transition from primary to secondary school, *Children and Society*, 19, 16–26.

Qualifications and Curriculum Authority (1998) *Can Do Better: Raising Boys' Achievement in English*. London: QCA.

Read, B. (2006) Gendered constructions of cooperation and competition by pupils, in: A. Ross, M. Fulop and M. Pergar Kuscer (eds), *Teachers' and Pupils' Constructions of Competition and Cooperation: A Three-Country Study of Slovenia, Hungary and England*. Ljubljana: University of Llubljana Press, pp. 174–185.

Read, B., Francis, B. and Skelton, C. (2011) Gender, popularity and notions of in/authenticity amongst 12–13 yr old school girls, *British Journal of Sociology of Education*, 32:2, 169–183.

Reay, D. (1998) Rethinking social class: Qualitative perspectives on class and gender, *Sociology*, 32:2, 259–75.

Reay, D. (2001) Spice girls, nice girls, girlies and tomboys – gender discourses, girls' cultures and femininities in the primary classroom, *Gender and Education*, 13:2, 153–166.

Reay, D. (2002) Shaun's story: Troubling discourses of white working-class masculinities, *Gender and Education*, 14:3, 221–233.

Reay, D. (2004a) Education and cultural capital: The implications of changing trends in education policies, *Cultural Trends*, 32:2, 73–86.

Reay, D. (2004b) Gendering Bourdieu's concept of capitals? Emotional capital, women and social class, in: L. Adkins and B. Skeggs (eds), *Feminism After Bourdieu*. London: Blackwell.

Reay, D. (2006) Gender and class in education, in: C. Skelton, B. Francis and L. Smulyan (eds), *The Sage Handbook of Gender and Education*. London and New York: Sage.

Reay, D. and Ball, S. (1998) 'Making up their minds': Family dynamics of school choice, *British Educational Research Journal*, 14:4, 431–448.

Reay, D. and Lucey, H. (2003) The limits of choice: Children and inner-city schooling, *Sociology*, 37, 121–143.

Reay, D., David, M. and Ball, S. (2005) *Degrees of Choice: Social Class, Race and Gender in Higher Education*. Stoke-on-Trent: Trentham Books.

Reay, D., Crozier, G. and Clayton, J. (2009) Strangers in Paradise: Working class students in elite universities, *Sociology* 43:6, 1103–1121.

Redman, P. and Mac an Ghail, M. (1997) Educating Peter, in: D.L. Steinberg, D. Epstein and R. Johnson (eds), *Border Patrols: Policing the Boundaries of Heterosexuality*. London: Cassell.

Renold, E. (2000) 'Coming out': Gender, (hetero)sexuality and the primary school, *Gender and Education*, 12:3, 309–326.

Renold, E. (2001) 'Square-girls', femininity and the negotiation of academic success in the primary school, *British Educational Research Journal*, 27: 5, 577–588.

Renold, E. (2005) *Girls, Boys and Junior Sexualities*. London: Routledge.

Renold, E. (2006) 'They Won't Let us Play . . . Unless You're Going Out with One of Them': Girls, boys, and Butler's 'heterosexual matrix' in the primary years, *British Journal of Sociology of Education*, 27:4, 491–511.

Renold, E. (2007) Primary school 'studs': (De)constructing young boys' heterosexual masculinities, *Men and Masculinities*, 9:3, 275–298.

Renold, E. (2008) Queering masculinity: Re-theorising contemporary tomboyism in the schizoid space of innocent/heterosexualized young femininities, *Girlhood Studies*, 1:2, 129–151.

Renold, E. and Allan, A. (2006) Bright and beautiful: High achieving girls, ambivalent femininities and the feminization of success in the primary school, *Discourse: Studies in the Cultural Politics of Education*, 27:4, 457–473.

Renold, E. and Ringrose, J. (forthcoming) Phallic girls? Girls' negotiation of phallogocentric power, in: N. Rodriguez (ed), *Queer Masculinities: A Critical Reader in Education*. Berlin: Springer.

Riddell, S. (1989) Pupils, resistance and gender codes: A study of classroom encounters, *Gender and Education*, 1:2, 183–197.

Riddell, S. (1992) *Politics and the Gender of the Curriculum*. London: Routledge.

Ringrose, J. (2007) Successful girls?: Complicating post-feminist, neo-liberal discourses of educational achievement and gender equality, *Gender and Education*, 19, 471–489.

Ringrose, J. (2008) 'Every time she bends over she pulls up her thong': Teen girls negotiating discourses of competitive, heterosexualized aggression, *Girlhood Studies*, 1:1, 33–59.

Sadker, M. and Sadker, D. (1994) *Failing at Fairness: How Our Schools Cheat Girls*. New York: Touchstone.

Salisbury, J. and Jackson, D. (1996) *Challenging Macho Values*. London, Falmer.

Sammons, P., Hillman, J. and Mortimore, P. (1995) *Key Characteristics of Effective Schools: A Review of School Effectiveness Research*. A report by the Institute of Education for the Office for Standards in Education. London: Office for Standards in Education.

Sayers, J. (1984) Psychology and gender divisions, in: S. Acker, J. Megarry, S. Nisbet and E. Hoyle, (eds), *World Yearbook of Education 1984: Women and Education*. London: Kogan Page.

Schippers, M. (2007) Recovering the feminine Other: Masculinity, femininity, and gender hegemony, *Theory and Society*, 36, 85–102.

Scott, S. (2007) *Shyness and Society: The Illusion of Competence*. Basingstoke: Palgrave.

Science Daily (2009) Gifted Children Shape Their Personalities According to Social Stigma (10 March, 2009) (http://www.sciencedaily.com/releases/2009/03/090303102614.htm) (Accessed 18 August 2010).

Seidler, V. (1989) *Rediscovering Masculinity*. London: Routledge.

Serbin, L. (1983) The hidden curriculum: Academic consequences of teacher expectations, in: M. Marland (ed), *Sex Differentiation and Schooling*. London: Heinemann.

Sewell, T. (1997) *Black Masculinities and Schooling: How Black Boys Survive Modern Schooling*. Stoke on Trent: Trentham Books.

Sharpe, S. (1976*) Just Like a Girl*. Harmondsworth, Penguin.

Skeggs, B. (1997) *Formations of Class and Gender*. London: Sage.

Skeggs, B. (2004) *Class, Self, Culture*. London: Routledge.

Skeggs, B. (2005a) Exchange, value and affect: Bourdieu and 'the Self', in: L. Adkins and B. Skeggs (eds), *Feminism After Bourdieu*. Oxford: Blackwell.

Skeggs, B. (2005b) The making of class and gender through visualizing moral subject formation, *Sociology*, 39:51, 965–982.

Skelton, C. (ed) (1989) *Whatever Happens to Little Women? Gender and Schooling*. Milton Keynes: Open University Press.

Skelton, C. (2001) *Schooling the Boys*. Buckingham: Open University Press.

Skelton, C. (2010) Gender and achievement: Are girls the 'success stories' of restructured education systems? *Educational Review*, 62:2, 131–142.

Skelton, C. and Francis, B. (2003) Introduction: Boys and girls in the primary classroom, in C. Skelton and B. Francis (eds) *Boys and Girls in the Primary Classroom*. Buckingham: Open University Press.

Skelton, C. and Francis, B. (2009) *Feminism and 'The Schooling Scandal'*. London: Routledge.

Skelton, C. and Francis, B. (2011) The 'renaissance child': High achievement and gender in late modernity, *International Journal of Inclusive Education* IFirst, http://www.tandfonline.com/doi/a bs/10.1080/13603116.2011.555098.

Skelton, C. and Read, B. (2006) Male and female teachers' evaluative responses to gender and the learning environments of primary age pupils, *International Studies in Sociology of Education*, 16:2, 105–120.

Skelton, C., Francis, B. & Read, B. (2010) 'Brains before 'beauty'?' High achieving girls, school and gender identities*, Educational Studies*, 36:2, 185–194.

Skelton, C., Carrington, B., Francis, B., Hutchings, M., Read, B. and Hall, I. (2009) Gender 'matters' in the primary classroom: Pupils' and teachers' perspectives, *British Educational Research Journal*, 35: 2, 187–204.

Slater, M. (2009) *Charles Dickens*. London: Yale University Press.

Smith, J. (2007) Ye've Got to 'ave Balls to Play this Game Sir!' Boys, peers and fears: the negative influence of school-based 'cultural accomplices' in constructing hegemonic masculinities, *Gender and Education* 19:2, 179–198.

Smith, C. and Lloyd, B. (1978) Maternal behaviour and perceived sex of infant: Revisited, *Child Development*, 49, 1263–1265.

Soper, K. (1990) *Troubled Pleasures*. London: Verso.

Spender , D. (1982) *Invisible Women: The Schooling Scandal*. London: Writers' and Readers Publishing Collective.

Stables, A. and Stables, S. (1995) Gender differences in students' approaches to a-level subject choices and perceptions of a-level subjects, *Educational Research*, 37:1, 39–51.

Stanworth, M. (1983) *Gender and Schooling*. London: Hutchinson.

Stoeger, H. (2008) Editorial, *High Ability Studies*, 19:1, 1–3.

Sutherland, M. (1981) *Sex Bias in Education*. Oxford: Blackwell.

Swain, J. (2000) The Money's good, the fame's good, the girls are good: The role of playground football in the construction of young boys' masculinities in a junior school, *British Journal of Sociology of Education*, 21:1, 95–109.

Swain, J. (2002) The resources and strategies boys use to establish status in a junior school without competitive sport, *Discourse: Studies in the Cultural Politics of Education*, 23:1, 91–107.

Thiessen, D. and Cook-Sather, A. (eds) (2007) *International Handbook of Student Experience in Elementary and Secondary School*. Dordrecht, The Netherlands: Springer.

Thornberg, R. (2008) It's not fair – voicing children's criticisms of school rules, *Children and Society*, 22:6, 418–428.

Tinklin, T., Croxford, L., Ducklin, A. and Frame, B. (2005) Gender and attitudes to work and family roles: The views of young people at the millennium, *Gender and Education*, 17:2, 129–142.

Tyre, P. (2008) *The Trouble With Boys*. New York: Crown Publishers.

US Department of Education (2010) *Accelerating Achievement and Ensuring Equity* (http://www2.ed.gov/about/overview/budget/budget11/justifications/b-aaee.pdf) (Accessed 9 February 2011).

Walden, R. and Walkerdine, V. (1985) *Girls and Mathematics*. Bedford Way Papers, 24. London: University of London, Institute of Education.

Waldrip, A., Malcolm, K.T. and Jensen-Campbell, L. A. (2008) with a little help from your friends: The importance of high-quality friendships on early adolescent adjustment, *Social Development*, 17:4, 832–852.

Walker, J.C. (1988) *Louts and Legends*. London: Unwin Hyman.

Walkerdine, V. (1988) *The Mastery of Reason*. Cambridge: Routledge and Kegan Paul.

Walkerdine, V. (1989) *Counting Girls Out*. London: Virago.

Walkerdine, V. (1990) *Schoolgirl Fictions*. London: Verso.

Walkerdine, V. (1997) *Daddy's Girl*. London: Verso.

Walkerdine, V. (2003) Reclassifying upward mobility: Femininity and the neo-liberal subject, *Gender and Education*, 15:3, 237–248.

Walkerdine, V. and Lucey, H. (1989) *Democracy in the Kitchen: Regulating Mothers and Socialising Daughters*. London, Virago.

Walkerdine, V., Lucey, H. and Melody, H. (2001) *Growing Up Girl: Psychosocial Explorations of Gender and Class*. London: Palgrave.

Warrington, M., Younger, M. and Bearne, E. (2006) *Raising Boys' Achievement in Primary Schools: Towards a Holistic Approach*. Maidenhead: Open University Press/McGraw Hill.

Weaver-Hightower, M. (2009) Issues of boys' education in the United States: diffuse contexts and futures, in: W. Martino, M. Kehler and M.B. Weaver-Hightower (eds), *The Problem with Boys' Education*. New York: Routledge.

Weiner, G. (1994) *Feminisms in Education*. Buckingham: Open University Press.

Weiner, G. (2006) Out of the ruins: Feminist pedagogy in recovery, in: C. Skelton, B. Francis and L. Smulyan (eds), *The Sage Handbook of Gender and Education*. London: Sage.

Weis, L. (2004) Gender, masculinity and the new economy, in L. Weis and M. Fine (eds), *Working Method: Research and Social Justice*. New York: Routledge, pp. 77–90.

Weis, L. (ed.) (2008) *The Way Class Works*. New York: Routledge.

Weiten, W. (2008) *Psychology: Themes and Variations* (8th edition). Belmont, CA: Wadsworth Publishing.

Weitz, R. (2001) Women and their hair: Seeking power through resistance and accommodation, *Gender and Society* 15, 667–686.

Wells, A.S. and Oakes, J. (1997) Tracking, detracking and the politics of educational reform: A sociological perspective, in: C. Torres (ed), *Emerging Issues in the Sociology of Education: Comparative Perspectives*. Albany, NY: SUNY Press.

Whitehead, J. and Clough, N. (2004) Pupils: the forgotten partners in Education Action Zones, *Journal of Education Policy* 19:2, 215–227.

Whitty, G., Power, S. and Halpin, D. (1998) *Devolution and Choice in Education*. Buckingham: Open University Press.

Whyte, J. (1983) *Beyond the Wendy House: Sex Role Stereotyping in Primary Schools*. York: Longman Press for Schools Council.

Willis, P. (1977) *Learning to Labour*. Aldershot: Saxon House Press.

Wing, A. (1997) How can children be taught to read differently? *Bill's New Frock and the Hidden Curriculum, Gender and Education*, 9:4, 491–504.

Woods, P. (1979) *The Divided School*. London: Routledge and Kegan Paul.

Woods, P. (1990) *The Happiest Days? How Pupils Cope With Schools*. Lewes: Falmer.

Wolf, A. (2010) Speech to 2020 Public Services Seminar, June 2010, The Royal Society of Arts, London.

Wright, C. (1987) The relations between teachers and Afro-Caribbean pupils: Observing multiracial classrooms, in: G. Weiner and M. Arnot (eds), *Gender Under Scrutiny*. London: Hutchinson.

Wright, C., Weekes, D. and McGlaughlin, A. (2000) *'Race', Class and Gender in Exclusion from School*. London: Falmer.

Youdell, D. (2004) Identity traps or how black students fail: The interactions between biographical, subcultural and learner identities, in: Gloria Ladson-Billings and David Gillborn (eds), *The Routledge Falmer Reader in Multicultural Education*. New York: Routledge Falmer, pp. 84–102.

Youdell, D. (2006) *Impossible Bodies, Impossible Selves: Exclusions and Student Subjectivities*. Secaucus, NJ: Springer.

Younger, M., Warrington, M. and Williams, J. (1999) The gender gap and classroom interactions: Reality and rhetoric? *British Journal of Sociology of Education*, 20, 325–341.

Younger, M., Warrington, M. and McLellan, R. (2005). *Raising Boys' Achievements in Secondary Schools: Issues, Dilemmas and Opportunities*. Maidenhead: Open University Press/McGraw Hill.

Zajda, J. (ed) (2005) *International Handbook on Globalisation, Education and Policy Research: Global Pedagogies and Policies*. Dordrecht, The Netherlands: Springer.

Index

Page numbers in **bold** denote figures/tables.